DATE DUE

Nov. 19, 2007	

SPANISH
BORDERLANDS
SOURCEBOOKS

Presenting Over Four Hundred and Fifty Scholarly Articles and Source
Materials Documenting Interactions Between Native Americans and
Europeans from California to Florida

Each Volume Edited with an Introduction by a Major Scholar

General Editor
David Hurst Thomas
American Museum of Natural History

A GARLAND SERIES

11

THE HERNANDO DE SOTO EXPEDITION

EXPEDITION

Edited with an Introduction by
Jerald T. Milanich

GARLAND PUBLISHING, INC.
NEW YORK & LONDON, 1991

Library of Congress Cataloging-in-Publication Data

The Hernando de Soto expedition / edited with an introduction by Jerald T. Milanich.

p. cm. — (The Spanish borderlands sourcebooks ; 11)

Includes bibliographical references.

Contents: Narratives of the career of Hernando de Soto in
the conquest of Florida as told by a Knight of Elvas and in a
relation by Luis Hernandez de Biedma, factor of the expedition (1866) / Buckingham Smith, translator — A Narrative of
de Soto's expedition based on the diary of Rodrigo Ranjel,
his private secretary, by Gonzalo Fernández de Oviedo y
Valdés (1904) / Edward Gaylord Bourne, translator — The
Cañete fragment: another narrative of Hernando de Soto
(1982) / Eugene Lyon, editor and translator.

ISBN 0-8240-1950-4 (alk. paper)

1. Soto, Hernando de. ca. 1500–1542—Manuscripts.   2.
Florida—Discovery and exploration—Spanish—Sources. 3.
Florida—History—To 1565—Sources. I. Milanich, Jerald T.
II. Knight of Elvas. Relacam verdadereira. English. 1991. III.
Fernández de Oviedo y Valdés, Gonzalo, 1478–1557. Historia
general y natural de las Indias. Selections. 1991. IV. Cañete,
Sebastián de, 16th cent. Selections. English. 1991. V. Series.

E125.S7H47 1991

970.1'6092—dc20

[B]

90-29269

Printed on acid-free, 250-year-life paper.
Manufactured in the United States of America

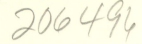

CONTENTS

SOURCES

BOURNE, EDWARD GAYLORD, TRANSLATOR

1904   A Narrative of de Soto's Expedition based on the Diary of Rodrigo Ranjel, his Private Secretary, by Gonzalo Fernandez de Oviedo y Valdés. In *Narratives of the Career of Hernando de Soto in the Conquest of Florida . . .*, Vol. II, Edward Gaylord Bourne, ed. Pp. 47–149. New York: A.S. Barnes and Co.

LYON, EUGENE, EDITOR AND TRANSLATOR

1982   The Cañete Fragment: Another Narrative of Hernando de Soto. Ms. on file, St. Augustine Foundation, St. Augustine. Reprinted by permission of the translator.

SMITH, BUCKINGHAM, TRANSLATOR

1866   *Narratives of the Career of Hernando de Soto in the Conquest of Florida as Told by a Knight of Elvas and in a Relation by Luys Hernandez de Biedma, Factor of the Expedition*, Vol. I. New York: Bradford Club.

INTRODUCTION

Twenty-one years after Christopher Columbus's initial voyage to the New World, Juan Ponce de León, the ex-governor of the Spanish colony of San Juan (Puerto Rico), sailed northward from that island and reached the Atlantic coast of North America, somewhere between the mouth of the St. Johns River and Cape Canaveral. He claimed the land for Spain and named it La Florida because his discovery was made during Holy Week preceding Easter, the time of the Feast of Flowers (Pascua Florida).

Over the next decade and a half Spanish sailors charted the coastlines of what they quickly realized was a vast land; La Florida was much more than the Florida peninsula whose southern portion Juan Ponce had navigated. By the late 1520s coastal explorers had mapped the Atlantic coast of La Florida from Labrador (and beyond) to the Florida Keys, as well as the entire Gulf of Mexico coast.

Sailors gave way to conquistadores and colonists as Spain attempted to explore the interior of this new land and to establish settlements. La Florida could provide Spain an overland route from New Spain (Mexico) to the Atlantic coast along which cargo could be transported before being loaded on ships and sent across the Atlantic Ocean to Spain. The sea route around the Gulf of Mexico, through the Straits of Florida, up the Atlantic coast to the Carolinas, and then across the Atlantic to Spain was dangerous because of shoals and storms, and many ships and sailors had been lost. Spain also expected to find wealth in interior La Florida, another stimulus to settlement. But the first attempts to establish a permanent colony in La Florida failed miserably. Lucas Vásquez de Ayllón's 1526 colony somewhere on the coast of Georgia or South Carolina and the expedition of Pánfilo de Narváez that went ashore near Tampa Bay in 1528 both ended in disaster.

The need for a protected overland route from Mexico to the Atlantic and the lure of riches would bring another conquistador to La Florida, Hernando de Soto. De Soto's expedition in La Florida would be Spain's most ambitious attempt; it was well supplied and well funded with de Soto's share of the wealth wrested from the Inca empire in the early 1530s. Although de Soto and his army would travel through the interior of La Florida for four years and provide history with extraordinary firsthand descriptions of the native societies of the region, they too failed to conquer the land. But, like the other early European explorers to La Florida, they did leave behind a lasting legacy that would spell the beginning of the end for hundreds of thousands of La Florida's native peoples: Old World diseases against which the indigenous population had no immunities.

HERNANDO DE SOTO, CONQUISTADOR

Much has been published about de Soto and his exploits in the New World. Biographies (Albornoz 1972, 1986; Solar y Taboada 1929) and novels and popular books and articles have been written about him and his exploits in Central and South America and La Florida (e.g., Abbott 1873; Blanco 1955; Brown 1975; Daly 1896; Graham 1903; Irving 1835; Jennings 1959; King 1898; Knoop 1940; Knowles 1912; Lefevre 1836; Lytle 1941; Malone 1914; Maynard 1930; Montgomery 1964; Ober 1906; Pérez Cabrera 1939; Posten 1967; Roig de Leuchsenring 1939; Simms 1888; Steele 1956; Syme 1957; Wilmer 1858). De Soto, for whom we have named counties, towns, streets, shopping malls, caverns, and even an automobile, became an American hero in the early nineteenth century, and he continues to be the focus of poems and verses (Herre 1868; Holford 1884; Mansell 1879; Peter 1983). As a hero, de Soto is a symbol of the brave and noble conquistador searching for wealth and conquering new lands, a romantic figure that helped to wrest our country from the wilderness (e.g., Pinckney 1899; Severin 1967; Von Hagen 1955). Perhaps a more correct image will emerge as current research focusing on the de Soto expedition and its impact on the native peoples of La Florida reaches the public.

Despite being the subject of many books and articles, the details of de Soto's early life remain shrouded in time. Much of the known information has been summarized in John Swanton's *De Soto Expedition Commission Report* first published in 1939 and reprinted in 1985. A modern scholarly biography of de Soto remains to be written.

Hernando de Soto was born about 1500 in Jerez de los Caballeros in Spain. Jerez is in Extremadura, an area of Spain that produced a number of New World conquistadores, including Vasco Núñez de Balboa, Hernándo Cortés, and Francisco Pizarro. De Soto's aristocratic family had received honors for military exploits during the *reconquista*, the wars against the Islamic peoples who had conquered the Hispanic peninsula in the eighth century. His family's military successes had embellished their crest and gained knighthood for various family members.

Almost nothing is known of de Soto's early years in Spain. Probably in 1514 he sailed to the New World in a fleet accompanying the newly named governor of Castillo del Oro, Spain's Central American colony in what is now Panama. He would remain in Central America for the next 17 years.

During the 1520s de Soto, as a captain, participated in military actions against both native peoples and rival Spanish factions in Panama and Nicaragua. He gradually amassed status and wealth, the latter derived in part from dealing in native slaves and from wealth taken from native peoples. With his successes he accumulated ships and a cadre of military aides, cavalry, and infantry. He had become a conquistador, who combined military prowess with business acumen and alliances. At times his military and business endeavors were carried out in partnership with Hernan Ponce de León and Francisco Pizarro.

In 1531 de Soto left Central America as a part of the Spanish army that looted the Inca civilization in highland South America. It was as a result of that conquest that Francisco Pizarro would etch his name on the list of New World conquistadores. By 1535, when he left Peru to return to Spain, de Soto had himself acquired great wealth and added to his reputation as a military force to be reckoned with.

In Spain he married Isabella de Bobadilla, the daughter of the Castillo del Oro governor whom he had first accompanied to Central America in 1514. De Soto was received at court and was probably lauded as a New World success story. Indeed, by the standards of the day he was a hero, having participated in military adventures that brought him status and wealth. But apparently he sought more wealth, and he petitioned the Spanish crown to allow him to explore and conquer additional New World lands. Initially he sought the rights to either lands in Ecuador and Colombia, located north of Pizarro's holdings, or in Guatemala. His requests were denied. Instead he negotiated a contract that charged him to conquer, pacify, and settle La Florida, the land first named by Juan Ponce de León a quarter century before and which thus far had thwarted Spanish ambitions.

THE LA FLORIDA EXPEDITION

The *asiento* or contract between Carlos V and Hernando de Soto is dated April 20, 1537. It is reprinted here as an appendix in Buckingham Smith's translations of the narratives of the Gentleman of Elvas and Luis Hernández de Biedma. The charter required de Soto to take men and supplies for 18 months and to settle 200 leagues of coastline as well as to build three stone forts. In return de Soto, who was named governor of Cuba to allow him to use that colony as a support base and staging area for the La Florida expedition, was to receive lands, titles, and a share of the profits from the Florida colony. Apparently de Soto funded the expedition with his own capital, wealth taken from the Inca.

Included in the army that de Soto and his aides organized were mounted knights with their entourages, field camps, and equipment; foot soldiers (including pikemen, crossbowmen, and arquebusiers); and a variety of craftsmen, including tailors, shoemakers, stocking-makers, notaries, farriers, and trumpeters. Catholic priests were members of the expedition as were two Spanish women, one of whom was killed on the route. Accounts of the number of Europeans that were on the expedition differ, but it seems certain that more than 600 people landed with de Soto; if that figure does not include servants, the actual number may be much higher. The army would swell to more than one thousand with the addition of native bearers who were forced to serve the Spanish.

The expedition was organized as an army, with officers and a chain of command and various units. Scout parties marched ahead to locate native villages with stored food supplies that could be used to feed the army. Other units reconnoitered along the army's flanks, exploring and raiding. The entrada would cut a wide swath through the territories of the native peoples, whose ancestors had lived in La Florida for thousands of years.

In 1538 the expedition sailed from Spain to Cuba, where de Soto assumed the governorship, organized and trained his army, and made final plans. A pilot was sent ahead to locate the debarkation point on the Gulf of Mexico coast, a large protected harbor called Bahia Honda (Tampa Bay). Bahia Honda had been known previously; it appears on pre-de Soto Spanish maps and is described in the pre-1540 Chaves derrotero (Castañeda, Cuesta, and Hernández 1983). Prior to sailing from Cuba with the main fleet, de Soto wrote his will and appointed his wife as acting governor of Cuba in his absence.

The ships carrying the army and its supplies anchored off the south end of the mouth of Bahia Honda in late May 1539; apparently they were a few miles south of the southernmost channel leading into the harbor. To locate the entrance, de Soto, his chief pilot, and Juan Añasco, who served the King as an auditor but whom de Soto appointed as a captain of cavalry, boarded a brigantine and went ashore to determine their location and, probably, to take possession of the land for their sovereign. Their initial landfall was probably just west or southwest of Bradenton.

Once ashore the winds shifted, and they became stranded for the night. By the time they were able to return to the fleet the next day, other boats had located the channel into Tampa Bay, and the fleet began to move into it, along the southern shore, to seek safe anchorage and a place to offload supplies and establish a basecamp. De Soto renamed the bay Espiritu Santo, a name that appears on later maps.

The camp was established within an Indian town, probably near the mouth of the Little Manatee River. Over the next six weeks the Spaniards scouted the surrounding territory, gathered intelligence, and organized their next move. In July, leaving behind perhaps more than 100 people at the base camp, de Soto, with at least 500 Spaniards, native bearers, horses, and a drove of pigs brought as food on the hoof and to stock the soon-to-be-established settlements, began their northward march.

During the late summer and early fall, the army traveled almost due north through peninsular Florida before turning west and marching through the territory of the Apalachee Indians to Anhaica, the principal town of the Apalachee. This town is the recently discovered and excavated Governor Martin archaeological site in downtown Tallahassee (Ewen 1988, 1989). At Anhaica, reached on October 6, 1539, de Soto and his army would spend their first La Florida winter.

A party was sent to the adjacent Gulf coast to mark a place where the supplies left behind at Espiritu Santo could be brought by ship and offloaded. Twenty cavalry were sent back along the overland route to Tampa Bay to order the camp to be broken, the supplies brought by ship to the coast near Anhaica, and the men from the base camp to march by land and join the main body of the army at their winter camp. All of these things were accomplished and by the end of the year the expedition, resupplied and with the reenforcements from Tampa Bay, set about planning their penetration into the interior of La Florida. Apparently de Soto was seeking Chicora, a rumored (and imaginary) rich native province believed by the Spanish to be located in interior South Carolina (see Hoffman 1984).

In March 1540, the army, led by native guides, broke camp and marched north-northeast across Georgia, crossing the Savannah River into South Carolina and reaching the province of Cofitachequi, where they found freshwater pearls but not the gold or silver they sought. They turned northwesterly and traveled into North Carolina and across the Appalachian mountains into the Tennessee River Valley in eastern Tennessee, reaching one end of the vast native province of Coosa. De Soto and his army then turned southwesterly, marching through Coosa, passing through one town after another for more than 200 miles before leaving Coosa territory. They traveled through the heartland of a province that was at its height; the Spaniards saw firsthand grandeur and native accomplishments that no European had ever seen before and that would never be seen again. By the time members of the Tristán de Luna expedition reached Coosa 20 years later, disease and the aftermath of de Soto's entrada had taken its toll. The native societies of La Florida had been changed forever.

In south-central Alabama the Spaniards were almost defeated by warriors of Chief Tuscaluza at his town of Mobila. The bloody battle resulted in 3000 natives slain and the destruction of much of the Spaniards' supplies. De Soto could have opted to march southward from that point to the Gulf coast where he had previously arranged a rendezvous with one of his ships. Instead he chose to turn north-northwest and seek the wealth that was proving so elusive.

They marched into Mississippi, where they spent the second winter in La Florida and where they fought another great battle. In May 1541 the army reached the Mississippi River.

The next year was spent in Arkansas, traveling from town to town, some of which were as large as the villages they had left behind in Spain. They saw remarkable things, and their firsthand accounts provide us with extraordinary information and descriptions of the native peoples. But Arkansas, like the lands east of the Mississippi River, did not contain large deposits of mineral wealth. De Soto was unable to find the mines that would furnish him with a location to establish settlements.

In late spring 1541, the army returned to the Mississippi River, where de Soto died, perhaps of malaria, on June 20, 1541. Luis de Moscoso took over as leader of the army. Tattered, torn, and unsuccessful in their quest to find wealth and establish a colony, the Spaniards turned from conquest to survival. The backswamps along the Mississippi thwarted their attempts to follow its banks southward to its mouth, from which point the army could have reached New Spain (Mexico) by marching along the Gulf of Mexico. Instead the Spaniards decided to march overland, across southern Arkansas, northwest Louisiana, and southern Texas to Mexico. But that attempt proved unsuccessful; the native societies of southern Texas did not have the stored food supplies that had sustained the Spaniards elsewhere in La Florida. Faced with possible starvation if they continued, Moscoso and his army turned around and retraced their footsteps to the Mississippi River. Six months, the last half of 1542, had been spent on the failed journey.

During the first six months of 1543, they camped adjacent to the river and built boats. In late June they set out, paddling down the Mississippi and reaching the Gulf of Mexico 20 days later. On September 10, 1543, the 311 survivors reached safe haven, a Spanish settlement on the River of Panuco, near present-day Tampico, Mexico. Their incredible odyssey of more than four years had ended.

The Hernando de Soto expedition was a failure; its leader and half the participants had died and not a single one of its chartered goals was accomplished. On the other hand, the expedition did provide Spain with a great deal of information on the interior of La Florida and its people. Had gold or silver mines been found, no doubt Spain would have eventually established the interior settlements and routes that were sought.

The expedition also provides us with our only accounts of many of the native societies of La Florida at the time of European contact; they contain rich information on the indigenous chiefdoms, information that is important to our understanding of Native American cultures (e.g., Swanton 1932). But it is a horrible irony that even while providing those unprecedented descriptions, this same expedition helped to introduce the various diseases and disruption that brought about the demise of the native societies. The European exploration and colonization of La Florida and the entire New World brought about the deaths of millions of Native Americans and the demise of their indigenous way of life.

RESEARCH ON THE DE SOTO EXPEDITION

Our knowledge of the de Soto expedition comes primarily from four documents, all of which are firsthand accounts recorded by participants. All four have been translated into English and all are reprinted in this sourcebook. The first was written by a Portuguese knight from the town of Elvas. It was first published in Portuguese in 1557 and has been available in an English translation since 1866. Information on various translations of the Gentleman of Elvas account (as well as the accounts of Biedma and Ranjel) can be found in James Robertson (1933: 2: 397–412) and in Swanton (1985). A shorter firsthand narrative is by Luis Hernández de Biedma, who accompanied the expedition as a representative of the Spanish crown.

The third narrative, the most detailed, was recorded by Rodrigo Ranjel, de Soto's personal secretary. Ranjel's account has been lost, but the noted Spanish historian Gonzalo Fernández de Oviedo y Valdéz had copied it in the sixteenth century, preserving what is clearly the most important single source of information on the expedition.

Portions of a fourth firsthand account were discovered earlier this decade in the Spanish archives by historian Eugene Lyon. The Cañete fragment, a portion of a more lengthy account written by a priest, Father Sabastián de Cañete, who accompanied the expedition, was found in papers pertaining to Pedro Menéndez de Avilés's later colonization of La Florida. Apparently Menéndez or an aide took the pages of the Cañete account because they included information on Cofitachequi, where the freshwater pearls had been found.

These four documents provide the basic corpus of information that must be used to reconstruct and interpret the route of the de Soto expedition and to pinpoint the specific locations of the native peoples encountered. We can supplement the information in them, however, with additional sources. One is a secondhand account of the expedition authored by Garcilaso de la Vega (nicknamed the Inca because his mother was a native woman from Peru) that is based on interviews with survivors and other sources of information (Garcilaso de la Vega 1951). Approximately one-quarter of the manuscript was completed by 1587, and it was not until 1599 that it was completed, more than a half-century after the expedition took place. Consequently, much of the information in the account is jumbled or exaggerated (for a critique, see Henige 1986). Unfortunately, the Garcilaso de la Vega account has been widely circulated and used by a number of people as the basis for their research on the expedition, resulting in erroneous conclusions. Many of the novels and books about de Soto and his La Florida expedition also have used Garcilaso as their major source of information.

Other information on the events of the expedition can also be found in two studies of the survivors. One, by Lockhardt (1972) contains information on members of the army who returned to Peru (some of de Soto's men were veterans of his activities among the Inca in the early 1530s). The second, by Ignacio Avellaneda (1989), presents information from testimonies provided by survivors in Mexico and elsewhere. One such document is included as an appendix in the Smith translation of the Gentleman of Elvas and the Biedma narratives reprinted in this volume. Avellaneda's excellent archival research points out the need for more such studies.

Additional documents pertinent to the expedition and, especially, its aftermath, are discussed in Robertson (1933: 2: 412–418). As might be expected, the failure of the expedition generated lawsuits and hearings whose official records, though containing little about the route per se, help us to understand the organization of Spanish expeditions to the New World.

These various documentary sources combined with cartographic information and geographical interpretations have provided various researchers with grist for their attempts to trace the de Soto expedition's route. Perhaps the earliest appeared in 1788 (*Columbian Magazine* 1788) and is based on the Elvas narrative, supplemented by Garcilaso de la Vega's account as published by the Spanish historian Antonio de Herrera y Tordesillas in the early seventeenth century. The author of the article traces the route and argues that de Soto and his army did not reach the Ohio River and could not be responsible for the earthworks observed there (viz. Webster 1788, who argues that the earthworks on the Ohio, as well as in Georgia, the Carolinas, and on the Mississippi

River, were built by de Soto's army; today it is known that the "fortifications" were made by prehistoric Native Americans).

During the nineteenth and early twentieth centuries, while de Soto was becoming an American hero, many individuals were using various of the narratives to reconstruct all or portions of his route (see Andrews 1917; Choate 1903; Jones 1880; Lewis 1903; Phinney 1925; Pickett 1849; Rowland 1927; Shipp 1881; Steck 1932; Westcott 1888). As the four hundredth anniversary of the de Soto expedition approached in 1939, still another generation of scholars went to work on reconstructions of the route (Boyd 1938; Swanton 1938). The federally mandated De Soto Expedition Commission, with John Swanton of the Smithsonian Institution as chair of the research committee, published its overview in 1939 (Swanton 1985). Over the years the report has generated a number of additional studies and dissenting interpretations (Baber 1942; Bullen 1952; Gibson 1968; Lankford 1977; McWilliams 1968; Pittman 1965; Schell 1966; Swanton 1952a, 1952b, 1953; True 1954; Weddle 1985; Wilkinson 1954; Williams 1986).

In 1954, John M. Goggin, an archaeologist, published a seminal article in de Soto studies entitled, "Are There de Soto Relics in Florida?" That study, although very out of date by today's standards, made clear the possibility of using archaeologically recovered artifacts to provide evidence of the route of the expedition. Studies of Spanish colonial artifacts and material culture that started in the 1960s (Fairbanks 1968a, 1968b; Goggin 1960, 1968), began to be applied to the study of de Soto in the 1970s (Brain 1975; Brown 1977, 1979). Today we have very good chronological controls for Spanish artifacts found in the southern United States and can define certain types associated with the de Soto expedition, items such as glass beads, hawks-bells, and iron tools given to the native peoples, and pieces of hardware and the like lost by the Spanish army (Brain 1985b; Deagan 1987; Mitchem 1989a, 1989b; Mitchem and Leader 1988; Mitchem and McEwan 1988; Smith 1982, 1983; Smith and Good 1982).

Artifact typologies are allowing archaeologists to associate specific archaeological sites with the de Soto expedition (see Smith 1987: 48–51 for a list of such sites; also, Curren 1987: 7–11; Ewen 1988, 1989: Little and Curren 1981; Mitchem 1989a, 1989b: 436–468; Mitchem and Hutchinson 1987; Mitchem and Leader 1988; Mitchem et al. 1985; Mitchem and Weisman 1984; Morse 1981). Such information, combined with cartographic and geographical data, has allowed new interpretations of the route tied to native villages which contain de Soto-related artifacts (Brain 1985a, 1985b; Curren 1986, 1987; DePratter, Hudson, and Smith 1985; Hudson 1989; Hudson, DePratter, and Smith 1984, 1989; Hudson and Milanich 1990; Milanich 1989; see Hudson

1987b and Knight 1988 for the methods by which these sources of data are used to interpret the route).

Reconstructions of the route of the de Soto expedition and the location of archaeological sites that correlate with native villages visited by the army are producing a gazetteer of native societies in La Florida at the time of European contact. Archaeologists can begin to use this "social geography" (Hudson, DePratter, and Smith 1989: 96) to study in detail the results of that contact on native cultures, using the de Soto era as a temporal baseline from which we can move backward and forward in time. The results are impressive. In the interior of La Florida, Marvin Smith (1987) has documented the archaeological correlates of the demise of chiefdoms. Other studies include Hudson (1987a); Hudson et al. (1985); Mitchem (1989b); Ramenofsky (1987); and Smith (1989).

The conclusions being generated by these and other studies point toward widespread depopulation and culture change in the sixteenth century. Both diseases and military actions were causal factors in the depopulation that occurred in La Florida (Blakely 1988; Mitchem and Hutchinson 1987; Mitchem 1989b: 483–498). As a result the native societies of La Florida in the early sixteenth century were greatly changed from those observed by Europeans and Americans in the late seventeenth and eighteenth centuries. The epidemics hypothesized by Dobyns (1983) did indeed take place and were devastating, although they might not have been pandemics that swept the New World; the jury is still out on that score (Blakely and Detweiler-Blakely 1989; Milner 1980; Snow and Lanphear 1988). Whatever the exact nature of the disease epidemics, the results were devastating.

The story of the Hernando de Soto expedition through La Florida in 1539–1543 that is contained in the primary documents reprinted here is much more than the story of an army's trek through unknown lands. It is also the story of the Native Americans of La Florida, peoples whose traditional ways of life underwent great changes in the sixteenth century. De Soto and the other conquistadores set the stage for European colonization of La Florida and the New World. But that colonization has been at the expense of the native peoples who lived here at the time.

REFERENCES

ABBOTT, JOHN S.C.
> 1873   *Ferdinand de Soto, the Discoverer of the Mississippi.* New York: Dodd, Mead & Co.

ALBORNOZ, MIGUEL
> 1972   *Hernando de Soto; el Amadís de la Florida.* Madrid: Ediciones de la Revista de Occidente.

> 1986   *Hernando de Soto: Knight of the Americas.* New York: F. Watts.

ANDREWS, DANIEL M.
> 1917   *De Soto's Route from Cofitachequi, in Georgia, to Cosa, in Alabama.* Lancaster, Pennsylvania: New Era Printing Company.

AVELLANEDA, IGNACIO
> 1989   *Los Sobrientos de la Florida: The Survivors of the de Soto Expedition.* Edited by Bruce D. Chappell. Research Publications of the P.K. Yonge Library of Florida History No. 2. University of Florida Libraries, Gainesville.

BABER, ADIN
> 1942   Food Plants of the De Soto Expedition. *Tequesta* 2: 34–40.

BLAKELY, ROBERT L., EDITOR
> 1988   *The King Site, Continuity and Contact in Sixteenth-Century Georgia.* Athens: University of Georgia Press.

BLAKELY, ROBERT L., AND BETTINA DETWEILER-BLAKELY
    1989   The Impact of European Diseases in the Sixteenth-Century Southeast: A Case Study. *Midcontinental Journal of Archaeology* 14: 62–89.

BLANCO, CASTILLA F.
    1955   *Hernando de Soto, el Centauro de las Indias.* Madrid: Editorial Carrera del Castillo.

BOYD, MARK F.
    1938   The Arrival of De Soto's Expedition in Florida. *Florida Historical Quarterly* 16: 188–22.

BRAIN, JEFFREY P.
    1975   Artifacts of the Adelantado. *Conference on Historic Site Archaeology Papers* 8: 129–138.

    1985a   Introduction: Update of de Soto Studies Since the United States de Soto Expedition Commission Report. In *Final Report of the United States De Soto Expedition Commission*, by John R. Swanton, pp. xi-lxxii. Washington, D.C.: Smithsonian Institution Press.

    1985b   The Archaeology of the Hernando de Soto Expedition. In *Alabama and Its Borderlands from Prehistory to Statehood*, edited by Reid Badger and Lawrence A. Clayton, pp. 96–107. University: University of Alabama Press.

BROWN, IAN W.
    1977   Historic Trade Bells. *Conference on Historic Archaeology Papers* 10: 69–82.

    1979   Bells. In *Tunica Treasure*, by Jeffrey Brain, pp. 197–205. Papers of the Peabody Museum of Archaeology and Ethnology, vol. 71. Harvard University, Cambridge, Massachusetts.

BROWN, VIRGINIA P.
1975   *The Gold Disc of Coosa.* Huntsville, Ala.: Strode Publishers.

BULLEN, RIPLEY P.
1952   De Soto's Uçita and the Terra Ceia Site. *Florida Historical Quarterly* 30: 317–323.

CASTAÑEDA, PAULINO, MARIANO CUESTA, AND PILAR HERNÁNDEZ
1983   *Transcripción, Estudio y Notas del "Espejo de Navegantes" de Alonso Chaves.* Madrid: Instituto de Historia y Cultura Naval.

CHOATE, CHARLES A.
1903   De Soto in Florida. *Gulf States Historical Magazine* 1: 342–344.

COLUMBIAN MAGAZINE
1788   Observations on the Travels and Transactions of Ferdinando de Soto in Florida; Intended to Prove that the Ancient Fortifications Discovered on the Banks of the Ohio, and other Inland Parts of America, were not Constructed by Him. September, vol. 2, no. 9, 477–489. Philadelphia.

CURREN, CALEB
1986   In Search of de Soto's Trail (a Hypothesis of the Alabama Route). *Bulletins of Discovery*, no. 1. Alabama-Tombigbee Commission, Camden.

1987   The Route of the de Soto Army through Alabama. *De Soto Working Paper* 3. Alabama De Soto Commission, University of Alabama, State Museum of Natural History.

DALY, DOMINICK
1896   *Adventures of Roger L'Estrange, sometime Captain in the Florida Army, of his Excellency the Marquis Hernando de Soto. . . an Autobiography translated from the Spanish.* London: Swan Sonnenschein & Co.

DEAGAN, KATHLEEN A.
1987   *Artifacts of the Spanish Colonies of Florida and the Caribbean, 1500–1800. Volume I: Ceramics, Glassware, and Beads.* Washington, D.C.: Smithsonian Institution Press.

DEPRATTER, CHESTER B., CHARLES HUDSON, AND MARVIN T. SMITH
1985   The Hernando de Soto Expedition: From Chiaha to Mabila. In *Alabama and Its Borderlands from Prehistory to Statehood,* edited by Reid Badger and Lawrence A. Clayton, pp. 108–126. University: University of Alabama Press.

DOBYNS, HENRY F.
1983   *Their Number Become Thinned: Native America Population Dynamics in Eastern North America.* Knoxville: University of Tennessee Press.

EWEN, CHARLES R.
1988   The Discovery of de Soto's First Winter Encampment in Florida. *De Soto Working Paper* 7. Alabama De Soto Commission, University of Alabama, State Museum of Natural History.

1989   Anhaica: Discovery of Hernando de Soto's 1539–1540 Winter Camp. In *First Encounters, Spanish Explorations in the Caribbean and the United States, 1492–1570,* edited by Jerald T. Milanich and Susan Milbrath, pp. 110–118. Gainesville: University of Florida Press.

FAIRBANKS, CHARLES H.

    1968a   Early Spanish Colonial Beads. *Conference on Historic Site Archaeology* 2: 3–21.

    1968b   Florida Coin Beads. *Florida Anthropologist* 21: 102–105.

GARCILASO DE LA VEGA

    1951   *The Florida of the Inca.* Translated and edited by John G. and Jeanette J. Varner. Austin: University of Texas Press.

GIBSON, JON L.

    1968   The DeSoto Expedition in the Mississippi Valley I: Evaluation of the Geographical Potential of the Lower Ouachita River Valley with Regard to the DeSoto-Moscoso Expedition. *Louisiana Studies* pp. 203–212.

GOGGIN, JOHN M.

    1954   Are There de Soto Relics in Florida? *Florida Historical Quarterly* 32: 151–162.

    1960   *The Spanish Olive Jar, an Introductory Study.* Yale University Publications in Anthropology 62. New Haven.

    1968   *Spanish Majolica in the New World.* Yale University Publications in Anthropology 72. New Haven.

GRAHAM, ROBERT B.C.

    1903   *Hernando de Soto: Together with an Account of one of his Captains, Goncalo Silvestre.* London: W. Heinemann.

HENIGE, DAVID

    1986   The Context, Content and Credibility of *La Florida del Ynca. The Americas* 43: 1–24.

HERRE, BENJAMIN G.
  1868   *De Soto's March: A Narrative Poem.* Lancaster, Pa.:
          Inquirer Steam Printing.

HOFFMAN, PAUL E.
  1984   The Chicora Legend and Franco-Spanish Rivalry. *Florida
          Historical Quarterly* 62: 419–438.

HOLFORD, CASTELLO N.
  1884   *Cofachiqui and Other Poems.* Wisc.: Bloomington.

HUDSON, CHARLES
  1987a   An Unknown South: Spanish Explorers and Southeastern
          Chiefdoms. In *Visions and Revisions, Ethnohistoric
          Perspectives on Southern Cultures,* edited by George
          Sabo III and William M. Schneider, pp. 6–24. Southern
          Anthropological Society Proceedings 20. Athens: Univer-
          sity of Georgia Press.

  1987b   The Uses of Evidence in Reconstructing the Route of the
          Hernando de Soto Expedition. *De Soto Working Paper* 1.
          Alabama De Soto Commission, University of Alabama,
          State of Museum of Natural History.

  1989   De Soto in Alabama. *De Soto Working Paper* 10. Alabama
          De Soto Commission, University of Alabama, State
          Museum of Natural History.

HUDSON, CHARLES, CHESTER DEPRATTER, AND MARVIN T. SMITH
  1984   The Hernando de Soto Expedition: From Apalachee to
          Chiaha. *Southeastern Archaeology* 3: 65–77.

  1989   Hernando de Soto's Expedition through the Southern
          United States. In *First Encounters, Spanish Explorations in
          the Caribbean and the United States, 1492–1570,* edited by
          Jerald T. Milanich and Susan Milbrath, pp. 77–98.
          Gainesville: University of Florida Press.

HUDSON, CHARLES, AND JERALD T. MILANICH
1990   *Hernando de Soto and the Florida Indians.* Gainesville: University of Florida Press.

HUDSON, CHARLES, MARVIN SMITH, DAVID HALLY, RICHARD POLHEMUS, AND CHESTER DEPRATTER
1985   Coosa: A Chiefdom in the Sixteenth Century Southeastern United States. *American Antiquity* 50: 723–737.

IRVING, THEODORE
1835   *The Conquest of Florida, by Hernando de Soto.* Philadelphia: Carey, Lea & Blanchard.

JENNINGS, JOHN EDWARD
1959   *The Golden Eagle; a Novel Based on the Fabulous Life and Times of the Great Conqistador Hernando de Soto, 1500–1542.* New York: Putnam.

JONES, CHARLES C.
1880   *Hernando de Soto. The Adventures Encountered and the Route Pursued by the Adelantado during his March through the . . . State of Georgia.* Savannah: J.H. Estill.

KING, GRACE E.
1898   *De Soto and his Men in the Land of Florida.* New York: Macmillan.

KNIGHT, VERNON J., JR.
1988   A Summary of Alabama's de Soto Mapping Project and Project Bibliography. *De Soto Working Paper* 9. Alabama De Soto Commission, University of Alabama, State Museum of Natural History.

KNOOP, FAITH Y.

1940   *Quest of the Cavaliers: De Soto and the Spanish Explorers.*
New York and Toronto: Longmans, Green and Co.

KNOWLES, CHARLES E.

1912   *In Quest of Gold; being a Romance Dealing with the Remarkable Expedition of Ferdinand De Soto and his
Cavaliers to Florida in the Year 1539.* New York: John Lane
and Co.

LANKFORD, GEORGE

1977   A New Look at de Soto's Route through Alabama. *Journal
of Alabama Archaeology* 23: 11–36.

LEFEVRE, EDWIN

1836   The Conquest of Florida. *Museum* 27: 130–132.

LEWIS, THEODORE H.

1903   The Chronicle of De Soto's Expedition. *Publications of the
Mississippi Historical Society* 7: 379–397.

LITTLE, KEITH, AND CALEB B. CURREN, JR.

1981   Site 1Ce308: A Protohistoric Site on the Upper Coosa River,
Alabama. *Journal of Alabama Archaeology* 27: 117–124.

LOCKHARDT, JAMES M.

1972   *The Men of Cajamarca; A Social and Biographical Study of
the First Conquerers of Peru.* Austin: University of Texas
Press.

LYTLE, ANDREW N.
1941   *At the Moon's Inn.* Indianapolis and New York: Bobbs-Merrill Company.

McWILLIAMS, TENNANT S.
1968   The DeSoto Expedition in the Mississippi Valley II: Armada on the Mississippi. *Louisiana Studies:* 213–227.

MALONE, WALTER
1914   *Hernando de Soto.* New York and London: G.P. Putnam's Sons.

MANSELL, THOMAS
1879   *DeSoto and Other Poems.* St. Louis: Hugh R. Hildreth Printing Company.

MAYNARD, THEODORE
1930   *De Soto and the Conquistadors.* New York and London: Longmans, Green and Co.

MILANICH, JERALD T.
1989   Hernando de Soto and the Expedition in Florida: An Overview. *Florida Anthropologist* 42:303–316.

MILNER, GEORGE R.
1980   Epidemic Disease in the Postcontact Southeast: An Appraisal. *Midcontinental Journal of Anthropology* 5: 39–56.

MITCHEM, JEFFREY M.

    1989a   Artifacts of Exploration: Archaeological Evidence from Florida. In *First Encounters, Spanish Explorations in the Caribbean and the United States, 1492–1570*, edited by Jerald T. Milanich and Susan Milbrath, pp. 99–109. Gainesville: University of Florida Press.

    1989b   *Redefining Safety Harbor: Late Prehistoric/Protohistoric Archaeology in West Peninsular Florida.* Ph.D. dissertation, University of Florida. Ann Arbor: University Microfilms.

MITCHEM, JEFFREY M., AND DALE L. HUTCHINSON

    1987   Interim Report on Archaeological Research at the Tatham Mound, Citrus County, Florida: Season III. *Miscellaneous Project Report Series* 30. Department of Anthropology, Florida Museum of Natural History, Gainesville.

MITCHEM, JEFFREY M., AND JONATHAN M. LEADER

    1988   Early Sixteenth Century Beads from Tatham Mound, Citrus County, Florida: Data and Interpretations. *Florida Anthropologist* 41: 42–60.

MITCHEM, JEFFREY M., AND BONNIE G. MCEWAN

    1988   New Data on Early Bells from Florida. *Southeastern Archaeology* 7: 39–48.

MITCHEM, JEFFREY M., MARVIN T. SMITH, ALBERT C. GOODYEAR, AND ROBERT R. ALLEN

    1985   Early Spanish Contact on the Florida Gulf Coast: The Weeki Wachee and Ruth Smith Mounds. In *Indians, Colonists, and Slaves: Essays in Memory of Charles H. Fairbanks*, edited by Kenneth W. Johnson, Jonathan M. Leader, and Robert C. Wilson, pp. 179–219. Florida Journal of Anthropology Special Publication 4, Gainesville.

Mitchem, Jeffrey M., and Brent R. Weisman
1984 Excavations at the Ruth Smith Mound (8C1200). *Florida Anthropologist* 37: 100–112.

Montgomery, Elizabeth R.
1964 *A World Explorer: Hernando de Soto.* Champaign, Ill.: Garrard Publishing Company.

Morse, Phyllis A.
1981 Parkin: The 1978–1979 Archeological Investigations of a Cross Country Arkansas Site. *Arkansas Archaeological Survey Series* 13.

Ober, Frederick A.
1906 *Ferdinand De Soto and the Invasion of Florida.* New York and London: Harper and Brothers.

Pérez Cabrera, José Manuel
1939 *El Capitán Hernando de Soto, Gobernador de la Isla Fernandina de Cuba, Adelantado de la Florida....* Havana.

Peter, Lily
1983 *The Great Riding: The Story of de Soto in America, Retold in Verse.* Fayetteville: University of Arkansas Press.

Phinney, A.H.
1925 Narvaez and DeSoto: Their Landing Places and the Town of Espiritu Santo. *Florida Historical Quarterly* 3: 15–21.

PICKETT, ALBERT J.
1849   *Invasion of the Territory of Alabama by One Thousand Spaniards, under Ferdinand de Soto, in 1540.* Montgomery: Brittan & De Wolf.

PINCKNEY, PAUL
1899   The Romance of de Soto. An Autumn Thought. *Southern Home Journal* 4(5): 10–24.

PITTMAN, WAYNE D
1965   History of Hernando de Soto and Panfilo de Narvaez, Suwannee County, Florida: with Suggestions for Sites of Historical Markers and Recommendations of Lettering for the Board of Directors, Suwannee County Chamber of Commerce. Live Oak, Florida. Manuscript, P.K. Yonge Library of Florida History, Gainesville.

POSTEN, MARGARET L.
1967   *The Gold Seekers: The Story of Hernando de Soto; the People and Incidents in the Life of One of Spain's Most Colorful Conquistadores.* Minneapolis: T.S. Denison.

RAMENOFSKY, ANN F.
1987   *Vectors of Death: The Archaeology of European Contact.* Albuquerque: University of New Mexico Press.

ROBERTSON, JAMES ALEXANDER, EDITOR AND TRANSLATOR
1933   *True Relation of the Hardships Suffered by Governor Hernando de Soto and Certain Portuguese Gentlemen during the Discovery of the Province of Florida. Now Newly Set Forth by a Gentleman of Elvas.* 2 vols. Florida State Historical Society, Deland.

ROIG DE LEUCHSENRING, EMILIO
1939   Hernando de Soto, Cuba y la Conquista de la Florida. IV Centenario de la Expedición a la Florida, 1539–1939. Sociedad Colombista Panamericana, La Habana.

ROWLAND, DUNBAR, EDITOR
1927   A Symposium on the Place of the Discovery of the Mississippi River by Hernando de Soto. *Special Bulletin 1, Mississippi Historical Society.*

SCHELL, ROLF F.
1966   *De Soto Didn't Land at Tampa.* Ft. Myers Beach, Fla.: Island Press.

SEVERIN, TIMOTHY
1967   The Passion of Hernando de Soto. *American Heritage* 3: 26–31, 91–97.

SHIPP, BERNARD
1881   *The History of Hernando de Soto and Florida; or, Record of the Events of Fifty-six Years, from 1512–1568.* Philadelphia: Collins Printer.

SIMMS, WILLIAM G.
1888   *Vasconcelos: A Romance of the New World.* Chicago, New York: Belford, Clarke & Co.

SMITH, MARVIN T.
1982   "Eye" Beads in the Southeast. *Conference on Historic Site Archaeology Papers 1979* 14: 116–127.

1983   Chronology from Glass Beads: The Spanish Period in the Southeast, 1513–1670. In *Proceedings of the 1982 Glass Trade Bead Conference,* edited by Charles F. Hayes III, pp.

147–158. Research Records 16. Research Division, Rochester Museum and Science Center, Rochester, New York.

1987   *Archaeology of Aboriginal Culture Change in the Interior Southeast: Depopulation during the Early Historic Period.* Gainesville: University of Florida Press.

1989   Indian Responses to European Contact: The Coosa Example. In *First Encounters, Spanish Explorations in the Caribbean and the United States, 1492–1570,* edited by Jerald T. Milanich and Susan Milbrath, pp. 135–149. Gainesville: University of Florida Press.

SMITH, MARVIN T., AND MARY ELIZABETH GOOD

1982   *Early Sixteenth Century Glass Beads in the Spanish Colonial Trade.* Cottonlandia Museum, Greenwood, Mississippi.

SNOW, DEAN R., AND KIM M. LANPHEAR

1988   European Contact and Indian Depopulation in the Northeast: The Timing of the First Epidemics. *Ethnohistory* 35: 15–33.

SOLAR Y TABOADA, ANTONIO DEL

1929   *El Adelantado Hernando de Soto; Breves Noticias, Nuevos Documentos para su Biografía y Relación de los que le Acompañaron a la Florida.* Badajoz: Ediciones Arqueros.

STECK, FRANCIS B.

1932   Neglected Aspects of the De Soto Expedition. *Mid-America* 15 [new series vol. 4]: 3–26.

STEELE, WILLIAM O.

1956   *DeSoto, Child of the Sun; the Search for Gold.* New York: Aladdin Books.

SWANTON, JOHN R.

1932   Ethnological Value of the DeSoto Narratives. *American Anthropologist* 34: 570–590.

1938   The Landing Place of DeSoto. *Florida Historical Quarterly* 16: 149–173.

1952a   De Soto's First Headquarters in Florida. *Florida Historical Quarterly* 30: 311–316.

1952b   Hernando de Soto's Route through Arkansas. *American Antiquity* 18: 156–162.

1953   De Soto and Terra Ceia. *Florida Historical Quarterly* 31: 196–207.

SWANTON, JOHN R., EDITOR

1985   *Final Report of the United States De Soto Expedition Commission.* United States House of Representatives Document 71, 76th Congress, 1st Session. Washington, D.C.: Smithsonian Institution Press. Originally published 1939.

SYME, RONALD

1957   *De Soto, Finder of the Mississippi.* New York: Morrow.

TRUE, DAVID O.

1954   The Narvaez and De Soto Landings in Florida. Manuscript, P.K. Yonge Library of Florida History, Gainesville.

VARNER, JOHN, AND JEANETTE VARNER, TRANSLATORS AND EDITORS

1951   *The Florida of the Inca.* Austin: University of Texas Press.

VON HAGEN, VICTOR W.

1955   De Soto and the Golden Road. *American Heritage* 6(5): 32–37, 102–103.

WEBSTER, NOAH

1788   Letter to the Rev. Dr. Stiles, President of Yale College, on
the Remains of Fortifications in the Western Country. *The
American Magazine*, February, pp. 146–156. [Reprinted in
The Late Prehistoric Southeast: A Sourcebook, edited by
Chester B. DePratter. 1986. New York and London:
Garland Publishing, Inc.]

WEDDLE, ROBERT S.

1985   *Spanish Sea, the Gulf of Mexico in North American Discovery, 1500–1685.* College Station: Texas A&M University
Press.

WESTCOTT, JOHN

1888   *DeSoto in Florida; an Itinerary of the Route of Hernando de
Soto through Florida, . . . , and in Georgia as far as the
Ocmulgee River.* Palatka, Florida: Palatka News Publ. Co.

WILKINSON, WARREN H.

1954   *Opening the Case against the U.S. de Soto Commission's
Report and other de Soto Papers.* Jacksonville Beach: Alliance for the Preservation of Florida Antiquities.

WILLIAMS, LINDSEY W.

1986   *Boldly Onward: A True History Mystery.* Charlotte Harbor,
Florida.

WILMER, LAMBERT A.

1858   *The Life, Travels and Adventures of Ferdinand de Soto,
Discoverer of the Mississippi.* Philadelphia: J.T. Lloyd.

TRUE RELATION

OF THE

VICISSITUDES THAT ATTENDED

THE

GOVERNOR DON HERNANDO DE SOTO

AND SOME

NOBLES OF PORTUGAL IN THE DISCOVERY

OF THE

PROVINCE OF FLORIDA,

NOW JUST GIVEN BY A

FIDALGO OF ELVAS.

VIEWED BY THE LORD INQUISITOR.

1

NARRATIVES

OF THE CAREER OF

HERNANDO DE SOTO

IN THE

CONQUEST OF FLORIDA

AS TOLD BY A KNIGHT OF ELVAS

AND IN A RELATION BY

Luys Hernandez de Biedma

FACTOR OF THE EXPEDITION

TRANSLATED BY

BUCKINGHAM SMITH

NEW YORK

M DCCC LXVI

3

Entered according to Act of Congress, in the year 1866,

By John B. Moreau,

FOR THE BRADFORD CLUB,

In the Clerk's Office of the District Court of the United States
for the Southern District of New York.

ONE HUNDRED AND TWENTY-FIVE COPIES PRINTED.

4

LIFE OF SOTO

HERNANDO DE SOTO, whose name is conspicuous among the early
enterprises of discovery and conquest in both American continents,
was born at Xeréz, in the Province of Estremadura. He was of
good origin; his blood what is called noble in Spain, and so derived
from the four quarterings of ancestry. In his early youth, probably
in Sevilla, at the time the splendid armament was prepared at the
royal cost that conveyed Pedrárias to Castilla del Oro, Soto joined
the Governor, as one, perhaps, of the fifteen hundred men whom he
conducted. In the year 1514 he arrived at Nombre de Dios, a little
while after Balboa, looking from Panamá, made discovery of the
South Sea, which Magallanes afterwards called Pacifico.

Soto, under Francisco Hernandez de Córdova, was one of the
first settlers of what was afterwards known as Leon in Nicaragua.
He was early sent to drive Gil Gonzalez Dávila from that territory;
but he being still young, and with little military experience, Dávila,
under pretext of treating, rose upon him at daylight. Although his
men made brave resistance, they were overcome by a much feebler
force, losing a large amount of gold with their arms. The danger
of keeping so many prisoners induced the victor to set them at liberty at the end of three days, restoring their property, having first
made sure of their peaceful return to Leon.

Subsequently, Francisco Hernandez, finding a large number of
men unemployed about him, and an abundance of every material
for his design, strove to bring about a revolt, intending afterward
to ask of the King the government of the country. For having

B

opposed the measure, with a dozen others, Soto was seized and sent to the fort at Granada. With nine men, the Captain Compañon went to his relief; and, having liberated him, took the field, armed and on horseback, where he awaited Hernandez, who, although he had sixty men, would not venture a conflict, knowing that his person would be sought out over every other. Not long afterwards, Pedrárias captured his ambitious lieutenant and beheaded him.

Towards the year 1524, Hernando de Soto, Francisco Compañon, and Hernan Ponçe de Leon resided in the same town, associates in all that they possessed. They were wealthy, and in the respectability of their standing were equal, as also in their rank in life. Having good apportionments of Indians, they employed them profitably as herdsmen, and in gathering gold. Of Compañon we hear little. He died early; and in the will of Soto, made many years afterward, a number of masses are ordered to be said for the repose of the soul of that Captain.

Such are some of the brief and scattered notices found in the old books respecting the early days of the future Adelantado of Florida. The incidents are blended with the subjugation and settlement of Central America, as the history of his later years is inseparably connected with that of the conquest of Peru.

While Pedrárias governed Castilla del Oro, he transferred the capital of the Province across the Isthmus, from Darien to Panamá, on the ocean which, in the year 1513, his predecessor had beheld. From this point, in the course of years, small expeditions were fitted out by the colonists, to go southward by sea for traffic, and on discoveries. Andagoya was another explorer; and, in 1524, Pizarro followed the coast, in sight of the Andes, to the ninth degree of latitude south of the equator. The result of these enterprises was the evidence of the existence of the precious metals in large amount among the natives, and of emeralds, with the knowledge of an extensive, populous, and opulent Indian empire.

Pizarro, supplied with means by the friends who had before assisted him, taking with him the portion of gold that belonged of right to the crown, with specimens of the cotton and fabrics of the region which he had visited, as also of the jewels, plumes, and people of Tumbez, went to Spain to ask for the government of that country. While absent, in the year 1529, his friends, fearing that the enterprise might be taken in hand by Pedrárias, applied to three of the richest citizens of Leon to take part in it with Pizarro and his companions, Luque and Almagro; and they received the word of Hernan Ponçe that either he, Soto, or Companon would come to Panama for that purpose, and there await the arrival of their leader.

Pizarro returned, bringing with him four brothers, born, like himself, out of wedlock, and one, Hernando, legitimate. Luque and Almagro, who had found the means and given him their assistance (the former as the agent of a silent partner), were not pleased with the addition to their numbers of this kindred of the new Adelantado, although for Luque, who was of the Church, a bishopric had been provided. Almagro remained inactive until Pizarro promised to assist him to a government as extensive as the one conceded, when the territory should be won, and that the treasure, slaves, and effects of every nature, acquired by him, should be shared among the three; and that nothing should be asked of the King in behalf of the brothers until the fulfilment of these stipulations. At this juncture, Ponçe arrived with two cargoes of slaves. The vessels were added to the common stock on condition of paying their charter, the bestowal on Ponçe of one of the largest apportionments of Indians that should be made, and appointing Soto to be captain of troops, and governor of the principal place the invaders might occupy.

One hundred and eighty-five capable men embarked, with thirty-seven horses, the men bearing bucklers made of the staves of wine-barrels, almost impenetrable to either dart or arrow. Almagro remained to collect and bring away any other forces that might arrive. After a few days' navigation the Spaniards landed, and despoiled the unsuspecting inhabitants of Quaque of twenty thousand *pesos'* worth of gold and a large amount of precious stones. The vessels were immediately sent to take back the news and bring more men and horses.

The troops remained in quiet seven months, scourged by a sharp and novel disease. At that time a vessel arrived with some additional strength, when, relying upon the promise of soon receiving more, the army was put in motion. The Indians, alas! soon began to have a different impression of the white men from that before received; they were now discovered to be neither good nor averse to robbery; but false, cruel, and destructive. The object was to reach Tumbez; but the invader had little idea of the vast forces that the contending brothers, Guascar and Atahualpa, Princes of Peru, had marshalled, though, fortunately for him, in view of each other they regarded his arrival as a matter too trivial for present thought.

On the mainland near the Island of Puna, where the Spaniards lived for a long while, the force was joined by Belalcázar, with a company of thirty men and twelve horses; and in -the year 1531, Hernando de Soto arrived with two ships, bringing infantry and cavalry. The original force, which had been wasting away by a strange malady, being thus strengthened, the Commander, believing that the people of Tumbez were sufficiently gratified by the outrages they had been allowed to commit on those of Puná to give his men a friendly reception, determined to remove to the main. Opportunely a note was found in the hands of one of the Indians of that city, written by a Castilian left there on the occasion of its discovery, which ran: "Ye who shall come to this land, know that there are more gold and silver in it than there is iron in Biscaya." The greater part of the soldiery, however, only laughed at the paper, as a device to give them encouragement.

The Spaniards were astonished at the ruin of the city, wrought by war with Puná, and, it was said, by pest; but the sorest disappointment was felt by those from Nicaragua, who thought they had exchanged a paradise for disease and desolation. Some Indians, seeking to save their property, drew near to the strangers, and in conversation spoke of Cuzco, Vilcas, Pachacamac; of edifices having ceilings of gold and silver plate—news ordered to be immediately spread throughout the camp. Not to remain in idleness, the troops ranged the arid country in the hot sun; discovered a river in a green vale, over which passed the great highway of the Incas; and visited-a royal caravansera, where they drank from the cool waters.

Cautious in advancing the next step, only after consultation with the officers was it resolved to make reconnoissance about the skirts of the mountains, where were said to be masses of population, and, if possible, to find Chillemasa, the lord of Tumbez. This duty being intrusted to Soto, he directly set about to perform it, with a company of sixty cavalry and a small body of foot. Shortly after, Juan de la Torre came back, saying that he had fled from the Captain, who proposed to mutiny with that troop, and return upon Quito. The Commander passed over the intelligence delicately, and Soto, having proceeded with his guides as far as Caxas, came back. He spoke of having seen large edifices, and numerous flocks of the sheep and camels of the country. Among the articles of plunder that were displayed, the soldiers were particularly pleased with some tablets of fine gold. A portion of the royal road of the Inca Guaynacapa, for its grandeur, had awakened the highest admiration. The inhabitants, astonished that these people should venture so far away from their companions, united for their destruction; but coming hand to hand, many of the Indians were left dead, while they did little injury.

The people, at hearing the report from Soto, were delighted, and began to receive with less distrust the story the Indians had told of the magnificence of Cuzco, in which the great lord held his court and was served from urns and beakers of gold; where the country was productive and populous; the fanes lined with the precious metals—a tale they had before attributed to the fancy only of their General. Still, there were those who did not believe in the reality of such riches; and Francisco Ysaga is recorded as one who gave his steed to procure releasement from the service. Nor should we smile at the incredulity of what might have been a swine-herd of the *dehesas* of Estremadura; since, a few years earlier, in the reign of Ysabel, the sacred mass-bells were of bronze, and the sceptre of Castilla, which waved Colón westward, to throw open the Portals of the Ocean, was light, and only silver-gilded. The prisoners brought by Soto were questioned, and the objects of spoil being carefully considered, it was thought best to establish on the spot a permanent foothold. This, formed of invalid soldiers, was the town of San Miguel, which became finally seated at the junction of several rivers, in the broad and fertile vale of Piúra.

Hernando de Soto now went forward with a troop of horsemen, to observe the passing of Atahualpa, who, with a large force, was rumoured to be marching from Quito to Caxamalca, to oppose his brother, advancing from Cuzco. The army was found to be very large, and the Spaniards, at sight of it, quailed in view of the poverty of their numbers. Atahualpa, on the other side, having heard about the invaders, through the stories in circulation, sent a lord to see what people they might be. Wheresoever this emissary went, the Spaniards were supplied with subsistence from that moment less willingly than before. Having attired himself in the costume of a countryman, he set out to visit the camp. With a basket of guavas as a gift, he presented himself before the Chief, to excuse the Cacique of Mayabelica for having failed in rendering him obedience; but Pizarro, displeased, cuffed the *Orejon*, who thereupon returned to the Prince, speaking disparagingly of what he had discovered. He said the intruders scarcely numbered two hundred men, were the wash of the sea, had beards, were thieves, and went about carried on a kind of sheep, like that of Callao. After hearing this statement, Atahualpa gave himself no more concern about the strange people.

While the invaders paused to make the new settlement, information was diligently sought concerning the political difficulties of Peru, the customs of the inhabitants, their arms, manner of fighting, and their military force. The treasure in hand having been divided, the General borrowed of his friends and sent a large sum to Almagro, renewing to him the assurances of good faith, and urging that the forces at his disposal should be sent; for he had suspected that it was the desire of his companion to push his own fortunes at a distance, and Pizarro stood in need of his liberality, energy, and promptitude.

In September, 1532, the troop took its departure from San Miguel, in quest of Atahualpa—who, having proved successful in repeated battles over the forces of the legitimate heir of the crimson *borla*, held him pent up in Cuzco—and, on the third day, it stopped in the valley of Piúra, to learn more particulars, and make further preparations. The entire force now consisted of only sixty-seven cavalry, with a hundred and ten infantry having swords and bucklers, some with crossbows, and three or four bearing fire-arms. The crossbow-men, numbering twenty, were placed apart, under an officer. The Commander now boldly proclaimed that if there were any who would go back they might return to the town, where servants would be allotted them to labour, the same as had been provided for others who remained there ; for the fame of the Indian strength had alarmed the timid, and it was desirable to have those only who were willing to go forward, trusting more to the valour of a few than to the show of many.

Thus provided, the army began its march, the boldness of the leader well sustained by the courage of his companions. The way was found to be open and undefended, left so purposely, it was supposed, to allow them to march as far as they would from support. Words of peace and greeting were continually received, with gifts from Atabualpa. A message was returned, to say that the Spaniards were marching to his assistance, and to make known to him from the Vicar of Christ, and from the great temporal prince, the King of Castilla and Leon, that there is a God in heaven and on earth.

After many days, the Spaniards arrived where from the direct road to Chincha one forks to Caxamalca, which was chosen, though less favourable than the other to movement, and where there were natural defences. The men were told that the success of the enterprise was dependent on action ; to keep the other road, where they should be lost in time and place, was not the way to their object ; and that, after all, men have to die, with this difference, that some leave a name to be famous, while others are forgotten. Stimulated by this address, and reminded that in such a cause, when the Holy Faith is to be planted, Christians should look for divine assistance, the soldiers declared their wish to be led, and that, when the occasion should present itself, they would be mindful of their duty.

After a journey through vales at the foot of the ridge, the troops were allowed to rest a day before ascending. Forty cavalry and sixty infantry were selected with which to advance, intrusted to the experience of guides, leaving the rest in charge of the luggage. The way was steep and difficult. Fortifications were passed, and places that might have been favourably held stood vacant. The war between the brothers alone seemed to awaken interest and occupy the attention.

After several days' march, through a region cold from elevation, in the beginning of the year 1533, Caxamalca being at hand, the force was drawn up in three divisions. The place the Inca occupied was exactly ascertained, as well as the strength and position of his troops. On the evening of the 14th of November, the Spaniards entered the town, but found it nearly uninhabited. In the midst of a great plaza, within a triangular wall, were only some women in houses, who gave utterance to their sympathy for the fate that to them appeared to await the strangers. Nothing anywhere presented a welcome, or bore a friendly aspect.

A messenger sent to Atahualpa did not return; and it was thought proper that his army should at once be scrutinized. Hernando de Soto, in the character of ambassador, went, attended by fifteen horsemen, to gain the presence of the great monarch, and ask a grant of leave for the General to appear before him, and deliver the words sent by the King. From a tower the Indian tents were seen extending the distance of more than a league, that of the Prince rising in the midst.

At this time Hernando de Soto was in about the thirty-third year of his age. In person he was of moderate size, with breeding and manner becoming his condition. A fine equestrian, he was also skilled in the use of arms. Passing along on his charger, he leaped the banks of a water-course, and amid an astonished multitude rode up to where the army lay. In number it was estimated at thirty thousand strong—the divisions composed of archers, slingers, lancers, and mace-men. He reached the royal tent, and, his presence being announced, the chief inmates appeared. Atahualpa, accompanied by a retinue, sat on a rich stool, the imperial tassel decorating his forehead. In a low voice, with eyes fixed on the ground, he required that the Christian should be asked his purpose. He was told that the General of the white men had sent him salutations, and an invitation to sup with him in Caxamalca, or, if that could not be, then to dine the next day. The Inca bade him take back the royal thanks, and promised to come the next day: he afterwards added that he should be attended by his army, but that it need excite no apprehension. At this moment, Hernan Pizarro coming up with an equal number of horsemen, hearing what was said, made obeisance to the Inca. He declared that his Highness would be very welcome, even though he should bring his men armed, for nothing so delighted Spaniards as military spectacles. Atahualpa, understanding this person to be the brother of the General, raised his eyes and said, that from the banks of the Turicara the *Curaca* had sent him an iron collar, with word that, for the ill-treatment the Caciques had received from the white men, he had killed three of their number and a horse. Pizarro denied the charge, called Maya-belica a great knave, and declared that, even though the Chiefs had been treated badly, the people there were as so many turkeys, and all on those plains were not enough to take the life of a single horse. The conversation having ceased, beautiful women handed drink of maize to the Prince and strangers, in golden cups. Soto, remount-ing with *donaire*, coursed his steed in the royal presence. He skirmished, he charged, wheeled, curvetted, and, returning, halted so nigh to the royal stool, that Atahualpa felt the impatient blast of the nostrils of the beast, and the heat of his strength; still the native remained as composed as though he were accustomed to such pas-time. Calling to him some people who had fled, he reproved their timidity, telling them that in the country whence those animals came, they were like the sheep in Peru. The time, until the morn-ing, was spent on both sides in watchfulness and care. The captains visited the guards, the soldiers made every thing ready, and passed words of encouragement. Indian priests offered sacrifices, uttering supplications in their temples to the Sun. A squadron of men, apt in the use of the *laso*, were added to the warriors.

The next day Atahualpa, in slow and imposing procession, marched up to where the impatient Spaniards were expecting him within the walls; and thence he sent word to their com-mander to tie his horses and bloodhounds, or otherwise he should come no farther. With a body of eight thousand men, he shortly afterward entered the plaza, in the middle of which Pizarro awaited him, having fifteen chosen men, armed with sword and buckler. The Friar Valverde went forward, exhorting the Inca to peace. He held up a cross and presented a Bible, in which he said the commands of God were inscribed. The Prince took the book, turned it over, examined the leaves, and cast it aside, telling the friar to bring back the treasure and the thousand things of which the inhabitants had been robbed.

At this moment a shout arose from the warriors, which was followed by the beating of drums; Pizarro then waved a white shawl, the signal preconcerted for action. Thereupon Captain Pedro de Candia caused a gun to be fired, and directly began the discharge of the arquebuses, followed by the blast of trumpets and roll of kettle-drums, carrying consternation and fearful panic among the native host. The charge of horse succeeded. Detached bodies, issuing from several directions where they had been concealed, were led upon the defenceless squadrons by Hernan Pizarro and Soto; while the infantry, under Belalcázar and Mena, joining in the war-cry of "Santiago," attacked them with sword and crossbow. The General approached the litter, and, with his band, struck down the bearers; these were directly replaced, and they again by others, who took successively the posts of the fallen; first one and then another soldier rushed upon Atahualpa, till Pizarro interposed for his safety. Two thousand Indians were slain within a brief period of time, no one pretending to offer resistance. The spoil was immense. Jars of silver, jewels of gold, and rich stuffs, strewed the ground. Many *Curacas* were killed about the royal litter; many princesses and priestesses were taken, as well as the wives of nobles.

The Inca, pondering upon the mutations of fortune, observed that within a day, as it were, he was a victor over Guascar, and himself was vanquished. Seeking to extricate himself from present troubles, the unhappy Prince appeared only to have fallen lower in misfortune. He reckoned on the avarice of the white man, but had not calculated his possible perfidy. Thinking to regain his liberty at a price so extraordinary that when named the payment was considered impossible, he secretly ordered his brother to be drowned in the River Andamarca, incited to this course, not unlikely, by the policy of Pizarro. The room, nevertheless, which was the measure of the purchase-money, was duly filled from the gold and silver of Cuzco, of its temple, *guacas*, or receptacles of deceased kings, and from the oratories. The Inca, notwithstanding, was still detained. In the mean time, Almagro, who had been made field-marshal by royal commission, approached the city, and after being greeted on the road by his old comrade, who came out to meet him, he went directly to call upon the prisoner.

The treasure did not long remain undivided. In the allotment, Almagro probably shared with Pizarro according to their agreement; the Lieutenant-General, Hernan Pizarro, took the second portion in magnitude, and Soto the third, in amount twenty-three thousand five hundred and thirty-two *pesos*, each of the value of an ounce of pure silver.

About this time there were rumours of a purpose on the part of the Inca to bring war upon the Christians. They appear, however, to have had no better foundation than the tales of servants and the apprehensions of timidity, if they were not altogether produced by the Adelantado, in seeking a pretext to place the succession to the *borla* in question, by the failure of both pretenders to the empire. Taking occasion of the absence of Hernan Pizarro on a mission to Spain, Soto and Guevara, with some others, were sent to ascertain the truth of the report, that an army was to be found at a distant point; but before they could get back to make known the falsity of the news, which had before been suspected, Atahualpa, on a variety of charges, and with the sanction of the Dominican Valverde, was beheaded. The officers, on their arrival, reproached the Chief for the wantonness and excess of the action. Some had sought the society of the Prince, being interested in him through his admirable conversation, in which they discovered a strong understanding and an acute intellect. In those personages he might have found friends. Soto, whom the Adelantado had just before made lieutenant-general, was one of the gentlemen who had most pleased the captive, having at times, with chess and dice, relieved some of his heavy hours.

With the death of the two Princes, government was suspended, and society became entirely disorganized. Distant Provinces and late territorial accessions withdrew their allegiance: old lords regained their possessions, or new masters usurped them. Law was at an end. Life was nowhere safe for the Indian: the highways became infested with thieves, as the mountains with robbers. The downfall of the extensive monarchy was complete. It had lasted, from its rise, according to some computations, nearly four centuries;

but the perfection and extent of the public works on the soil attest for its civilization a much higher antiquity. In extent, along the sea, it measured from nigh the equator, southward, a distance of about thirty-five degrees of coast. One of kin, on the side of Guascar, was permitted to receive the crimson tassel.

The Spaniards, having tarried seven months in Caxamalca, advanced towards Cuzco with the newly appointed sovereign, Almagro conducting the vanguard. As they passed through Yanamarca, there lay the unburied corses of three thousand men, slain in a contest between the native factions. Approaching the beautiful valley of Xauxa, the Marshal was directed to advance with Soto and other officers. After traversing some distance they met a large body of Indians, who bade them begone from their country, and charged them with the murder of their King. · The stream was crossed, the Indians dispersed, and the Spaniards, weary of killing, returned to find that Pizarro had arrived. Provisions, deposits of fine cloth, and a large amount of gold in a temple, were the booty.

Belalcázar had been sent to command in San Miguel. Finding himself with considerable force from Panamá, he became ambitious to go back to make the conquest of Quito. A rumour prevailed that the Indians to the north were preparing an independency; and this, joined to the news brought by the late comers, that the Adelantado of Guatemala was making ready to subdue the Provinces of Quito, was enough to satisfy any scruples that might exist in the conscience of a *conquistador* as to what should be his proper course in the face of such temptation; so that when importuned to undertake the adventure, Belalcázar found no difficulty in acceding to the desire of his men, who believed the treasure of Caxamalca was as nothing compared with that of Quito, where the Court once had been held. One hundred and fifty well-appointed infantry and cavalry were got in readiness to march; but, as the event proved, to contend with no other enemies than cold, hunger, and severe fatigue.

Hernando de Soto went forward from Xauxa with sixty cavalry towards Cuzco. The soldiers distrusting their abilities to cope with the Indians in sight, and the Captain, who was considered to be a man of no less judgment than courage, finding himself surrounded,

16

addressed his men. He declared their only safety to be in giving battle; that their enemies were preparing, counting the strength they should meet, and increasing their numbers every hour. The Spaniards had hitherto met the inhabitants of the plains: these people were the Ayllos, living on the first ascent to the mountains. They appeared along the heights in masses, with clubs, darts, and slings, swearing by the Sun and the Earth to destroy this band of robbers, or to die themselves. Soto went foremost into action, the Indians, with yells, holding the ground with desperate firmness. Five Christians were slain outright, and two horses. The Captain, with one other, fought his way toward the eminences. Some who fell in the passage-way impeded the ascent of the rest, until two, having dismounted, placed themselves one on either side for defence, thus enabling others to get by. With these succours, the first that passed returned to assist those advancing; when the Indians, weary of the contest, drew off to a little distance, and the Spaniards betook themselves to the margin of a brook at hand. Eleven men and fourteen horses were injured. That night Almagro reached the pass, and, sounding a trumpet, was answered from Soto. In the morning the forces united, and easily scattered the natives. This rencontre appears to have been the severest the Spaniards experienced in the subjugation of the Incas.

In the year 1534, Pedro de Alvarado, having ships in readiness on the Pacific coast of Guatemala to go on discoveries in the west, according to the royal permission, hearing of the wealth of Quito, and considering it not within the limits of country assigned to Pizarro, directed his ambitious course thither by sea, with five hundred soldiers, of whom nearly the half were mounted. Among those he brought in his company was Captain Luis de Moscoso de Alvarado, the same personage who some years later, on the death of Soto, successfully conducted the retreat of his followers down the Mississippi to the shores of Mexico.

Alvarado, having arrived with his army on the coast of Peru, near the equator, marched into the interior. For a time he met no serious interruption. Towns of importance were surprised, and large quantities of gold procured from them. In ascending the Andes, the severity of the weather caused the loss of eighty-three soldiers: many negroes and natives of Guatemala likewise perished by the way. Three and four thousand *pesos* were given at first for a horse; but treasure itself was at last abandoned among the snows, with armour, and the victims of the elements. The mountains, nevertheless, were pierced, and the Adelantado halted not far from the River Bamba.

While Alvarado thus contended with hunger and cold, toiling along the rugged ascent to Quito, Pizarro was approaching Cuzco. Having overtaken Almagro and Soto, he sent them forward to meet a force reported to be advancing. It was encountered, and soon dispersed. Mango Inca, who had been raised by the natives in those parts to be their sovereign, finding no escape, delivered himself in state to the victors. The pillage of the city took place before the arrival of the Spaniards. When Soto entered Cuzco the Temple of the Sun had been rifled, and valuables to an immense amount carried away. Nevertheless, the plate remaining was considerable. Other things than the precious metals were now neglected; from their abundance losing all esteem in the eyes of the conquerors. Even silver, for the time, appeared to be unimportant. Soto had already shodden with it the horses of his troops. Of the precious stones, they who wished took what most pleased them.

Wild was the lament of the people on the occupation of their city by the strangers. Thousands bemoaned the loss of friends and homes, crying out to their gods, and cursing the dissension of Guascar and Atahualpa, who had brought desecration to their temples, and laid waste their most cherished possessions.

The news of the arrival and march of Alvarado having come to the knowledge of Almagro, he determined at once to oppose him. He sent word to Pizarro of what was passing, and then set out for San Miguel. Finding Belalcázar gone, there were not wanting those to intimate distrust of him—that he had marched to unite with Alvarado. The resolution of the Marshal was to follow on; and he came to Quito directly after the arrival of Belalcázar, while he was yet fruitlessly searching for treasure. Having tenderly chided the Captain for leaving his post, with a part of his well-disciplined soldiery he went to look for Alvarado, and found him near the Rio Bamba.

The fading fortunes of the Adelantado of Guatemala were too manifest for him to put them at issue even with the feebler force of Almagro, whose possession already of Quito, and his well-known liberality, were more than a match for the strength of his adversary. Several days of conference ensued, in which the Marshal insisted upon nothing less than an abandonment of the expedition, and the return of Alvarado whence he came. This was finally assented to on the part of Moscoso and Cladera, with the condition that one hundred and twenty thousand castellanos should be paid to the Adelantado, in recompense for the ships, outfit, and men to be left,—terms to which Almagro acceded.

Pizarro was well pleased with the treaty; but some unquiet spirits sought to awaken distrust of Almagro in his mind, with fears of the consequences of the friendship said to exist between him and Alvarado, that had for its object to unseat him in his government. From this time begin the factions and conflicts of the Pizarros and Almagros. Some of the best minded of their companions sought to restrain them, but only with occasional or momentary success. The conduct of the brothers of Pizarro was found insufferable to many, and the arrogance of Hernando was regarded to be as lofty as his aspirations. Soto prominently attempted to quiet the gathering storm, and, failing of success, prepared to remove from the scene.

Almagro made ready to accomplish the conquest of Chili, and Soto had the promise of the post of lieutenant-general; but, dissatisfied, he withdrew at length from the enterprise. This being the condition of affairs, in the year 1535, some gentlemen and soldiers, finding themselves in good circumstances of wealth, thought to fix a limit to their desires and return to their native land, warned by the rising passions among the conquerors. The love of riches, having been satisfied, was giving way to ambition of rule; and the Indian *borla*, now torn in fragments, no longer held them in brotherhood, as before, for safety, wealth, and renown.

In Spain Soto appears to have resided in Xeréz, and at court, probably, he met the widow of Pedrárias, with whom he had been acquainted in Nicaragua, first cousin to the celebrated Marchioness of Moya, lady of honour and life-long favourite of Ysabel of Castilla.

With her he contracted for espousals with her daughter, named,
after her, Ysabel de Bobadilla, and sent her in marriage-pledge six
thousand ducats. He became a knight of the Order of Santiago.
Being now in the vigour of life, he sought for a government beyond
sea. His first desire was to obtain one over the country extending
from Panamá to San Miguel; though he deemed that the most sterile
and unprofitable territory in the New World, yet he supposed the
unknown region lying to the east of Quito—the country of Canela—
might be made available; and if that concession could not be
secured, then he desired to have the *Adelantamiento* of Nicaragua,
with the privilege of sailing west towards the Spice Islands of the
South Sea, and the right to one-tenth of whatever he should discover in that direction, at his own cost.

About this time, the news of the utter loss of the armament
which set out to conquer Florida having arrived, Soto obtained the
grant of that country, from the River Palmas eastwardly to the
"Island of Florida," once ceded to Narvaez, with the Tierra-Nueva
adjoining it on the ocean, before conferred on Ayllón, having no
specific limit to the northward, but geographically bounded by the
Land of Estevan Gomez. Within four years from the time of landing in the country, he was to receive two hundred leagues of shore,
to be selected by him from what he might conquer and colonize,
where he should be Governor and Captain-General, with the dignity
of Adelantado for life, and High-Sheriff in perpetuity to his heirs.
Within that territory he had the right to select twelve leagues square
by the sea for his possession. Fifty negro slaves, of which one-
third should be female, were permitted to be taken to Cuba, and,
also by him, other fifty to Florida. If a king or cacique should
be taken, the Adelantado was to receive one-seventh part from his
ransom and the spoil of his goods; but if he should be killed in
any manner, either before or after capture, the King should receive
one-half, after deducting the fifth due to the Crown. These terms
appear to have been imposed to restrain atrocities such as were
committed by the conquerors on the native sovereigns of México,
Mechoacán, and Perú.

The better to command and afford whatever might be necessary
in the progress of this great undertaking, Soto was made Governor

of Cuba during the pleasure of the sovereign. In consequence, he subsequently took up stock-farms on the Island, whence to draw supplies, whether as invader or colonist—a feature in the plan of subjugation laid down with breadth to be carried out by the suggestions of experience, sustained by the General's individual resources.

It is to the testament of Soto that we are to look for more of his character than can be learned from those who have written rather of his actions than of his mind, or the kindliness of his heart. The endowments bespeak his pride, his piety, religious feeling, and magnificence: the bequests mark the munificence with which it was in his power to bestow. Portions were set apart for five maids of his wife, dependent on her kind favour; and from a source in perpetual rents, to be bought by amounts aloof from the hazards of his adventure, provision is made for marrying annually three destitute orphans, daughters of persons of his line to the fifth degree, "the poorest that can be found;" and if there should be none such, then those of noble ancestry in the same condition, "the poorest in the City of Xeréz." An equal rental is bequeathed to Doña Ysabel, and, when it can no longer avail her, to the marriage yearly of other damsels, in number and under circumstances like the first. The body of his mother, his own tomb and private chapel, his friends and dependents, with the repose of souls, are provided for.

The history of the life of Hernando de Soto while in Spain, as a man of fame and fortune, as well as of his subsequent career in America, may be read in the following account of his attempted conquest. The author, although a foreigner, has no more than any other writer allowed a word to fall from his pen disrespectful of the Adelantado. By him was he seen first in a position of affluence and splendor; then as he accompanied him thrice through the circle of the seasons, amid privations, anxieties, and bitter disappointment. If, in the course of that protracted march over the soil of our country, Soto should in instances be thought cruel,—as there were acts of severity he deemed necessary for "pacification," and the safety of his command,—they are not in excess of those of other captains of that age; nor must it be forgotten that the people of his country were as refined, enlightened, and humane as any of Europe.

D

By those who knew him was he deemed brave, prudent, and magnanimous. The estate which beckoned to his ambition was in extent a principality, the title accessory, a marquisate. These, in the prime of life, with still greater riches and wider honours than he possessed, appeared to sway temptingly towards his hand.

Such is an imperfect sketch of some of the more conspicuous passages in the life of Hernando de Soto, Captain in Nicaragua, Lieutenant-General in the conquest of Peru, Governor of Cuba, and Adelantado of Florida.

PROEM.

This book is a translation of the original Portuguese *Relaçam verdadeira dos trabalhos q̄ ho gouernador dõ Fernãdo de souto e certos fidalgos portuguezes passarom no descubrimẽto da prouincia da Frolida. Agora nouamẽte feita per hũ fidalgo Deluas*, printed at Evora in the year 1557, copies of which are very rare. Two translations into English have been published at London: the earlier, made by Richard Hakluyt, was first printed in 1609, with the title, "Virginia richly valued, by the description of the mainland of Florida, her next neighbour;" the later was printed in 1686, one year after the first edition in French was issued, of which it is a translation. The book was also printed in Dutch, in 1706.

The author of the *Relaçam* is unknown. At the time of making the original publication, as appears from the printer's notice, he was yet living. No doubt, he was one of the eight Portuguese gentlemen, spoken of in the text, who went from Elvas to join Soto at Sevilla, three of whom lost their lives in Florida. In the order they are mentioned, it is perhaps worth the remark, as possibly indicating the writer, that two named Fernandez are placed last; first Benito, who was drowned near Achese, then Alvaro, a survivor.

The narrative, as an early record of the country, and condition of the inhabitants, merits attention and study. The facts are stated with clearness and evident care. It is likewise an outward picture of affairs as they stood in the camp, or appeared from the marquee of the Adelantado. Some hints of their inner working, up to the

23

time of the death of Soto, may be learned from the *Historia General y Natural de las Indias.* Documents of the age, now published, attest the exactness of many statements, and time simply has unveiled the truthfulness of others.

The digression, giving a history of Ortiz among the Indians from whom he fled, probably the Calosa, a people living about the Capes of Florida at the earliest day,—to the country of Outina, as appears from some trace of the language of the people among whom the Spaniards landed, speaking the Timuqua tongue—is a happy union of incidents in native life, customs, and superstition.

The speeches of the Indians, however clothed in words, are after the Indian manner of thought, as they were probably rendered into Spanish by the ability of the Andaluz, long a captive among them. In more simple language, the ideas would have been brought nigher to nature.

That this account, fraught with instructive incident, has come to us untouched from the hand that wrote it, is matter for gratulation; since in two chronicles we have to lament over ruins that mark as many narratives to have existed, possessing a scope and interest not inferior to the present one. The production of Rodrigo Rangel, the private secretary of the Adelantado, afforded the material for the chapters, now incomplete, of Oviedo; and an account, composed by a captain who remained in America,—for which pictures in colours of the battle-scenes with the Indians of Florida were at one time in the cabinet of Philip II.—was the source whence Herrera drew supplies; while the dry and brief itinerary of Biedma has escaped to us undisturbed in the same official repository—the Council of the Indias. The *Florida* of the Ynca, on the same subject, belongs less to history than to romance.

To avoid confusion and error as to persons, the names of the Spaniards are given in the translation spelled in their own language, such as Soto and Añasco, instead of Souto and Dambusco. On the other hand, the reader is entitled to find the variety in the orthography of Indian proper names preserved in their irregularity, for observation and the benefit of criticism.

DISCOVERY OF FLORIDA.

RELATION OF THE TOILS AND HARDSHIPS THAT ATTENDED
DON HERNANDO DE SOTO. GOVERNOR OF FLORIDA, IN THE
CONQUEST OF THAT COUNTRY; IN WHICH IS SET FORTH
WHO HE WAS, AND ALSO WHO WERE OTHERS WITH HIM;
CONTAINING SOME ACCOUNT OF THE PECULIARITIES AND
DIVERSITIES OF THE COUNTRY, OF ALL THAT THEY SAW
AND OF WHAT BEFELL THEM.

CHAPTER I.

Who Soto was, and how he came to get the Government of Florida.

Hernando de Soto was the son of an esquire of Xerez
de Badajóz, and went to the Indias of the Ocean Sea,
belonging to Castilla, at the time Pedrárias Dávila was
the Governor. He had nothing more than blade and
buckler: for his courage and good qualities Pedrárias
appointed him to be captain of a troop of horse, and he
went by his order with Hernando Pizarro to conquer
Peru. According to the report of many persons who
were there, he distinguished himself over all the captains
and principal personages present, not only at the seizure
of Atabalipa, lord of Peru, and in carrying the City of

2

25

Cuzco, but at all other places wheresoever he went and found resistance. Hence, apart from his share in the treasure of Atabalipa, he got a good amount, bringing together in time, from portions falling to his lot, one hundred and eighty thousand cruzados, which he brought with him to Spain. Of this the Emperor borrowed a part, which was paid; six hundred thousand reaes in duties on the silks of Granada, and the rest at the Casa de Contratacion.

In Sevilla, Soto employed a superintendent of house-hold, an usher, pages, equerry, chamberlain, footmen, and all the other servants requisite for the establishment of a gentleman. Thence he went to Court, and while there was accompanied by Juan de Añasco of Sevilla, Luis Moscoso de Alvarado, Nuño de Tobár, and Juan Rodri-guez Lobillo. All, except Añasco, came with him from Peru; and each brought fourteen or fifteen thousand cruzados. They went well and costly apparelled; and Soto, although by nature not profuse, as it was the first time he was to show himself at Court, spent largely, and went about closely attended by those I have named, by his dependents, and by many others who there came about him. He married Doña Ysabel de Bobadilla, daughter of Pedrárias Dávila, Count of Puñonrostro. The Emperor made him Governor of the Island of Cuba and Adelantado of Florida, with title of Marquis to a certain part of the territory he should conquer.

CHAPTER. II.

How Cabeca de Vaca arrived at Court, and gave account of the country of Florida; and of the persons who assembled at Sevilla to accompany Don Hernando de Soto.

After Don Hernando had obtained the concession, a fidalgo arrived at Court from the Indias, Cabeça de Vaca by name, who had been in Florida with Narvaez; and he stated how he with four others had escaped, taking the way to New Spain; that the Governor had been lost in the sea, and the rest were all dead. He brought with him a written relation of adventures, which said in some places: Here I have seen this; and the rest which I saw I leave to confer of with His Majesty: generally, however, he described the poverty of the country, and spoke of the hardships he had undergone. Some of his kinsfolk, desirous of going to the Indias, strongly urged him to tell them whether he had seen any rich country in Florida or not; but he told them that he could not do so; because he and another (by name Orantes, who had remained in New Spain with the purpose of returning into Florida) had sworn not to divulge certain things which they had seen, lest some one might beg the government in advance of them, for which he had come to

27

Spain; nevertheless, he gave them to understand that it was the richest country in the world.

Don Hernando de Soto was desirous that Cabeça de Vaca should go with him, and made him favorable proposals; but after they had come upon terms they disagreed, because the Adelantado would not give the money requisite to pay for a ship that the other had bought. Baltasar de Gallegos and Cristóbal de Espindola told Cabeça de Vaca, their kinsman, that as they had made up their minds to go to Florida, in consequence of what he had told them, they besought him to counsel them; to which he replied, that the reason he did not go was because he hoped to receive another government, being reluctant to march under the standard of another; that he had himself come to solicit the conquest of Florida, and though he found it had already been granted to Don Hernando de Soto, yet, on account of his oath, he could not divulge what they desired to know; nevertheless, he would advise them to sell their estates and go,—that in so doing they would act wisely.

As soon as Cabeça de Vaca had an opportunity he spoke with the Emperor; and gave him an account of all that he had gone through with, seen, and could by any means ascertain. Of this relation, made by word of mouth, the Marquis of Astorga was informed. He determined at once to send his brother, Don Antonio Osorio; and with him Francisco and Garcia Osorio, two of his kinsmen, also made ready to go. Don Antonio disposed of sixty thousand reaes income that he received of the Church, and Francisco of a village of vassals he owned in Campos. They joined the Adelantado at Sevilla, as did also Nuño de Tobár. Luis de Moscoso, and Juan Rcdriguez Lobillo. Moscoso took two brothers; there went likewise Don Carlos, who had married the Governor's niece, and he carried her with him. From Badajóz went Pedro Calderon, and three kinsmen of the Adelantado : Arias Tinoco, Alonso Romo, and Diego Tinoco.

As Luis de Moscoso passed through Elvas, André de Vasconcelos spoke with him, and requested him to speak to Don Hernando de Soto in his behalf; and he gave him warrants, issued by the Marquis of Vilareal, conferring on him the captaincy of Ceuta, that he might show them; which when the Adelantado saw, and had informed himself of who he was, he wrote to him that he would favour him in and through all, and would give him a command in Florida. From Elvas went André de Vasconcelos, Fernan Pegado, Antonio Martinez Segurado, Men Royz Pereyra, Ioam Cordeiro, Estevan Pegado, Bento Fernandez, Alvaro Fernandez; and from Salamanca, Jaen, Valencia, Albuquerque, and other parts of Spain, assembled many persons of noble extraction in Sevilla; so much so that many men of good condition, who had sold their lands, remained behind in Sanlúcar for want of shipping, when for known countries and rich it was usual to lack men : and the cause of this was what Cabeça de Vaca had told the Emperor, and given persons to understand who conversed with him respecting that country. He went for Governor to Rio de la Plata, but his kinsmen followed Soto.

Baltasar de Gallegos received the appointment of chief Castellan, and took with him his wife. He sold houses, vineyards, a rent of wheat, and ninety geiras of olive-field in the Xarafe of Sevilla. There went also many other persons of mark. The offices, being desired of many, were sought through powerful influence: the place of Factor was held by Antonio de Biedma, that of Comptroller by Juan de Añasco, and that of Treasurer by Juan Gaytan, nephew of the Cardinal of Ciguenza.

CHAPTER III.

How the Portugues went to Sevilla and thence to Sanlúcar; and how the Captains were appointed over the Ships, and the People distributed among them.

The Portugues left Elvas the 15th day of January, and came to Sevilla on the vespers of Saint Sebastian. They went to the residence of the Governor; and entering the court, over which were some galleries in which he stood, he came down and met them at the foot of the stairs, whence they returned' with him; and he ordered chairs to be brought, in which they might be seated. André de Vasconcelos told him who he was, and who the others were; that they had all come to go with him and aid in his enterprise. The Adelantado thanked him, and appeared well pleased with their coming and proffer. The table being already laid, he invited them to sit down; and, while at dinner, he directed his majordomo to find lodgings for them near his house.

From Sevilla the Governor went to Sanlúcar, with all the people that were to go. He commanded a muster to be made, to which the Portugues turned out in polished armor, and the Castilians very showily, in silk over silk, pinked and slashed. As such luxury did not appear to him becoming on such occasion, he ordered a review to be called for the next day, when every man should appear with his arms; to which the Portugues came as at first; and the Governor set them in order near the standard borne by his ensign. The greater number of the Castilians were in very sorry and rusty shirts of mail; all wore steel caps or helmets, but had very poor lances. Some of them sought to get among the Portugues. Those that Soto liked and accepted of were passed, counted, and enlisted; six hundred men in all followed him to Florida. He had bought seven ships; and the necessary subsistence was already on board. He appointed captains, delivering to each of them his ship, with a roll of the people he was to take with him.

CHAPTER IIII.

How the Adelantado with his People left Spain, going to the Canary Islands, and afterward arrived in the Antillas.

In the month of April, of the year 1538 of the Christian era, the Adelantado delivered the vessels to their several captains, took for himself a new ship, fast of sail, and gave another to André de Vasconcelos, in which the Portugues were to go. He passed over the bar of Sanlúcar on Sunday, the morning of Saint Lazarus, with great festivity, commanding the trumpets to be sounded and many charges of artillery to be fired. With a favourable wind he sailed four days, when it lulled, the calms continuing for eight days, with such rolling sea that the ships made no headway.

The fifteenth day after our departure we came to Gomera, one of the Canaries, on Easter Sunday, in the morning. The Governor of the Island was apparelled all in white, cloak, jerkin, hose, shoes, and cap, so that he looked like a governor of Gypsies. He received the Adelantado with much pleasure, lodging him well and the rest with him gratuitously. To Doña Ysabel he gave a natural daughter of his to be her waiting-maid. For our money we got abundant provision of bread, wine,

3

and meats, bringing off with us what was needful for the ships. Sunday following, eight days after arrival, we took our departure.

On Pentecost we came into the harbour of the City of Santiago, in Cuba of the Antillas. Directly a gentleman of the town sent to the seaside a splendid roan horse, well caparisoned, for the Governor to mount, and a mule for his wife; and all the horsemen and footmen in town at the time came out to receive him at the landing. He was well lodged, attentively visited and served by all the citizens. Quarters were furnished to every one without cost. Those who wished to go into the country were divided among the farm-houses, into squads of four and six persons, according to the several ability of the owners, who provided them with food.

CHAPTER V.

Of the Inhabitants there are in the City of Santiago and other Towns of the Island,—the Character of the Soil and of the Fruit.

The City of Santiago consists of about eighty spacious and well-contrived dwellings. Some are built of stone and lime, covered with tiles: the greater part have the sides of board and the roofs of dried grass. There are extensive country seats, and on them many trees, which differ from those of Spain. The fig-tree bears fruit as big as the fist, yellow within and of little flavour: another tree with a delicious fruit, called anane, is of the shape and size of a small pine-apple, the skin of which being taken off, the pulp appears like a piece of curd. On the farms about in the country are other larger pines, of very agreeable and high flavour, produced on low trees that look like the aloe. Another tree yields a fruit called mamei, the size of a peach, by the islanders more esteemed than any other in the country. The guayaba is in the form of a filbert, and is the size of a fig. There is a tree, which is a stalk without any branch, the height of a lance, each leaf the length of a javelin, the fruit of the size and form of a cucumber, the bunch having twenty or thirty of them, with which the tree goes on bending down more and more as they grow: they are called plantanos in that country, are of good flavour, and

will ripen after they are gathered, although they are
better when they mature on the tree. The stalks yield
fruit but once, when they are cut down, and others, which
spring up at the butt, bear in the coming year. There is
another fruit called batata, the subsistence of a multitude
of people, principally slaves, and now grows in the Island
of Terceira, belonging to this kingdom of Portugal. It is
produced in the earth, and looks like the ynhame, with
nearly the taste of chestnut. The bread of the country
is made from a root that looks like the batata, the stalk
of which is like alder. The ground for planting is prepared in hillocks; into each are laid four or five stalks, and
a year and a half after they have been set the crop is fit
to be dug. Should any one, mistaking the root for batata,
eat any of it, he is in imminent danger; as experience
has shown, in the case of a soldier, who died instantly
from swallowing a very little. The roots being peeled
and crushed, they are squeezed in a sort of press; the
juice that flows has an offensive smell; the bread is of
little taste and less nourishment. The fruit from Spain
are figs and oranges, which are produced the year round,
the soil being very rich and fertile.

There are numerous cattle and horses in the country,
which find fresh grass at all seasons. From the many
wild cows and hogs, the inhabitants everywhere are abundantly supplied with meat. Out of the towns are many
fruits wild over the country; and, as it sometimes hap-
pens, when a Christian misses his way and is lost for fifteen or twenty days, because of the many paths through
the thick woods made by the herds traversing to and fro,

he will live on fruit and on wild cabbage, there being many and large palm-trees everywhere which yield nothing else available beside.

The Island of Cuba is three hundred leagues long from east to southeast, and in places thirty, in others forty leagues from north to south. There are six towns of Christians, which are, Santiago, Baracoa, the Báyamo, Puerto Principe, Sancti Spiritus, and Havana. They each have between thirty and forty householders, except Santiago and Havana, which have some seventy or eighty dwellings apiece. The towns have all a chaplain to hear confession, and a church in which to say mass. In Santiago is a monastery of the order of Saint Francis; it has few friars, though well supported by tithes, as the country is rich. The Church of Santiago is endowed, has a cura, a prebend, and many priests, as it is the church of the city which is the metropolis.

Although the earth contains much gold, there are few slaves to seek it, many having destroyed themselves because of the hard usage they receive from the Christians in the mines. The overseer of Vasco Porcallo, a resident of the Island, having understood that his slaves intended to hang themselves, went with a cudgel in his hand and waited for them in the place at which they were to meet, where he told them that they could do nothing, nor think of any thing, that he did not know beforehand; that he had come to hang himself with them, to the end that if he gave them a bad life in this world, a worse would he give them in that to come. This caused them to alter their purpose and return to obedience.

CHAPTER VI.

How THE GOVERNOR SENT DOÑA YSABEL WITH THE
SHIPS FROM SANTIAGO TO HAVANA, WHILE HE WITH
SOME OF THE MEN WENT THITHER BY LAND.

THE Governor sent Don Carlos with the ships, in
company with Doña Ysabel, to tarry for him at Havana,
a port in the eastern end of the Island, one hundred and
eighty leagues from Santiago. He and those that remained, having bought horses, set out on their journey,
and at the end of twenty-five leagues came to Báyamo,
the first town. They were lodged, as they arrived, in
parties of four and six, where their food was given to
them; and nothing was paid for any other thing than
maize for the beasts; because the Governor at each town
assessed tax on the tribute paid, and the labour done, by
the Indians.

A deep river runs near Báyamo, larger than the
Guadiana, called Tanto. The monstrous alligators do
harm in it sometimes to the Indians and animals in the
crossing. In all the country there are no wolves, foxes,
bears, lions, nor tigers: there are dogs in the woods,
which have run wild from the houses, that feed upon the
swine: there are snakes, the size of a man's thigh, and
even bigger; but they are very sluggish and do no kind

of injury. From that town to Puerto Principe there are fifty leagues. The roads throughout the Island are made by cutting out the undergrowth, which if neglected to be gone over, though only for a single year, the shrubs spring up in such manner that the ways disappear: and so numerous likewise are the paths made by cattle, that no one can travel without an Indian of the country for a guide, there being everywhere high and thick woods.

From Puerto Principe the Governor went by sea in a canoe to the estate of Vasco Porcallo, near the coast, to get news of Doña Ysabel, who, at the time, although not then known, was in a situation of distress, the ships having parted company, two of them being driven in sight of the coast of Florida, and all on board were suffering for lack of water and subsistence. The storm over, and the vessels come together, not knowing where they had been tossed, Cape San Antonio was descried, an uninhabited part of the Island, where they got water; and at the end of forty days from the time of leaving Santiago, they arrived at Havana. The Governor presently received the news and hastened to meet Doña Ysabel. The troops that went by land, one hundred and fifty mounted men in number, not to be burdensome upon the Islanders, were divided into two squadrons, and marched to Sancti Spiritus, sixty leagues from Puerto Principe. The victual they carried was the caçabe bread I have spoken of, the nature of which is such that it directly dissolves from moisture; whence it happened that some ate meat and no bread for many days. They took dogs with them, and a man of the country, who hunted as they journeyed, and who killed the hogs at night found further necessary for provision where they stopped; so that they had abundant supply both of beef and pork. They found immense annoyance from mosquitos, particularly in a lake called Bog of Pia, which they had much ado in crossing between midday and dark, it being more than half a league over, full half a bow-shot of the distance swimming, and all the rest of the way the water waist deep, having clams on the bottom that sorely cut the feet, for not a boot nor shoe sole was left entire at half way. The clothing and saddles were floated over in baskets of palm-leaf. In this time the insects came in great numbers and settled on the person where exposed, their bite raising lumps that smarted keenly, a single blow with the hand sufficing to kill so many that the blood would run over the arms and body. There was little rest at night, as happened also afterwards at like seasons and places.

They came to Sancti Spiritus, a town of thirty houses, near which passes a little river. The grounds are very fertile and pleasant, abundant in good oranges, citrons, and native fruit. Here one half the people were lodged; the other half went on twenty-five leagues farther, to a town of fifteen or twenty householders, called Trinidad. There is a hospital for the poor, the only one in the Island. They say the town was once the largest of any; and that before the Christians came into the country a ship sailing along the coast had in her a very sick man, who begged to be set on shore, which the captain directly ordered, and the vessel kept on her way. The inhabitants, finding him where he had been left, on that shore which had never yet been hunted up by Christians, carried him home, and took care of him until he was well. The Chief of the town gave him a daughter; and being at war with the country round about, through the prowess and exertion of the Christian he subdued and reduced to his control all the people of Cuba. A long time after, when Diego Velasquez went to conquer the Island, whence he made the discovery of New Spain, this man, then among the natives, brought them, by his management, to obedience, and put them under the rule of that Governor.

From Trinidad they travelled a distance of eighty leagues without a town, and arrived at Havana in the end of March. They found the Governor there, and the rest of the people who had come with him from Spain. He sent Juan de Añasco in a caravel, with two pinnaces and fifty men, to explore the harbour in Florida, who brought back two Indians taken on the coast. In consequence, as much because of the necessity of having them for guides and interpreters, as because they said, by signs, that there was much gold in Florida, the Governor and all the company were greatly rejoiced, and longed for the hour of departure—that land appearing to them to be the richest of any which until then had been discovered.

4

CHAPTER VII.

How we left Havana and came to Florida, and
what other Matters took place.

Before our departure, the Governor deprived Nuño
de Tobár of the rank of Captain-General, and conferred it
on a resident of Cuba, Vasco Porcallo de Figueroa, which
caused the vessels to be well provisioned, he giving a great
many hogs and loads of caçabe bread. That was done
because Nuño de Tobár had made love to Doña Ysabel's
waiting-maid, daughter of the Governor of Gomera; and
though he had lost his place, yet, to return to Soto's
favour, for she was with child by him, he took her to wife
and went to Florida. Doña Ysabel remained, and with
her the wife of Don Carlos, of Baltasar de Gallegos, and
of Nuño de Tobár. The Governor left, as his lieutenant
over the Island, Juan de Rojas, a fidalgo of Havana.

On Sunday, the 18th day of May, in the year 1539,
the Adelantado sailed from Havana with a fleet of nine
vessels, five of them ships, two caravels, two pinnaces;
and he ran seven days with favourable weather. On the
25th of the month, being the festival of Espiritu Santo,
the land was seen, and anchor cast a league from shore,
because of the shoals. On Friday, the 30th, the army
landed in Florida, two leagues from the town of an

Indian chief named Ucita. Two hundred and thirteen horses were set on shore, to unburthen the ships, that they should draw the less water; the seamen only remained on board, who going up every day a little with the tide, the end of eight days brought them near to the town.

So soon as the people were come to land, the camp was pitched on the sea-side, nigh the bay, which goes up close to the town. Presently the Captain-General, Vasco Porcallo, taking seven horsemen with him, beat up the country half a league about, and discovered six Indians, who tried to resist him with arrows, the weapons they are accustomed to use. The horsemen killed two, and the four others escaped, the country being obstructed by bushes and ponds, in which the horses bogged and fell, with their riders, of weakness from the voyage. At night the Governor, with a hundred men in the pinnaces, came upon a deserted town; for, so soon as the Christians appeared in sight of land, they were descried, and all along on the coast many smokes were seen to rise, which the Indians make to warn one another. The next day, Luis de Moscoso, master of the camp, set the men in order. The horsemen he put in three squadrons—the vanguard, battalion, and rearward; and thus they marched that day and the next, compassing great creeks which run up from the bay; and on the first of June, being Trinity Sunday, they arrived at the town of Ucita, where the Governor tarried.

The town was of seven or eight houses, built of timber, and covered with palm-leaves. The Chief's house stood near the beach, upon a very high mount made by

hand for defence; at the other end of the town was a
temple, on the top of which perched a wooden fowl with
gilded eyes, and within were found some pearls of small
value, injured by fire, such as the Indians pierce for
beads, much esteeming them, and string to wear about
the neck and wrists. The Governor lodged in the house
of the Chief, and with him Vasco Porcallo and Luis de
Moscoso; in other houses, midway in the town, was
lodged the Chief Castellan, Baltasar de Gallegos, where
were set apart the provisions brought in the vessels.
The rest of the dwellings, with the temple, were thrown
down, and every mess of three or four soldiers made a
cabin, wherein they lodged. • The ground about was very
fenny, and encumbered with dense thicket and high trees.
The Governor ordered the woods to be felled the distance
of a crossbow-shot around the place, that the horses might
run, and the Christians have the advantage, should the
Indians make an attack at night. In the paths, and at
proper points, sentinels of foot-soldiers were set in couples, who watched by turns; the horsemen, going the
rounds, were ready to support them should there be an
alarm.

The Governor made four captains of horsemen and
two of footmen : those of the horse were André de Vasconcelos, Pedro Calderon of Badajóz, and the two Carde-
ñosas his kinsmen (Arias Tinoco and Alfonso Romo),
also natives of Badajóz; those of the foot were Francisco
Maldonado of Salamanca, and Juan Rodriguez Lobillo.
While we were in this town of Ucita, the Indians which
Juan de Añasco had taken on that coast, and were with

the Governor as guides and interpreters, through the carelessness of two men who had charge of them, got away one night. For this the Governor felt very sorry, as did every one else ; for some excursions had already been made, and no Indians could be taken, the country being of very high and thick woods, and in many places was marshy.

CHAPTER VIII.

OF SOME INROADS THAT WERE MADE, AND HOW A CHRIS-
TIAN WAS FOUND WHO HAD BEEN A LONG TIME IN THE
POSSESSION OF A CACIQUE.

FROM the town of Ucita the Governor sent the Chief
Castellan, Baltasar de Gallegos, into the country, with
forty horsemen and eighty footmen, to procure an Indian
if possible. In another direction he also sent, for the
same purpose, Captain Juan Rodriguez Lobillo, with fifty
infantry: the greater part were of sword and buckler;
the remainder were crossbow and gun men. The command of Lobillo marched over a swampy land, where
horses could not travel; and, half a league from camp,
came upon some huts near a river. The people in them
plunged into the water; nevertheless, four women were
secured; and twenty warriors, who attacked our people,
so pressed us that we were forced to retire into camp.

The Indians are exceedingly ready with their weapons,
and so warlike and nimble, that they have no fear of footmen; for if these charge them they flee, and when they
turn their backs they are presently upon them. They
avoid nothing more easily than the flight of an arrow.
They never remain quiet, but are continually running,
traversing from place to place, so that neither crossbow

nor arquebuse can be aimed at them. Before a Christian can make a single shot with either, an Indian will discharge three or four arrows; and he seldom misses of his object. Where the arrow meets with no armour, it pierces as deeply as the shaft from a crossbow. Their bows are very perfect; the arrows are made of certain canes, like reeds, very heavy, and so stiff that one of them, when sharpened, will pass through a target. Some are pointed with the bone of a fish, sharp and like a chisel; others with some stone like a point of diamond: of such the greater number, when they strike upon armour, break at the place the parts are put together; those of cane split, and will enter a shirt of mail, doing more injury than when armed.

Juan Rodriguez Lobillo got back to camp with six men wounded, of whom one died, and he brought with him the four women taken in the huts, or cabins. When Baltasar de Gallegos came into the open field, he discovered ten or eleven Indians, among whom was a Christian, naked and sun-burnt, his arms tattooed after their manner, and he in no respect differing from them. As soon as the horsemen came in sight, they ran upon the Indians, who fled, hiding themselves in a thicket, though not before two or three of them were overtaken and wounded. The Christian, seeing a horseman coming upon him with a lance, began to cry out: "Do not kill me, cavalier; I am a Christian! Do not slay these people; they have given me my life!" Directly he called to the Indians, putting them out of fear, when they left the wood and came to him. The horsemen took up the Christian and Indians behind them on their beasts, and, greatly rejoicing, got back to the Governor at night-fall. When he and the rest who had remained in camp heard the news, they were no less pleased than the others.

CHAPTER IX.

How the Christian came to the Land of Florida, who he was, and of what passed at his Interview with the Governor.

The name of the Christian was Juan Ortiz, a native of Sevilla, and of noble parentage. He had been twelve years among the Indians, having gone into the country with Pánphilo de Narvaez, and returned in the ships to the Island of Cuba, where the wife of the Governor remained; whence, by her command, he went back to Florida, with some twenty or thirty others, in a pinnace; and cóming to the port in sight of the town, they saw a cane sticking upright in the ground, with a split in the top, holding a letter, which they supposed the Governor had left there, to give information of himself before marching into the interior. They asked it, to be given to them, of four or five Indians walking along the beach, who, by signs, bade them come to land for it, which Ortiz and another did, though contrary to the wishes of the others. No sooner had they got on shore, when many natives came out of the houses, and, drawing near, held them in such way that they could not escape. One, who would have defended himself, they slew on the spot; the other they seized by the hands, and took him to Ucita,

5

their chief. The people in the pinnace, unwilling to
land, kept along the coast and returned to Cuba.

By command of Ucita, Juan Ortiz was bound hand
and foot to four stakes, and laid upon scaffolding, beneath
which a fire was kindled, that he might be burned ; but a
daughter of the Chief entreated that he might be spared.
Though one Christian, she said, might do no good, cer-
tainly he could do no harm, and it would be an honour to
have one for a captive; to which the father acceded,
directing the injuries to be healed. When Ortiz got
well, he was put to watching a temple, that the wolves,
in the night-time, might not carry off the dead there,
which charge he took in hand, having commended himself to God. One night they snatched away from him
the body of a little child, son of a principal man ; and,
going after them, he threw a dart at the wolf that was
escaping, which, feeling itself wounded, let go its hold,
and went off to die ; and he returned, without knowing
what he had done in the dark. In the morning, finding
the body of the little boy gone, he became very sober ;
and Ucita, when he heard what had happened, determined he should be killed ; but having sent on the trail
which Ortiz pointed out as that the wolves had made, the
body of the child was found, and a little farther on a
dead wolf; at which circumstance the Chief became well
pleased with the Christian, and satisfied with the guard
he had kept, ever after taking much notice of him.

Three years having gone by since he had fallen into
the hands of this Chief, there came another, named Mocoço, living two days' journey distant from that port, and

burnt the town, when Ucita fled to one he had in another
seaport, whereby Ortiz lost his occupation, and with it
the favour of his master. The Indians are worshippers of
the Devil, and it is their custom to make sacrifices of the
blood and bodies of their people, or of those of any other
they can come by; and they affirm, too, that when he
would have them make an offering, he speaks, telling
them that he is athirst, and that they must sacrifice to
him. The girl who had delivered Ortiz from the fire,
told him how her father had the mind to sacrifice him
the next day, and that he must flee to Mocoço, who she
knew would receive him with regard, as she had heard
that he had asked for him, and said he would like to see
him: and as he knew not the way, she went half a league
out of town with him at dark, to put him on the road,
returning early so as not to be missed.

Ortiz travelled all night, and in the morning came to
a river, the boundary of the territory of Mocoço, where
he discovered two men fishing. As this people were at
war with those of Ucita, and their languages different, he
did not know how he should be able to tell them who he
was, and why he came, or make other explanation, that
they might not kill him as one of the enemy. It was
not, however, until he had come up to where their arms
were placed that he was discovered, when they fled towards the town; and though he called out to them to
wait, that he would do them no injury, they only ran the
faster for not understanding him. As they arrived, shouting, many Indians came out of the town, and began surrounding, in order to shoot him with their arrows, when

he, finding himself pressed, took shelter behind trees, crying aloud that he was a Christian fled from Ucita, come to visit and serve Mocoço. At the moment, it pleased God that an Indian should come up, who, speaking the language, understood him and quieted the others, telling them what was said. Three or four ran to carry the news, when the Cacique, much gratified, came a quarter of a league on the way to receive him. He caused the Christian immediately to swear to him, according to the custom of his country, that he would not leave him for any other master; and, in return, he promised to show him much honour, and if at any time Christians should come to that land, he would let him go freely, and give him his permission to return to them, pledging his oath to this after the Indian usage.

Three years from that time, some people fishing out at sea, three leagues from land, brought news of having seen ships; when Mocoço, calling Ortiz, gave him permission to depart, who, taking leave, made all haste possible to the shore, where, finding no vessels, he supposed the story to be only a device of the Cacique to discover his inclination. In this way he remained with him nine years, having little hope of ever seeing Christians more; but no sooner had the arrival of the Governor in Florida taken place, when it was known to Mocoço, who directly told Ortiz that Christians were in the town of Ucita. The captive, thinking himself jested with, as he had supposed himself to be before, said that his thoughts no longer dwelt on his people, and that his only wish now was to serve him. Still the Cacique assured him that it was even as he stated, and gave him leave to go, telling him that if he did not, and the Christians should depart, he must not blame him, for he had fulfilled his promise.

Great was the joy of Ortiz at this news, though still doubtful of its truth; however, he thanked Mocoço, and went his way. A dozen principal Indians were sent to accompany him; and on their way to the port, they met Baltasar de Gallegos, in the manner that has been related. Arrived at the camp, the Governor ordered that apparel be given to him, good armour, and a fine horse. When asked if he knew of any country where there was either gold or silver, he said that he had not been ten leagues in any direction from where he lived; but that thirty leagues distant was a chief named Paracoxi, to whom Mocoço, Ucita, and all they that dwelt along the coast paid tribute, and that he perhaps had knowledge of some good country, as his land was better than theirs, being more fertile, abounding in maize. Hearing this, the Governor was well pleased, and said he only desired to find subsistence, that he might be enabled to go inland with safety; for that Florida was so wide, in some part or other of it, there could not fail to be a rich country. The Cacique of Mocoço came to the port, and calling on the Governor, he thus spoke:—

Most High and Powerful Chief:—

Though less able, I believe, to serve you than the least of these under your control, but with the wish to do more than even the greatest of them can accomplish, I appear before you in the full confidence of receiving your favour, as much so as though I deserved it, not in requital of the trifling service I rendered in setting free the Christian while he was in my power, which I did, not for the sake

of my honour and of my promise, but because I hold that great
men should be liberal.   As much as in your bodily perfections you
exceed all, and in your command over fine men are you superior to
others, so in your nature are you equal to the full enjoyment of
earthly things.   The favour I hope for, great Lord, is that you will
hold me to be your own, calling on me freely to do whatever may
be your wish.

The Governor answered him, that although it were
true, in freeing and sending him the Christian, he had
done no more than to keep his word and preserve his
honour, nevertheless he thanked him for an act so valuable,
that there was no other for him that could be compared
to it; and that, holding him henceforth to be a brother,
he should in all, and through all, favour him.   Then a
shirt and some other articles of clothing were directed to
be given to the Chief, who, thankfully receiving them,
took leave and went to his town.

CHAPTER X.

How the Governor, having sent the Ships to Cuba, marched Inland, leaving one hundred Men at the Port.

From the port of Espiritu Santo, where the Governor was, he sent the Chief Castellan, with fifty cavalry and thirty or forty infantry, to the Province of Paracoxi, to observe the character of the country, inquire of that farther on, and to let him hear by message of what he should discover; he also sent the vessels to Cuba, that, at an appointed time, they might return with provisions. As the principal object of Vasco Porcallo de Figueroa in coming to Florida had been to get slaves for his plantation and mines, finding, after some incursions, that no seizures could be made, because of dense forest and extensive bogs, he determined to go back to Cuba; and in consequence of that resolution, there grew up such a difference between him and Soto, that neither of them treated nor spoke to the other kindly. Still, with words of courtesy, he asked permission of him to return, and took his leave.

Baltasar de Gallegos having arrived at Paracoxi, thirty Indians came to him on the part of the absent Cacique, one of whom said: "King Paracoxi, lord of this

Province, whose vassals we are, sends us to ask of you what it is you seek in his country, and in what he can serve you;" to which the Chief Castellan replied, that he much thanked the Cacique for his proffer, and bade them tell him to return to his town, where they would talk together of a peace and friendship he greatly desired to establish. They went off, and came again the next day, reporting that as their lord could not appear, being very unwell, they had come in his stead to see what might be wanted. They were asked if they had knowledge or information of any country where gold and silver might be found in plenty; to which they answered yes; that towards the sunset was a Province called Cale, the inhabitants of which were at war with those of territories where the greater portion of the year was summer, and where there was so much gold, that when the people came to make war upon those of Cale, they wore golden hats like casques.

As the Cacique had not come, Gallegos, reflecting, suspected the message designed for delay, that he might put himself in a condition of safety; and fearing that, if those men were suffered to depart, they might never return, he ordered them to be chained together, and sent the news to camp by eight men on horseback. The Governor, hearing what had passed, showed great pleasure, as did the rest who were with him, believing what the Indians said might be true. He left thirty cavalry and seventy infantry at the port, with provisions for two years, under command of Captain Calderon, marching with the others inland to Paracoxi; thence, having united with the force already there, he passed through a small town named Acela, and came to another called Tocaste, whence he advanced with fifty of foot and thirty horse towards Cale; and having gone through an untenanted town, some natives were seen in a lake, to whom having spoken by an interpreter, they came out and gave him a guide. From there he went to a river of powerful current, in the midst of which was a tree, whereon they made a bridge. Over this the people passed in safety, the horses being crossed swimming to a hawser, by which they were drawn to the other bank, the first that entered the water having been drowned for the want of one.

The Governor sent two men on horseback, with word to those in the rear that they should advance rapidly, for that the way was becoming toilsome and the provisions were short. He came to Cale and found the town abandoned; but he seized three spies, and tarried there until the people should arrive, they travelling hungry and on bad roads, the country being very thin of maize, low, very wet, pondy, and thickly covered with trees. Where there were inhabitants, some water-cresses could be found, which they who arrived first would gather, and, cooking them in water with salt, ate them without other thing; and they who could get none, would seize the stalks of maize and eat them, the ear, being young, as yet containing no grain. Having come to the river, which the Governor had passed, they got cabbage from the low palmetto growing there, like that of Andaluzia. There they were met by the messengers, who, reporting a great deal of maize in Cale, gave much satisfaction.

6

While the people should be coming up, the Governor ordered all the ripe grain in the fields, enough for three months, to be secured. In gathering it three Christians were slain. One of two Indians who were made prisoners stated that seven days' journey distant was a large Province, abounding in maize, called Apalache. Presently, with fifty cavalry and sixty infantry, he set out from Cale, leaving Luis de Moscoso, the Field Marshal, in command, with directions not to move until he should be ordered. Up to that time, no one had been able to get servants who should make his bread; and the method being to beat out the maize in log mortars with a one-handed pestle of wood, some also sifting the flour afterward through their shirts of mail, the process was found so laborious, that many, rather than crush the grain, preferred to eat it parched and sodden. The mass was baked in clay dishes, set over fire, in the manner that I have described as done in Cuba.

CHAPTER XI.

How the Governor arrived at Caliquen, and thence, taking the Cacique with him, came to Napetaca, where the Indians, attempting to rescue him, had many of their number killed and captured.

On the eleventh day of August, in the year 1539, the Governor left Cale, and arrived to sleep at a small town called Ytara, and the next day at another called Potano, and the third at Utinama, and then at another named Malapaz. This place was so called because one, representing himself to be its Cacique, came peacefully saying, that he wished to serve the Governor with his people, and asked that he would cause the twenty-eight men and women, prisoners taken the night before, to be set at liberty; that provisions should be brought, and that he would furnish a guide for the country in advance of us; whereupon, the Governor having ordered the prisoners to be let loose, and the Indian put under guard, the next day in the morning came many natives close to a scrub surrounding the town, near which the prisoner asked to be taken, that he might speak and satisfy them, as they would obey in whatever he commanded; but no sooner had he found himself close to them, than he boldly started away, and fled so swiftly that no one could overtake him, going off with the rest into the woods. The Governor ordered a bloodhound, already fleshed upon him, to be let loose, which, passing by many, seized upon the faithless Cacique, and held him until the Christians had come up.

From this town the people went to sleep at the one of Cholupaha, which, for its abundance of maize, received the name of Villafarta; thence, crossing a river before it, by a bridge they had made of wood, the Christians marched two days ~~through an~~ uninhabited country.

On the seventeenth day of August they arrived at Caliquen, where they heard of the Province of Apalache, of Narvaez having been there and embarked, because no road was to be found over which to go forward, and of there being no other town, and that water was on all sides. Every mind was depressed at this information, and all counselled the Governor to go back to the port, that they might not be lost, as Narvaez had been, and to leave the land of Florida; that, should they go further, they might not be able to get back, as the little maize that was yet left the Indians would secure: to which Soto replied, that he would never return until he had seen with his own eyes what was asserted, things that to him appeared incredible. Then he ordered us to be in readiness for the saddle, sending word to Luis de Moscoso to advance from Cale, that he waited for him; and, as in the judgment of the Field Marshal, and of many others, they should have to return from Apalache, they buried in Cale some iron implements with other things. They reached Caliquen through much suffering; for the land over which the Governor had marched lay wasted and was without maize.

All the people having come up, a bridge was ordered to be made over a river that passed near the town, whereon we crossed, the tenth day of September, taking with us the Cacique. When three days on our journey, some Indians arrived to visit their lord; and every day they came out to the road, playing upon flutes, a token among them that they come in peace. They stated that further on there was a Cacique named Uzachil, kinsman of the Chief of Caliquen, their lord, who waited the arrival of the Governor, prepared to do great services; and they besought him to set their Cacique free, which he feared to do, lest they should go off without giving him any guides; so he got rid of them from day to day with specious excuses.

We marched five days, passing through some small towns, and arrived at Napetaca on the fifteenth day of September, where we found fourteen or fifteen Indians who begged for the release of the Cacique of Caliquen, to whom the Governor declared that their lord was no prisoner, his attendance being wished only as far as Uzachil. Having learned from Juan Ortiz, to whom a native had made it known, that the Indians had determined to assemble and fall upon the Christians, for the recovery of their Chief, the Governor, on the day for which the attack was concerted, commanded his men to be in readiness, the cavalry to be armed and on horseback, each one so disposed of in his lodge as not to be seen of the Indians, that they might come to the

town without reserve. Four hundred warriors, with bows
and arrows, appeared in sight of the camp; and, going
into a thicket, they sent two of their number to demand
the Cacique: the Governor, with six men on foot, taking
the Chief by the hand, conversing with him the while to
assure the Indians, went towards the place where they
were, when, finding the moment propitious, he ordered
a trumpet to be sounded: directly, they who were in
the houses, foot as well as horse, set upon the natives,
who, assailed unexpectedly, thought only of their safety.
Of two horses killed, one was that of the Governor,
who was mounted instantly on another. From thirty
to forty natives fell by the lance; the rest escaped
into two very large ponds, situated some way apart,
wherein they swam about; and, being surrounded by the
Christians, they were shot at with crossbow and arquebuse, although to no purpose, because of the long distance
they were off.

At night, one of the lakes was ordered to be guarded,
the people not being sufficient to encircle both. The Indians, in attempting to escape in the dark, would come
swimming noiselessly to the shore, with a leaf of water-
lily on the head, that they might pass unobserved; when
those mounted, at sight of any ruffle on the surface, would
dash into the water up to the breasts of the horses, and
the natives would again retire. In such way passed the
night, neither party taking any rest. Juan Ortiz told
them that, as escape was impossible, they would do well
to give up; which they did, driven by extreme chillness
of the water; and one after another, as cold overpowered,

called out to him, asking not to be killed—that he was coming straightway to put himself in the hands of the Governor. At four o'clock in the morning they had all surrendered, save twelve of the principal men, who, as of more distinction and valiant than the rest, preferred to die rather than yield: then the Indians of Paracoxi, who were going about unshackled, went in after them, swimming, and pulled them out by the hair. They were all put in chains, and, on the day following, were divided among the Christians for their service.

While captives, these men determined to rebel, and gave the lead to an interpreter, one reputed brave, that when the Governor might come near to speak with him, he should strangle him; but no sooner was the occasion presented, and before his hands could be thrown about the neck of Soto, his purpose was discovered, and he received so heavy a blow from him in the nostrils, that they gushed with blood. The Indians all rose together. He who could only catch up a pestle from a mortar, as well he who could grasp a weapon, equally exerted himself to kill his master, or the first one he met; and he whose fortune it was to light on a lance, or a sword, handled it in a manner as though he had been accustomed to use it all his days. One Indian, in the public yard of the town, with blade in hand, fought like a bull in the arena, until the halberdiers of the Governor, arriving, put an end to him. Another got up, with a lance, into a maize crib, made of cane, called by Indians barbacoa, and defended the entrance with the uproar of ten men, until he was stricken down with a battleaxe. They who were subdued may have been in all two hundred men: some of the youngest the Governor gave to those who had good chains and were vigilant; all the rest were ordered to execution, and, being bound to a post in the middle of the town yard, they were shot to death with arrows by the people of Paracoxi.

CHAPTER XII.

How the Governor arrived at Palache, and was informed that there was much Gold inland.

On the twenty-third day of September the Governor left Napetaca, and went to rest at a river, where two Indians brought him a deer from the Cacique of Uzachil; and the next day, having passed through a large town called Hapaluya. he slept at Uzachil. He found no person there; for the inhabitants, informed of the deaths at Napetaca, dared not remain. In the town was found their food, much maize, beans, and pumpkins, on which the Christians lived. The maize is like coarse millet; the pumpkins are better and more savoury than those of Spain.

Two captains having been sent in opposite directions, in quest of Indians, a hundred men and women were taken, one or two of whom were chosen out for the Governor, as was always customary for officers to do after successful inroads, dividing the others among themselves and companions. They were led off in chains, with collars about the neck, to carry luggage and grind corn, doing the labour proper to servants. Sometimes it happened that, going with them for wood or maize, they would kill the Christian, and flee, with the chain on,

7

which others would file at night with a splinter of stone, in the place of iron, at which work, when caught, they were punished, as a warning to others, and that they might not do the like. The women and youths, when removed a hundred leagues from their country, no longer cared, and were taken along loose, doing the work, and in a very little time learning the Spanish language.

From Uzachill the Governor went towards Apalache, and at the end of two days' travel arrived at a town called Axille. After that, the Indians having no knowledge of the Christians, they were come upon unawares, the greater part escaping, nevertheless, because there were woods near town. The next day, the first of October, the Governor took his departure in the morning, and ordered a bridge to be made over a river which he had to cross. The depth there, for a stone's throw, was over the head, and afterward the water came to the waist, for the distance of a crossbow-shot, where was a growth of tall and dense forest, into which the Indians came, to ascertain if they could assail the men at work and prevent a passage; but they were dispersed by the arrival of crossbow-men, and some timbers being thrown in, the men gained the opposite side and secured the way. On the fourth day of the week, Wednesday of St. Francis, the Governor crossed over and reached Uitachuco, a town subject to Apalache, where he slept. He found it burning, the Indians having set it on fire.

Thenceforward the country was well inhabited, producing much corn, the way leading by many habitations like villages. Sunday, the twenty-fifth of October, he arrived at the town of Uzela, and on Monday at Anhayca Apalache, where the lord of all that country and Province resided. The Camp-master, whose duty it is to divide and lodge the men, quartered them about the town, at the distance of half a league to a league apart. There were other towns which had much maize, pumpkins, beans, and dried plums of the country, whence were brought together at Anhaica Apalache what appeared to be sufficient provision for the winter. These ameixas are better than those of Spain, and come from trees that grow in the fields without being planted.

Informed that the sea was eight leagues distant, the Governor directly sent a captain thither, with cavalry and infantry, who found a town called ·Ochete, eight leagues on the way; and, coming to the coast, he saw where a great tree had been felled, the trunk split up into stakes, and with the limbs made into mangers. He found also the skulls of horses. With these discoveries he returned, and what was said of Narvaez was believed to be certain, that he had there made boats, in which he left the country, and was lost in them at sea. Presently, Juan de Añasco made ready to go to the port of Espiritu Santo, taking thirty cavalry, with orders from the Governor to Calderon, who had remained there, that he should abandon the town, and bring all the people to Apalache.

In Uzachil, and other towns on the way, Añasco found many people who had already become careless; still, to avoid detention, no captures were made, as it was not well to give the Indians sufficient time to come together. He went through the towns at night, stopping at a distance from the population for three or four hours, to rest, and at the end of ten days arrived at the port. He dispatched two caravels to Cuba, in which he sent to Doña Ysabel twenty women brought by him from Ytara and Potano, near Cale; and, taking with him the foot-soldiers in the brigantines, from point to point along the coast by sea, he went towards Palache. Calderon with the cavalry, and some crossbow-men of foot, went by land. The Indians at several places beset him, and wounded some of the men. On his arrival, the Governor ordered planks and spikes to be taken to the coast for building a piragua, into which thirty men entered well armed from the bay, going to and coming from sea, waiting the arrival of the brigantines, and sometimes fighting with the natives, who went up and down the estuary in canoes. On Saturday, the twenty-ninth of November, in a high wind, an Indian passed through the sentries undiscovered, and set fire to the town, two portions of which, in consequence, were instantly consumed.

On Sunday, the twenty-eighth of December, Juan de Añasco arrived; and the Governor directed Francisco Maldonado, Captain of Infantry, to run the coast to the westward with fifty men, and look for an entrance; proposing to go himself in that direction by land on discoveries. The same day, eight men rode two leagues about the town in pursuit of Indians, who had become so bold that they would venture up within two crossbow-shot of the camp to kill our people. Two were discovered engaged in picking beans, and might have escaped, but a woman being present, the wife of one of them, they stood to fight. Before they could be killed, three horses were wounded, one of which died in a few days. Calderon going along the coast near by, the Indians came out against him from a wood, driving him from his course, and capturing from many of his company a part of their indispensable subsistence.

Three or four days having elapsed beyond the time set for the going and return of Maldonado, the Governor resolved that, should he not appear at the end of eight days, he would go thence and wait no longer; when the Captain arrived, bringing with him an Indian from a Province called Ochus, sixty leagues from Apalache, and the news of having found a sheltered port with a good depth of water. The Governor was highly pleased, hoping to find a good country ahead; and he sent Maldonado to Havana for provisions, with which to meet him at that port of his discovery, to which he would himself come by land; but should he not reach there that summer, then he directed him to go back to Havana and return there the next season to await him, as he would make it his express object to march in quest of Ochus.

Francisco Maldonado went, and Juan de Guzman remained instead, Captain of his infantry. Of the Indians taken in Napetuca, the treasurer, Juan Gaytan, brought a youth with him, who stated that he did not belong to that country, but to one afar in the direction of the sun's rising, from which he had been a long time absent visiting other lands; that its name was Yupaha, and was governed by a woman, the town she lived in being of astonishing size, and many neighboring lords her tributaries, some of whom gave her clothing, others gold in quantity. He showed how the metal was taken from the earth, melted, and refined, exactly as though he had seen it all done, or else the Devil had taught him how it was; so that they who knew aught of such matter declared it impossible that he could give that account without having been an eye-witness; and they who beheld the signs he made credited all that was understood as certain.

CHAPTER XIII.

How the Governor went from Apalache in quest of Yupaha, and what befell him.

On Wednesday, the third of March, in the year 1540, the Governor left Anhaica Apalache to seek Yupaha. He had ordered his men to go provided with maize for a march through sixty leagues of desert. The cavalry carried their grain on the horses, and the infantry theirs on the back; because the Indians they brought with them for service, being naked and in chains, had perished in great part during the winter. On the fourth day of the journey they arrived at a deep river, where a piragua was made; and, in consequence of the violence of the current, a cable of chains was extended from shore to shore, along which the boat passed, and the horses were drawn over, swimming thereto, by means of a windlass to the other side.

A day and a half afterwards, they arrived at a town by the name of Capachiqui, and on Friday, the eleventh, the inhabitants were found to have gone off. The following day, five Christians, going in the rear of the camp to search for mortars, in which the natives beat maize, went to some houses surrounded by a thicket, where many Indians lurked as spies, an equal number of whom, separating from the rest, set upon our men, one of whom flea back, crying out to arms. When they who could first answer to the call reached the spot, they found one of the Christians killed, and the three others badly wounded, the Indians fleeing into a sheet of water, full of woods, into which the horses could not go. The Governor left Capachiqui, passing through a desert; and on Wednesday, the twenty-first of the month, came to Toalli.

The houses of this town were different from those behind, which were covered with dry grass; thenceforward they were roofed with cane, after the fashion of tile. They are kept very clean: some have their sides so made of clay as to look like tapia. Throughout the cold country every Indian has a winter house, plastered inside and out, with a very small door, which is closed at dark, and a fire being made within, it remains heated like an oven, so that clothing is not needed during the night-time. He has likewise a house for summer, and near it a kitchen, where fire is made and bread baked. Maize is kept in barbacoa, which is a house with wooden sides, like a room, raised aloft on four posts, and has a floor of cane. The difference between the houses of the masters, or principal men, and those of the common people is, besides being larger than the others, they have deep balconies on the front side, with cane seats, like benches; and about are many large barbacoas, in which they bring together the tribute their people give them of maize, skins of deer, and blankets of the country. These are like shawls, some of them made from the inner bark of trees, and others of a grass resembling nettle, which, by treading out, becomes like flax. The women use them for covering, wearing one about the body from the waist downward, and another over the shoulder, with the right arm left free, after the manner of the Gypsies: the men wear but one, which they carry over the shoulder in the same way, the loins being covered with a bragueiro of deer-skin, after the fashion of the.woollen breech-cloth that was once the custom of Spain. The skins are well dressed, the colour being given to them that is wished, and in such perfection, that, when of vermilion, they look like very fine red broadcloth; and when black, the sort in use for shoes, they are of the purest. The same hues are given to blankets.

The Governor left Toalli on the twenty-fourth day of March, and arrived on Thursday, in the evening, at a little stream where a small bridge was made, and the people passed to the opposite side. Benito Fernandes, a Portuguese, fell off from it, and was drowned. So soon as the Governor had crossed, he found a town, a short way on, by the name of Achese, the people of which, having had no knowledge of the Christians, plunged into a river; nevertheless, some men and women were taken, among whom was found one who understood the youth, the guide to Yupaha, which rather confirmed what he stated, as they had come through regions speaking different languages, some of which he did not understand. By one of the Indians taken there, the Governor sent to call the Cacique from the farther side of the river, who, having come to him, thus spoke:—

8

Very High, Powerful, and Good Master:—

The things that seldom happen bring astonishment. Think, then, what must be the effect on me and mine, the sight of you and your people, whom we have at no time seen, astride .the fierce brutes, your horses, entering with such speed and fury into my country, that we had no tidings of your coming—things so altogether new, as to strike awe and terror to our hearts, which it was not nature to resist, so that we should receive you with the sobriety due to so kingly and famous a lord. Trusting to your greatness and personal qualities, I hope no fault will be found in me, and that I shall rather receive favours, of which one is that with my person, my country, and my vassals, you will do as with your own things; and another, that you tell me who you are, whence you come, whither you go, and what it is you seek, that I may the better serve you.

The Governor responded, that he greatly thanked him for his good-will, as much so as though he had given him a great treasure. He told him that he was the child of the sun, coming from its abode, and that he was going about the country, seeking for the greatest prince there, and the richest province. The Cacique stated that farther on was a great lord, whose territory was called Ocute. He gave him a guide, who understood the language, to conduct him thither; and the Governor commanded his subjects to be released. A high cross, made of wood, was set up in the middle of the town-yard; and, as time did not allow more to be done, the Indians were instructed that it was put there to commemorate the suffering of Christ, who was God and man; that he had created the skies and the earth, and had suffered for the salvation of all, and therefore that they should revere that sign; and they showed by their manner that they would do so.

The Governor set out on the first day of April, and advanced through the country of the Chief, along up a river, the shores of which were very populous. On the fourth he went through the town of Altamaca, and on the tenth arrived at Ocute. The Cacique sent him a present, by two thousand Indians, of many conies and partridges, maize bread, many dogs, and two turkeys. On account of the scarcity of meat, the dogs were as much esteemed by the Christians as though they had been fat sheep. There was such want of salt also, that oftentimes, in many places, a sick man having nothing for his nourishment, and was wasting away to bone, of some ail that elsewhere might have found a remedy, when sinking under pure debility he would say: "Now, if I had but a slice of meat, or only a few lumps of salt, I should not thus die."

The Indians never lack meat. With arrows they get abundance of deer, turkeys, conies, and other wild animals, being very skilful in killing game, which the Christians were not; and even if they had been, there was not the opportunity for it, they being on the march the greater part of their time; nor did they, besides, ever dare to straggle off. Such was the craving for meat, that when the six hundred men who followed Soto arrived at a town, and found there twenty or thirty dogs, he who could get sight of one and kill him, thought he had done no little; and he who proved himself so active, if his Captain knew of it, and he forgot to send him a quarter, would show his displeasure, and make him feel it in the watches, or in any matter of labour that came along, with which he could bear upon him.

On Tuesday, the twelfth of April, the Governor took his departure, the Cacique of Ocute giving him four hundred tamemes, the Indians that carry burdens. He passed through a town, the lord of which was called Cofaqui, and came to the province of another, named Patofa, who, being at peace with the Chief of Ocute and other neighbouring lords, had heard of the Governor for a long time, and desired to see him. He went to call on him, and made this speech:—

POWERFUL LORD:—

Not without reason, now, will I ask that some light mishap befall me, in return for so great good fortune, and deem my lot a happy one; since I have come to what I most wished in life, to behold and have the opportunity in some way to serve you. Thus the tongue casts the shadow of the thought; but I, nevertheless, am as unable to produce the perfect image of my feelings as to control the appearances of my contentment. By what circumstance has this your land, which I govern, deserved to be seen by one so superior and excellent that all on earth should obey and serve as prince? and those who here inhabit being so insignificant, how can they forget, in receiving this vast enjoyment, that, in the order of things, will follow upon it some great adversity? If we are held worthy of being yours, we can never be other than favoured, nor less than protected in whatsoever is reasonable and just; for they that fail of deserving either, with the name of men can only be considered brutes. From the depth of my heart, and with the respect due to such a chief, I make mine offer; and pray that, in return for so sincere good-will, you dispose of me, my country, and my vassals.

The Governor answered that his offers and good-will, shown in works, would greatly please him, and which he should ever bear in memory, to honour and favour him as he would a brother. From this Province of Patofa, back to the first Cacique we found at peace, a distance of fifty leagues, the country is abundant, picturesque, and luxuriant, well watered, and having good river margins; thence to the harbour of Espiritu Santo, where we first arrived, the land of Florida, which may be three hundred leagues in length, a little more or less, is light, the greater part of it of pine-trees, and low, having many ponds; and in places are high and dense forest, into which the Indians that were hostile betook themselves, where they could not be found; nor could horses enter there, which, to the Christians, was the loss of the food they carried away, and made it troublesome to get guides.

CHAPTER XIIII.

How the Governor left the Province of Patofa, marching into a Desert Country, where he, with his People, became exposed to great Peril and underwent severe Privation.

In the town of Patofa, the youth, whom the Governor brought with him for guide and interpreter, began to froth at the mouth, and threw himself on the ground as if he were possessed of the Devil. An exorcism being said over him, the fit went off. He stated that four days' journey from there, towards the sunrise, was the Province he spoke of: the Indians at Patofa said that they knew of no dwellings in that direction, but that towards the north-west there was a province called Coça, a plentiful country having very large towns. The Cacique told the Governor that if he desired to go thither he would give him a guide and Indians to carry burdens, and if he would go in the direction pointed out by the youth, he would furnish him with every thing necessary for that also.

With words of love, and tendering each other services, they parted, the Governor receiving seven hundred ta-memes. He took maize for the consumption of four days, and marched by a road that, gradually becoming less, on the sixth day it disappeared. Led by the youth, they forded two rivers, each the breadth of two shots of a crossbow, the water rising to the stirrups of the saddles, and passing in a current so powerful, that it became necessary for those on horseback to stand one before another, that they on foot, walking near, might cross along above them: then came to another of a more violent current, and larger, which was got over with more difficulty, the horses swimming for a lance's length at the coming out, into a pine-grove. The Governor menaced the youth, motioning that he would throw him to the dogs for having lied to him in saying that it was four days' journey, whereas they had travelled nine, each day of seven or eight leagues; and that the men and horses had become very thin, because of the sharp economy practised with the maize. The youth declared that he knew not where he was. Fortunately for him, at the time, there was not another whom Juan Ortez understood, or he would have been cast to the dogs.

The Governor, leaving the camp among the pine-trees, marched that day, with some cavalry and infantry, five or six leagues, looking for a path, and came back at night very cast down, not having found any sign of inhabitants. The next day there was a variety of opinion about the course proper to take, whether to return or do otherwise. The country through which they had come remained wasted and without maize; the grain they had so far brought with them was spent; the beasts, like the men, were become very lean; and it was held very doubtful whether relief was anywhere to be found: moreover, it was the opinion that they might be beaten by any Indians whatsoever who should venture to attack them, so that continuing thus, whether by hunger or in strife, they must inevitably be overcome. The Governor determined to send thence in all directions on horseback, in quest of habitations; and the next day he dispatched four captains to as many points, with eight of cavalry to each. They came back at night leading their beasts by the bridle, unable to carry their masters, or driven before them with sticks, having found no road, nor any sign of a settlement. He sent other four again the next day, with eight of cavalry apiece, men who could swim, that they might cross any ponds and rivers in the way, the horses being chosen of the best that were; Baltasar de Gallegos ascending by the river, Juan de Añasco going down it, Alfonso Romo and Juan Rodriguez Lobillo striking into the country.

The Governor had brought thirteen sows to Florida, which had increased to three hundred swine; and the maize having failed for three or four days, he ordered to be killed daily, for each man, half a pound of pork, on which small allowance, and some boiled herbs, the people with much difficulty lived. There being no food to give to the Indians of Patofa, they were dismissed, though they still wished to keep with the Christians in their extremity, and showed great regret at going back before leaving them in a peopled country. Juan de Añasco came in on Sunday, in the afternoon, bringing with him a woman and a youth he had taken, with the report that he had found a small town twelve or thirteen leagues off; at which the Governor and his people were as much delighted as though they had been raised from death to live.

On Monday, the twenty-sixth of April, the Governor set out for Aymay, a town to which the Christians gave the name of Socorro. At the foot of a tree, in the camp, they buried a paper, and in the bark, with a hatchet, they cut these words: "Dig here; at the root of this pine you will find a letter;" and this was so fixed that the Captains, who had gone in quest of an inhabited country, should learn what the Governor had done and the direction he had taken. There was no other road than the one Juan de Añasco had made moving along through the woods.

On Monday the Governor arrived at the town, with those the best mounted, all riding the hardest possible; some sleeping two leagues off, others three and four, each as he was able to travel and his strength held out. A barbacoa was found full of parched meal and some maize, which were distributed by allowance. Four Indians were taken, not one of whom would say any thing else than that he knew of no other town. The Governor ordered one of them to be burned; and thereupon another said, that two days' journey from there was a province called Cutifachiqui.

On Wednesday the three Captains came up: they had found the letter and followed on after the rest. From the command of Juan Rodriguez two men remained behind, their horses having given out, for which the Governor reprimanded him severely, and sent him to bring them. While they should be coming on he set out for Cutifachiqui, capturing three Indians in the road, who stated that the mistress of that country had already information of the Christians, and was waiting for them in a town. He

9

sent to her by one of them, offering his friendship, and announcing his approach. Directly as the Governor arrived, four canoes came towards him, in one of which was a kinswoman of the Cacica, who, coming near, addressed him in these words:—

EXCELLENT LORD:—

My sister sends me to salute you, and to say, that the reason why she has not come in person is, that she has thought to serve you better by remaining to give orders on the other shore; and that, in a short time, her canoes will all be here, in readiness to conduct you thither, where you may take your repose and be obeyed.

The Governor thanked her, and she returned to cross the river. After a little time the Cacica came out of the town, seated in a chair, which some principal men having borne to the bank, she entered a canoe. Over the stern was spread an awning, and in the bottom lay extended a mat where were two cushions, one above the other, upon which she sate; and she was accompanied by her chief men, in other canoes, with Indians. She approached the spot where the Governor was, and, being arrived, thus addressed him:—

EXCELLENT LORD:—

Be this coming to these your shores most happy. My ability can in no way equal my wishes, nor my services become the merits of so great a prince; nevertheless, good wishes are to be valued more than all the treasures of the earth without them. With sincerest and purest good-will I tender you my person, my lands, my people, and make you these small gifts.

The Cacica presented much clothing of the country, from the shawls and skins that came in the other boats; and drawing from over her head a large string of pearls, she threw them about his neck, exchanging with him many gracious words of friendship and courtesy. She directed that canoes should come to the spot, whence the Governor and his people passed to the opposite side of the river. So soon as he was lodged in the town, a great many turkeys were sent to him. The country was delightful and fertile, having good interval lands upon the streams; the forest was open, with abundance of walnut and mulberry trees. The sea was stated to be distant two days' travel. About the place, from half a league to a league off, were large vacant towns, grown up in grass, that appeared as if no people had lived in them for a long time. The Indians said that, two years before, there had been a pest in the land, and the inhabitants had moved away to other towns. In the barbacoas were large quantities of clothing, shawls of thread, made from the bark of trees, and others of feathers, white, gray, vermilion, and yellow, rich and proper for winter. There were also many well-dressed deer-skins, of colors drawn over with designs, of which had been made shoes, stockings, and hose. The Cacica, observing that the Christians valued the pearls, told the Governor that, if he should order some sepulchres that were in the town to be searched, he would find many; and if he chose to send to those that were in the uninhabited towns, he might load all his horses with them. They examined those in the town, and found three hundred and fifty pounds' weight of pearls, and figures of babies and birds made of them.

The inhabitants are brown of skin, well formed and

proportioned. They are more civilized than any people seen in all the territories of Florida, wearing clothes and shoes. This country, according to what the Indians stated, had been very populous. It appeared that the youth who was the guide had heard of it; and what was told him he declared to have seen, and magnified such parts as he chose, to suit his pleasure. He told the Governor that they had begun to enter upon the country he had spoken to him about, which, because of its appearance, with his being able to understand the language of the people, gained for him some credit. He wished to become a Christian, and asked to be baptized, which was done, he receiving the name of Pedro; and the Governor commanded the chain to be struck off that he had carried until then.

In the town were found a dirk and beads that had belonged to Christians, who, the Indians said, had many years before been in the port, distant two days' journey. He that had been there was the Governor-licentiate Ayllon, who came to conquer the land, and, on arriving at the port, died, when there followed divisions and murders among the chief personages, in quarrels as to who should have the command; and thence, without knowing any thing of the country, they went back to Spain.

To all it appeared well to make a settlement there, the point being a favourable one, to which could come all the ships from New Spain, Peru, Sancta Marta, and Tierra-Firme, going to Spain; because it is in the way thither, is a good country, and one fit in which to raise supplies; but Soto, as it was his object to find another treasure like that of Atabalípa, lord of Peru, would not be content with good lands nor pearls, even though many of them were worth their weight in gold (and if the country were divided among Christians, more precious should those be the Indians would procure than these they have, being bored with heat, which causes them to lose their hue): so he answered them who urged him to make a settlement, that in all the country together there was not support for his troops a single month; that it was necessary to return to Ochus, where Maldonado was to wait; and should a richer country not be found, they could always return to that who would, and in their absence the Indians would plant their fields and be better provided with maize. The natives were asked if they had knowledge of any great lord farther on, to which they answered, that twelve days' travel thence was a province called Chiaha, subject to a chief of Coça.

The Governor then resolved at once to go in quest of that country, and being an inflexible man, and dry of word, who, although he liked to know what the others all thought and had to say, after he once said a thing he did not like to be opposed, and as he ever acted as he thought best, all bent to his will; for though it seemed an error to leave that country, when another might have been found about it, on which all the people could have been sustained until the crops had been made and the grain gathered, there were none who would say a thing to him after it became known that he had made up his mind.

CHAPTER XV.

How the Governor went from Cutifachiqui in quest of Coça, and what occurred to him on the Journey.

On the third day of May the Governor set out from Cutifachiqui; and, it being discovered that the wish of the Cacica was to leave the Christians, if she could, giving them neither guides nor tamemes, because of the outrages committed upon the inhabitants, there never failing to be men of low degree among the many, who will put the lives of themselves and others in jeopardy for some mean interest, the Governor ordered that she should be placed under guard, and took her with him. This treatment, which was not a proper return for the hospitable welcome he had received, makes true the adage, For well doing . . ; and thus was she carried away on foot, with her female slaves.

This brought us service in all the places that were passed, she ordering the Indians to come and take the loads from town to town. We travelled through her territories a hundred leagues, in which, according to what we saw, she was greatly obeyed, whatsoever she ordered being performed with diligence and efficacy. Perico, the guide, said she was not the suzeraine, but her niece, who had come to that town by her command to punish capitally some principal Indians who had seized upon the tribute; but to this no credit was given, because of the falsehoods in which he had been taken, though all was put up with, from the necessity of having some one whereby to understand what the Indians said.

In seven days the Governor arrived at the Province of Chelaque, the country poorest off for maize of any that was seen in Florida, where the inhabitants subsisted on the roots of plants that they dig in the wilds, and on the animals they destroy there with their arrows. They are very domestic people, are slight of form, and go naked. One lord brought the Governor two deer-skins as a great gift. Turkeys were abundant; in one town they presented seven hundred, and in others brought him what they had and could procure. He was detained in going from this province to that of Xualla five days, where they found little grain, but remained two days, because of the weariness of the men and the leanness of the horses.

From Ocute to Cutifachiqui are one hundred and thirty leagues, of which eighty are desert; from Cutifa to Xualla are two hundred and fifty of mountainous country; thence to Guaxule, the way is over very rough and lofty ridges.

One day while on this journey, the Cacica of Cutifachi, whom the Governor brought with him, as has been stated, to the end of taking her to Guaxule, the farthest limit of her territories, conducted by her slaves, she left the road, with an excuse of going into a thicket, where, deceiving them, she so concealed herself that for all their search she could not be found. She took with her a cane box, like a trunk, called petaca, full of unbored pearls, of which, those who had the most knowledge of their value said they were very precious. They were carried for her by one of the women; and the Governor, not to give offence, permitted it so, thinking that in Guaxule he would beg them of her when he should give her leave to depart; but she took them with her, going to Xualla, with three slaves who had fled from the camp. A horseman, named Alimamos, who remained behind, sick of a fever, wandering out of the way, got lost; and he laboured with the slaves to make them leave their evil design. Two of them did so, and came on with him to the camp. They overtook the Governor, after a journey of fifty leagues, in a province called Chiaha; and he reported that the Cacica remained in Xualla, with a slave of André de Vasconcelos, who would not come with him, and that it was very sure they lived together as man and wife, and were to go together to Cutifachiqui.

At the end of five days the Governor arrived at Guaxule. The Christians being seen to go after dogs, for their flesh, which the Indians do not eat, they gave them three hundred of those animals. Little maize was found there, or anywhere upon that route. The Governor sent a native with a message to the Cacique of Chiaha, begging that he would order some maize to be brought together at his town, that he might sojourn there some time. He left Guaxule, and after two days' travel arrived at Canasagua, where twenty men came out from the town on the road, each laden with a basket of mulberries. This fruit is abundant and good, from Cutifachique to this place, and thence onward in other provinces, as are the walnut and the amexa; the trees growing about over the country, without planting or pruning, of the size and luxuriance they would have were they cultivated in orchards, by hoeing and irrigation. Leaving Canasagua, he marched five days through a desert.

Two leagues before coming to Chiaha, fifteen men met the Governor, bearing loads of maize, with word from the Cacique that he waited for him, having twenty barbacoas full; that, moreover, himself, his lands, and his vassals, were subject to his orders. On the fifth day of July the Governor entered Chiaha. The Cacique received him with great pleasure, and, resigning to him his dwellings for his residence, thus addressed him :—

POWERFUL AND EXCELLENT MASTER:—

Fortunate am I that you will make use of my services. Nothing could happen that would give me so great contentment, or which I should value more. From Guaxule you sent to have maize for you in readiness to last two months: you have in this town twenty barbacoas full of the choicest and the best to be found in all this country. If the reception I give is not worthy of so great a prince, consider my youth, which will relieve me of blame, and receive my good-will, which, with true loyalty and pure, shall ever be shown in all things that concern your welfare.

The Governor answered him, that his gifts and his kindness pleased him greatly, and that he should ever consider him to be his brother.

There was abundance of lard in calabashes, drawn like olive oil, which the inhabitants said was the fat of

10

bear. There was likewise found much oil of walnuts, which, like the lard, was clear and of good taste; and also a honey-comb, which the Christians had never seen before, nor saw afterwards, nor honey, nor bees, in all the country.

The town was isolated, between two arms of a river, and seated near one of them. Above it, at the distance of two crossbow-shot, the water divided, and united again a league below. The vale between, from side to side, was the width in places of a crossbow-shot, and in others of two. The branches were very wide, and both were fordable: along their shores were very rich meadow-lands, having many maize-fields.

As the Indians remained at home, no houses were taken save those of the Chief, in which the Governor lodged; the people lived out, wherever there happened to be shelter, each man having his tree. In this manner the army lay, the men out of order, and far apart. The Governor passed it over, as the Indians were peaceful, and the weather very calm: the people would have suffered greatly had they been required to do differently. The horses arrived so worn out, that they could not bear their riders from weakness; for they had come all the way having only a little maize to live on, travelling, hungry and tired, even from beyond the desert of Ocute; so, as the greater part of them were unfit to be mounted, even in the necessary case of battle, they were turned out at night to graze, about a quarter of a league from the camp. The Christians were greatly exposed, so much so that if at that time the Indians had set upon them, they would have been in bad way to defend themselves.

The duration of the sojourn was thirty days, in which time, the soil being covered with verdure, the horses fattened. At the departure, in consequence of the importunity of some who wanted more than was in reason, the Governor asked thirty women of the Chief for slaves, who replied that he would confer with his principal men; when one night, before giving an answer, all went off from the town with their women and children. The next day, having made up his mind to go in search of them, the Cacique arrived, and, approaching, thus addressed him:—

POWERFUL LORD:—

Because of my shame, and out of fear of you, discovering that my subjects, contrary to my wishes, had chosen to absent themselves, I left without your permission; but, finding the error of my way, I have returned like a true vassal, to put myself in your power, that you may do with my person as shall seem best to you. My people will not obey me, nor do any thing that an uncle of mine does not command: he governs this country, in my place, until I shall be of mature age. If you would pursue and punish them for disobedience, I will be your guide, since my fate at present forbids me doing more.

The Governor then, with thirty mounted men and as many footmen, went in search of the people. Passing by the towns of some of the chiefs who had gone off, he cut down and destroyed the great maize-fields; and going along up the stream where the natives were, on an islet, to which the cavalry could not go, he sent word to them, by an Indian, that they should put away all their fears, and, returning to their abodes, give him tamemes, as had been done all the way along, since he did not wish to have women, finding how very dear they were to them. The Indians judged it well to come and make their excuses to him, so they all went back to the town.

A Cacique of Acoste, who came to see the Governor, after tendering his services, and they had exchanged compliments and proffers of friendship, was asked if he had any information of a rich land; he answered yes: that towards the north there was a province called Chisca, and that a forge was there for copper, or other metal of that colour, though brighter, having a much finer hue, and was to appearances much better, but was not so much used, for being softer; which was the statement that had been given in Cutifachiqui, where we had seen some chopping-knives that were said to have a mixture of gold. As the country on the way was thinly peopled, and it was said there were mountains over which the beasts could not go, the Governor would not march directly thither, but judged that, keeping in an inhabited territory the men and animals would be in better condition, while he would be more exactly informed of what there was, until he should turn to it through the ridges and a region which he could more easily travel. He sent two Christians to the country of Chisca, by Indians who spoke the language, that they might view it, and were told that he would await their return at Chiaha for what they should have to say.

CHAPTER XVI.

How the Governor left Chiaha, and, having run a hazard of falling by the Hands of the Indians at Acoste, escaped by his Address: what occurred to him on the Route, and how he came to Coça.

When the Governor had determined to move from Chiaha towards Coste, he sent for the Cacique to come before him, and with kind words took his leave, receiving some slaves as a gift, which pleased him. In seven days the journey was concluded. On the seventh day of July, the camp being pitched among the trees, two crossbow-shot distant from the town, he went with eight men of his guard toward where the Cacique was, who received him evidently with great friendship. While they were conversing, some infantry went into the town after maize, and, not satisfied with what they got, they rummaged and searched the houses, taking what they would; at which conduct the owners began to rise and arm; some of them, with clubs in their hands, going at five or six men who had given offence, beat them to their satisfaction. The Governor, discovering that they were all bent upon some mischief, and himself among them with but few Christians about him, turned to escape from the difficulty by a stratagem much against his nature, clear and reliable

as it was, and the more unwillingly as it grieved him that
an Indian should presume, either with or without cause,
to offer any indignity to a Christian : he seized a stave
and took part with the assailants against his own people,
which while it gave confidence, directly he sent a message
secretly to the camp, that armed men should approach
where he was ; then taking the Chief by the hand, speaking to him with kind words, drew him with some principal men away from the town, out into an open road in
sight of the encampment, where cautiously the Christians
issued and by degrees surrounded them.   In this manner
they were conducted within the tents ; and when near his
marquee the Governor ordered them to be put under
guard.   He told them that they could not go thence without giving him a guide and Indians for carrying loads,
nor until the sick men had arrived whom he had ordered
to come down by the river in canoes from Chiaha, and so
likewise those he had sent to the Province of Chisca.   He
feared that both the one and the other had been killed by
the Indians.   In three days they that went to Chisca got
back, and related that they had been taken through a
country so scant of maize, and with such high mountains,
that it was impossible the army should march in that
direction ; and finding the distance was becoming long,
and that they should be back late, upon consultation they
agreed to return, coming from a poor little town where
there was nothing of value, bringing a cow-hide as delicate as a calf-skin the people had given them, the hair
being like the soft wool on the cross of the merino with
the common sheep.

The Cacique having furnished the guide and tamemes, by permission of the Governor he went his way. The Christians left Coste the ninth day of July, and slept that night at Tali. The Cacique had come from the town to meet the Governor on the road, and made him this speech :—

EXCELLENT GREAT PRINCE :—

Worthy are you of being served and obeyed by all the princes of the world, for by the face can one judge far of the inner qualities. Who you are I knew, and also of your power, before your coming here. I wish not to draw attention to the lowliness in which I stand before you, to make my poor services acceptable and agreeable, since, where the strength fails, the will should instead be praised and taken. Hence, I dare to ask that you will only consider and attend to what you will command me to do here in your country.

The Governor answered, that his good-will and offer pleased him as much as though he had tendered him all the treasures of the earth: that he would always be treated by him as a true brother, favoured and esteemed. The Cacique ordered provision to be brought for two days' use, the time the Governor should be present; and on his departure, gave him the use of two men and four women, who were wanted to carry burdens.

They travelled six days, passing by many towns subject to the Cacique of Coca; and, as they entered those territories, numerous messengers came from him on the road every day to the Governor, some going, others coming, until they arrived at Coça, on Friday, the sixteenth of July. The Cacique came out to receive him at the distance of two crossbow-shot from the town, borne in a

litter on the shoulders of his principal men, seated on a
cushion, and covered with a mantle of marten-skins, of
the size and shape of a woman's shawl: on his head he
wore a diadem of plumes, and hc was surrounded by
many attendants playing upon flutes and singing. Coming to where the Governor was, he made his obeisance,
and followed it by these words:—

POWERFUL LORD, SUPERIOR TO EVERY OTHER OF THE EARTH:—
    Although I come but now to meet you, it is a long time since I
have received you in my heart. That was done the first day I
heard of you, with so great desire to serve, please, and give you
contentment, that this, which I express, is nothing in comparison
with that which is within me. Of this you may be sure, that to
have received the dominion of the world would not have interested
me so greatly as the sight of you, nor would I have held it for so
great a felicity. Do not look for me to offer you that which is your
own—this person, these lands, these vassals. My only desire is to
employ myself in commanding these people, that, with all diligence
and befitting respect, they conduct you hence to the town in festivity of voices and with flutes, where you will be lodged and waited
upon by me and them, where all I possess you will do with as with
your own, and in thus doing you will confer favour.

The Governor gave him thanks, and with mutual
satisfaction they walked on toward the place conferring,
the Indians giving up their habitations by order of their
Cacique, and in which the General and his men took
lodging. In the barbacoas was a great quantity of maize
and beans: the country, thickly settled in numerous and
large towns, with fields between, extending from one to
another, was pleasant, and had a rich soil with fair river
margins. In the woods were many amexeas, as well those of
Spain as of the country; and wild grapes on vines growing
up into the trees, near the streams; likewise a kind that

grew on low vines elsewhere, the berry being large and sweet, but, for want of hoeing and dressing, had large stones.

It was the practice to keep watch over the Caciques that none should absent themselves, they being taken along by the Governor until coming out of their territories; for by thus having them the inhabitants would await their arrival in the towns, give a guide, and men to carry the loads, who before leaving their country would have liberty to return to their homes, as sometimes would the tamemes, so soon as they came to the domain of any chief where others could be got. The people of Coça, seeing their lord was detained, took it amiss, and, going off, hid themselves in the scrub, as well those of the town of the Cacique as those of the towns of the principal men his vassals. The Governor dispatched four captains in as many directions to search for them : many men and women were taken who were put in chains. Seeing how much harm they received, and how little they gained by going off, they came in, declaring that they desired to serve in all that it were possible. Of the prisoners, some of the chiefs, whom the Cacique interceded for, were let go ; of the rest, each one took away with him as slaves those he had in chains, none returning to their country save some whose fortune it was to escape, laboring diligently to file off their irons at night; or, while on the march, could slip out of the way, observing the carelessness of those who had them in charge, sometimes taking off with them in their chains the burdens and the clothing with which they were laded.

11

CHAPTER XVII.

OF HOW THE GOVERNOR WENT FROM COÇA TO TASTALUCA.

THE Governor rested in Coça twenty-five days. On Friday, the twentieth of August, he set out in quest of a province called Tastaluca, taking with him the Cacique of Coça. The first day he went through Tallimuchase, a great town without inhabitants, halting to sleep half a league beyond, near a river-bank. The following day he came to Ytaua, a town subject to Coça. He was detained six days, because of a river near by that was then swollen: so soon as it could be crossed he took up his march, and went towards Ullibahali. Ten or twelve chiefs came to him on the road, from the Cacique of that province, tendering his service, bearing bows and arrows and wearing bunches of feathers.

The Governor having arrived at the town with a dozen cavalry and several of his guard, he left them at the distance of a crossbow-shot and entered the town. He found all the Indians with their weapons, and, according to their ways, it appeared to him in readiness for action: he understood afterwards that they had determined to wrest the Cacique of Coça from his power, should that chief have called on them. The place was enclosed, and near by ran a small stream. The fence, which was like that seen afterwards to other towns, was of large timber sunk deep and firmly into the earth, having many long poles the size of the arm, placed crosswise to nearly the height of a lance, with embrasures, and coated with mud inside and out, having loop-holes for archery. The Governor ordered all his men to enter the town. The Cacique, who at the moment was at a town on the opposite shore, was sent for, and he came at once. After some words between him and the Governor, proffering mutual service, he gave the tamemes that were requisite and thirty women as slaves. Mançano, a native of Salamanca, of noble ancestry, having strayed off in search of the grapes, which are good here, and plenty, was lost.

The Christians left, and that day they arrived to sleep at a town subject to the lord of Ullibahali, and the next day they came to pass the night at the town of Toasi, where the inhabitants gave the Governor thirty women and the tamemes that were wanted. The amount of travel usually performed was five or six leagues a day, passing through settled country; and when through desert, all the haste possible was made, to avoid the want of maize. From Toasi, passing through some towns subject to the lord of the Province of Tallise, he journeyed five days, and arrived at the town the eighteenth day of September.

Tallise was large, situated by the side of a great river, other towns and many fields of maize being on the opposite shore, the country on both sides having the greatest abundance of grain. The inhabitants had gone off. The Governor sent to call the Cacique, who, having arrived, after an interchange of kind words and good promises, lent him forty men. A chief came to the Governor in behalf of the Cacique of Tastaluca, and made the following address :—

VERY POWERFUL, VIRTUOUS, AND ESTEEMED LORD :—

The grand Cacique of Tastaluca, my master, sends me to salute you. He bids me say, that he is told how all, not without reason, are led captive by your perfections and power; that wheresoever lies your path you receive gifts and obedience, which he knows are all your due; and that he longs to see you as much as he could desire for the continuance of life. Thus, he sends me to offer you his person, his lands, his subjects; to say, that wheresoever it shall please you to go through his territories, you will find service and obedience, friendship and peace. In requital of this wish to serve you, he asks that you so far favour him as to say when you will come; for that the sooner you do so, the greater will be the obligation, and to him the earlier pleasure.

The Governor received and parted with the messenger graciously, giving him beads (which by the Indians are not much esteemed), and other articles, that he should take them to his lord. He dismissed the Cacique of Coça, that he might return to his country: he of Tallise gave him the tamemes that were needed; and, having sojourned twenty days, the Governor set out for Tastaluca. He slept the night at a large town called Casiste, and the next day, passing through another, arrived at a village in the Province of Tastaluca; and the following night he rested in a wood, two leagues from the town where the Cacique resided, and where he was then present. He sent the Field-Marshal, Luis de Moscoso, with fifteen cavalry, to inform him of his approach.

The Cacique was at home, in a piazza. Before his

dwelling, on a high place, was spread a mat for him, upon which two cushions were placed, one above another, to which he went and sat down, his men placing themselves around, some way removed, so that an open circle was formed about him, the Indians of the highest rank being nearest to his person. One of them shaded him from the sun with a circular umbrella, spread wide, the size of a target, with a small stem, and having deer-skin extended over cross-sticks, quartered with red and white, which at a distance made it look of taffeta, the colours were so very perfect. It formed the standard of the Chief, which he carried into battle. His appearance was full of dignity: he was tall of person, muscular, lean, and symmetrical. He was the suzerain of many territories, and of a numerous people, being equally feared by his vassals and the neighbouring nations. The Field-Marshal, after he had spoken to him, advanced with his company, their steeds leaping from side to side, and at times towards the Chief, when he, with great gravity, and seemingly with indifference, now and then would raise his eyes, and look on as in contempt.

The Governor approached him, but he made no movement to rise; he took him by the hand, and they went together to seat themselves on the bench that was in the piazza. The Cacique addressed him these words:—

POWERFUL CHIEF:—

Your lordship is very welcome. With the sight of you I receive as great pleasure and comfort as though you were an own brother whom I dearly loved. It is idle to use many words here, as it is not well to speak at length where a few may suffice. The greater

the will the more estimable the deed ; and acts are the living witnesses of truth. You shall learn how strong and positive is my
will, and how disinterested my inclination to serve you. The gifts
you did me the favour to send I esteem in all their value, but most
because they were yours. See in what you will command me.

The Governor satisfied the Chief with a few brief
words of kindness. On leaving he determined, for certain
reasons, to take him along. The second day on the road
he came to a town called Piache : a great river ran near,
and the Governor asked for canoes. The Indians said
they had none, but that they could have rafts of cane and
dried wood, whereon they might readily enough go over,
which they diligently set about making, and soon completed. They managed them ; and the water being calm,
the Governor and his men easily crossed.

From the port of Espiritu Santo to Palache, a march
of about a hundred leagues, the course was west ; from
Apalache to Cutifachiqui, which may be four hundred and
thirty leagues, it was northeast ; from thence to Xualla,
two hundred and fifty leagues, it was towards the north ;
and thence to Tastaluca, which may be some other two
hundred and fifty leagues, one hundred and ninety of
them were toward the west, going to the Province of
Coça, and the sixty southwardly, in going thence to Tastaluca.

After crossing the river of Piache, a Christian having
gone to look after a woman gotten away from him, he had
been either captured or killed by the natives, and the
Governor pressed the Chief to tell what had been done;
threatening, that should the man not appear, he would

never release him. The Cacique sent an Indian thence to Mauilla, the town of a chief, his vassal, whither they were going, stating that he sent to give him notice that he should have provisions in readiness and Indians for loads; but which, as afterwards appeared, was a message for him to get together there all the warriors in his country.

The Governor marched three days, the last one of them continually through an inhabited region, arriving on Monday, the eighteenth day of October, at Mauilla. He rode forward in the vanguard, with fifteen cavalry and thirty infantry, when a Christian he had sent with a message to the Cacique, three or four days before, with orders not to be gone long, and to discover the temper of the Indians, came out from the town and reported that they appeared to him to be making preparation; for that while he was present many weapons were brought, and many people came into the town, and work had gone on rapidly to strengthen the palisade. Luis de Moscoso said that, since the Indians were so evil disposed, it would be better to stop in the woods; to which the Governor answered, that he was impatient of sleeping out, and that he would lodge in the town.

Arriving near, the Chief came out to receive him, with many Indians singing and playing on flutes, and after tendering his services, gave him three cloaks of marten-skins. The Governor entered the town with the Caciques, seven or eight men of his guard, and three or four cavalry, who had dismounted to accompany them; and they seated themselves in a piazza. The Cacique of Tas-taluca asked the Governor to allow him to remain there, and not to weary him any more with walking; but, finding that was not to be permitted, he changed his plan, and, under pretext of speaking with some of the chiefs, he got up from where he sate, by the side of the Governor, and entered a house where were many Indians with their bows and arrows. The Governor, finding that he did not return, called to him; to which the Cacique answered that he would not come out, nor would he leave that town; that if the Governor wished to go in peace, he should quit at once, and not persist in carrying him away by force from his country and its dependencies.

CHAPTER XVIII.

How the Indians rose upon the Governor, and what followed upon that Rising.

The Governor, in view of the determination and furious answer of the Cacique, thought to soothe him with soft words; to which he made no answer, but, with great haughtiness and contempt, withdrew to where Soto could not see nor speak to him. The Governor, that he might send word to the Cacique for him to remain in the country at his will, and to be pleased to give him a guide, and persons to carry burdens, that he might see if he could pacify him with gentle words, called to a chief who was passing by. The Indian replied, loftily, that he would not listen to him. Baltasar de Gallegos, who was near, seized him by the cloak of marten-skins that he had on, drew it off over his head, and left it in his hands; whereupon, the Indians all beginning to rise, he gave him a stroke with a cutlass, that laid open his back, when they, with loud yells, came out of the houses, discharging their bows.

The Governor, discovering that if he remained there they could not escape, and if he should order his men, who were outside of the town, to come in, the horses might be killed by the Indians from the houses,

12

and great injury done, he ran out ; but before he could
get away he fell two or three times, and was helped to
rise by those with him. He and they were all badly
wounded : within the town five Christians were instantly
killed. Coming forth, he called out to all his men to get
farther off, because there was much harm doing from the
palisade. The natives discovering that the Christians
were retiring, and some, if not the greater number, at
more than a walk, the Indians followed with great boldness, shooting at them, or striking down such as they could
overtake. Those in chains having set down their burdens near the fence while the Christians were retiring,
the people of Mauilla lifted the loads on to their backs,
and, bringing them into the town, took off their irons,
putting bows and arms in their hands, with which to
fight. Thus did the foe come into possession of all the
clothing, pearls, and whatsoever else the Christians had
beside, which was what their Indians carried. Since
the natives had been at peace to that place, some of us,
putting our arms in the luggage, went without any;
and two, who were in the town, had their swords and
halberds taken from them, and put to use.

The Governor, presently as he found himself in the
field, called for a horse, and, with some followers, returned and lanced two or three of the Indians; the rest,
going back into the town, shot arrows from the palisade.
Those who would venture on their nimbleness came out
a stone's throw from behind it, to fight, retiring from
time to time, when they were set upon.

At the time of the affray there was a friar, a clergyman, a servant of the Governor, and a female slave in the town, who, having no time in which to get away, took to a house, and there remained until after the Indians became masters of the place. They closed the entrance with a lattice door; and there being a sword among them, which the servant had, he put himself behind the door, striking at the Indians that would have come in; while, on the other side, stood the friar and the priest, each with a club in hand, to strike down the first that should enter. The Indians, finding that they could not get in by the door, began to unroof the house: at this moment the cavalry were all arrived at Mauilla, with the infantry that had been on the march, when a difference of opinion arose as to whether the Indians should be attacked, in order to enter the town; for the result was held doubtful, but finally it was concluded to make the assault.

CHAPTER XIX

How the Governor set his Men in order of Battle
and entered the town of Mauilla.

So soon as the advance and the rear of the force were
come up, the Governor commanded that all the best
armed should dismount, of which he made four squadrons
of footmen. The Indians, observing how he was going
on arranging his men, urged the Cacique to leave, telling
him, as was afterwards made known by some women who
were taken in the town, that as he was but one man, and
could fight but as one only, there being many chiefs
present very skilful and experienced in matters of war,
any one of whom was able to command the rest, and as
things in war were so subject to fortune, that it was never
certain which side would overcome the other, they wished
him to put his person in safety; for if they should con-
clude their lives there, on which they had resolved rather
than surrender, he would remain to govern the land : but
for all that they said, he did not wish to go, until, from
being continually urged, with fifteen or twenty of his own
people he went out of the town, taking with him a scarlet
cloak and other articles of the Christians' clothing, being
whatever he could carry and that seemed best to him.

The Governor, informed that the Indians were leaving

the town, commanded the cavalry to surround it; and
into each squadron of foot he put a soldier, with a brand,
to set fire to the houses, that the Indians might have no
shelter. His men being placed in full concert, he ordered
an arquebuse to be shot off: at the signal the four squadrons, at their proper points, commenced a furious onset,
and, both sides severely suffering, the Christians entered
the town. The friar, the priest, and the rest who were
with them in the house, were all saved, though at the cost
of the lives of two brave and very able men who went
thither to their rescue. The Indians fought with so great
spirit that they many times drove our people back out of
the town. The struggle lasted so long that many Christians, weary and very thirsty, went to drink at a pond near
by, tinged with the blood of the killed, and returned to the
combat. The Governor, witnessing this, with those who
followed him in the returning charge of the footmen,
entered the town on horseback, which gave opportunity
to fire the dwellings; then breaking in upon the Indians
and beating them down, they fled out of the place, the
cavalry and infantry driving them back through the gates,
where, losing the hope of escape, they fought valiantly;
and the Christians getting among them with cutlasses,
they found themselves met on all sides by their strokes,
when many, dashing headlong into the flaming houses,
were smothered, and, heaped one upon another, burned to
death.

They who perished there were in all two thousand
five hundred, a few more or less: of the Christians there
fell two hundred, among whom was Don Carlos, brother-

in-law of the Governor; one Juan de Gamez, a nephew; Men. Rodriguez, a Portugues; and Juan Vazquez, of Villanueva de Barcarota, men of condition and courage; the rest were infantry. Of the living, one hundred and fifty Christians had received seven hundred wounds from the arrow; and God was pleased that they should be healed in little time of very dangerous injuries. Twelve horses died, and seventy were hurt. The clothing the Christians carried with them, the ornaments for saying mass, and the pearls, were all burned there; they having set the fire themselves, because they considered the loss less than the injury they might receive of the Indians from within the houses, where they had brought the things together.

The Governor learning in Manilla that Francisco Maldonado was waiting for him in the port of Ochuse, six days' travel distant, he caused Juan Ortiz to keep the news secret, that he might not be interrupted in his purpose; because the pearls he wished to send to Cuba for show, that their fame might raise the desire of coming to Florida, had been lost, and he feared that, hearing of him without seeing either gold or silver, or other thing of value from that land, it would come to have such reputation that no one would be found to go there when men should be wanted: so he determined to send no news of himself until he should have discovered a rich country.

CHAPTER XX.

How the Governor set out from Mauilla to go to Chicaça, and what befell him.

From the time the Governor arrived in Florida until he went from Mauilla, there died one hundred and two Christians, some of sickness, others by the hand of the Indians. Because of the wounded, he stopped in that place twenty-eight days, all the time remaining out in the fields. The country was a rich soil, and well inhabited: some towns were very large, and were picketed about. The people were numerous everywhere; the dwellings standing a crossbow-shot or two apart.

On Sunday, the eighteenth of November, the sick being found to be getting on well, the Governor left Mauilla, taking with him a supply of maize for two days. He marched five days through a wilderness, arriving in a province called Pafallaya, at the town Taliepataua; and thence he went to another, named Cabusto, near which was a large river, whence the Indians on the farther bank shouted to the Christians that they would kill them should they come over there. He ordered the building of a piragua within the town, that the natives might have no knowledge of it; which being finished in four days, and ready, he directed it to be taken on sleds

half a league up stream, and in the morning thirty men
entered it, well armed. The Indians discovering what
was going on, they who were nearest went to oppose the
landing, and did the best they could; but the Christians
drawing near, and the piragua being about to reach the
shore, they fled into some cane-brakes. The men on
horses went up the river to secure a landing-place, to
which the Governor passed over, with the others that
remained. Some of the towns were well. stored with
maize and beans.

Thence towards Chicaça the Governor marched five
days through a desert, and arrived at a river, on the
farther side of which were Indians, who wished to arrest
his passage. In two days another piragua was made,
and when ready he sent an Indian in it to the Cacique, to
say, that if he wished his friendship he should quietly
wait for him; but they killed the messenger before his
eyes, and with loud yells departed. He crossed the river
the seventeenth of December, and arrived the same day
at Chicaça, a small town of twenty houses. There the
people underwent severe cold, for it was already winter,
and snow fell: the greater number were then lying in
the fields, it being before they had time to put up habitations. The land was thickly inhabited, the people living
about over it as they do in Mauilla; and as it was fertile, the greater part being under cultivation, there was
plenty of maize. So much grain was brought together
as was needed for getting through with the season.

Some Indians were taken, among whom was one the
Cacique greatly esteemed. The Governor sent an Indian

to the Cacique to say, that he desired to see him and have his friendship. He came, and offered him the services of his person, territories, and subjects: he said that he would cause two chiefs to visit him in peace. In a few days he returned with them, they bringing their Indians. They presented the Governor one hundred and fifty conies, with clothing of the country, such as shawls and skins. The name of the one was Alimamu, of the other Niculasa.

The Cacique of Chicaça came to visit him many times: on some occasions he was sent for, and a horse taken, on which to bring and carry him back. He made complaint that a vassal of his had risen against him, withholding tribute; and he asked for assistance, desiring to seek him in his territory, and give him the chastisement he deserved. The whole was found to be feigned, to the end that, while the Governor should be absent with him, and the force divided, they would attack the parts separately—some the one under him, others the other, that remained in Chicaça. He went to the town where he lived, and came back with two hundred Indians, bearing bows and arrows.

The Governor, taking thirty cavalry and eighty infantry, marched to Saquechuma, the Province of the Chief whom the Cacique said had rebelled. The town was untenanted, and the Indians, for greater dissimulation, set fire to it; but the people with the Governor being very careful and vigilant, as were also those that had been left in Chicaça, no enemy dared to fall upon them. The Governor invited the caciques and some chiefs to dine with him, giving them pork to eat, which they so

13

relished, although not used to it, that every night Indians would come up to some houses where the hogs slept, a crossbow-shot off from the camp, to kill and carry away what they could of them. Three were taken in the act: two the Governor commanded to be slain with arrows, and the remaining one, his hands having first been cut off, was sent to the Cacique, who appeared grieved that they had given offence, and glad that they were punished.

This Chief was half a league from where the Christians were, in an open country, whither wandered off four of the cavalry: Francisco Osorio, Reynoso, a servant of the Marquis of Astorga, and two servants of the Governor,—the one Ribera, his page, the other Fuentes, his chamberlain. They took some skins and shawls from the Indians, who made great outcry in consequence, and abandoned their houses. When the Governor heard of it, he ordered them to be apprehended, and condemned Osorio and Fuentes to death, as principals, and all of them to lose their goods. The friars, the priests, and other principal personages solicited him to let Osorio live, and moderate the sentence; but he would do so for no one. When about ordering them to be taken to the town-yard to be beheaded, some Indians arrived, sent by the Chief to complain of them. Juan Ortiz, at the entreaty of Baltasar de Gallegos and others, changed their words, telling the Governor, as from the Cacique, that he had understood those Christians had been arrested on his account; that they were in no fault, having offended him in nothing, and that if he would do him a favour, to let them go free: then Ortiz said to the Indians, that the Governor had the persons in custody, and would visit them with such punishment as should be an example to the rest. The prisoners were ordered to be released.

So soon as March had come, the Governor, having determined to leave Chicaça, asked two hundred tamemes of the Cacique, who told him that he would confer with his chiefs. Tuesday, the eighth, he went where the Cacique was, to ask for the carriers, and was told that he would send them the next day. When the Governor saw the Chief, he said to Luis de Moscoso that the Indians did not appear right to him; that a very careful watch should be kept that night, to which the Field Marshal paid little attention. At four o'clock in the morning the Indians fell upon them in four squadrons, from as many quarters, and directly as they were discovered, they beat a drum. With loud shouting, they came in such haste, that they entered the camp at the same moment with some scouts that had been out; of which, by the time those in the town were aware, half the houses were in flames. That night it had been the turn of three horsemen to be of the watch,—two of them men of low degree, the least value of any in the camp, and the third a nephew of the Governor, who had been deemed a brave man until now, when he showed himself as great a coward as either of the others; for they all fled, and the Indians, finding no resistance, came up and set fire to the place. They waited outside of the town for the Christians, behind the gates, as they should come out of the doors, having had no opportunity to put on their arms; and as they ran in all directions, bewildered by the noise, blinded by the smoke and the brightness of the flame, knowing not whither they were going, or were able to find their arms, or put saddles on their steeds, they saw not the Indians who shot arrows at them. Those of the horses that could break their halters got away, and many were burned to death in the stalls.

The confusion and rout were so great that each man fled by the way that first opened to him, there being none to oppose the Indians: but God, who chastiseth his own as he pleaseth, and in the greatest wants and perils hath them in his hand, shut the eyes of the Indians, so that they could not discern what they had done, and believed that the beasts running about loose were the cavalry gathering to fall upon them. The Governor, with a soldier named Tápia, alone got mounted, and, charging upon the Indians, he struck down the first of them he met with a blow of the lance, but went over with the saddle, because in the haste it had not been tightly drawn, and he fell. The men on foot, running to a thicket outside of the town, came together there: the Indians imagining, as it was dark, that the horses were cavalry coming upon them, as has been stated, they fled, leaving only one dead, which was he the Governor smote.

The town lay in cinders. A woman, with her husband, having left a house, went back to get some pearls that had remained there; and when she would have come out again the fire had reached the door, and she could not, neither could her husband assist her, so she was consumed. Three Christians came out of the fire in so bad plight, that one of them died in three days from that time, and the two others for a long while were carried in their pallets, on poles borne on the shoulders of Indians, for otherwise they could not have got along. There died in this affair eleven Christians, and fifty horses. One hundred of the swine remained, four hundred having been destroyed, from the conflagration of Mauilla.

If, by good luck, any one had been able to save a garment until then, it was there destroyed. Many remained naked, not having had time to catch up their skin dresses. In that place they suffered greatly from cold, the only relief being in large fires, and they passed the night long in turning, without the power to sleep; for as one side of a man would warm, the other would freeze. Some contrived mats of dried grass sewed together, one to be placed below, and the other above them : many who laughed at this expedient were afterwards compelled to do the like. The Christians were left so broken up, that what with the want of the saddles and arms which had been destroyed, had the Indians returned the second night, they might, with little effort, have been overpowered. They removed from that town to the one where the Cacique was accustomed to live, because it was in the open field. In eight days' time they had constructed many saddles from the ash, and likewise lances, as good as those made in Biscay.

CHAPTER XXI.

How the Indians returned to attack the Christians,
and how the Governor went to Alimamu, and they
tarried to give him Battle in the Way.

On Wednesday, the fifteenth day of March, in the
year 1541, eight days having passed since the Governor
had been living on a plain, half a league from the place
where he wintered, after he had set up a forge, and tem-
pered the swords which in Chicaça had been burned, and
already had made many targets, saddles, and lances, [on
Tuesday night,] at four o'clock in the morning, while it
was still dark, there came many Indians, formed in three
squadrons, each from a different direction, to attack the
camp, when those who watched beat to arms. In all
haste he drew up his men in three squadrons also, and
leaving some for the defence of the camp, he went out to
meet them. The Indians were overthrown and put to
flight. The ground was plain, and in a condition advan-
tageous to the Christians. It was now daybreak; and
but for some disorder, thirty or forty more enemies
might have been slain. It was caused by a friar raising great shouts in the camp, without any reason, crying, "To the camp! To the camp!" In consequence the

Governor and the rest went thither, and the Indians had time to get away in safety.

From some prisoners taken, the Governor informed himself of the region in advance. On the twenty-fifth day of April he left Chicaça and went to sleep at a small town called Alimamu. Very little maize was found ; and as it became necessary to attempt thence to pass a desert, seven days' journey in extent, the next day the Governor ordered that three captains, each with cavalry and foot, should take a different direction, to get provision for the way. Juan de Añasco, the Comptroller, went with fifteen horse and forty foot on the course the Governor would have to march, and found a staked fort where the Indians were awaiting them. Many were armed, walking upon it, with their bodies, legs, and arms painted and ochred, red, black, white, yellow, and vermilion in stripes, so that they appeared to have on stockings and doublet. Some wore feathers, and others horns on the head, the face blackened, and the eyes encircled with vermilion, to heighten their fierce aspect. So soon as they saw the Christians draw nigh they beat drums, and, with loud yells, in great fury came forth to meet them. As to Juan de Añasco and others it appeared well to avoid them, and to inform the Governor, they retired, over an even ground in sight, the distance of a crossbow-shot from the enclosure, the footmen, the crossbow-men, and targeteers putting themselves before those on horseback, that the beasts might not be wounded by the Indians, who came forth by sevens and eights to discharge their bows at them and retire. In sight of the Christians they made a fire, and, taking an Indian by the head and feet, pretended to give him many blows on the head and cast him into the flames, signifying in this way what they would do with the Christians.

A message being sent with three of the cavalry to the Governor, informing him of this, he came directly. It was his opinion that they should be driven from the place. He said that if this was not done they would be emboldened to make an attack at some other time, when they might do him more harm: those on horseback were commanded to dismount, and, being set in four squadrons, at the signal charged the Indians. They resisted until the Christians came up to the stakes; then, seeing that they could not defend themselves, they fled through that part near which passed a stream, sending back some arrows from the other bank; and because, at the moment, no place was found where the horses might ford, they had time to make their escape. Three Indians were killed and many Christians wounded, of whom, after a few days, fifteen died on the march. Every one thought the Governor committed a great fault in not sending to examine the state of the ground on the opposite shore, and discover the crossing-place before making the attack; because, with the hope the Indians had of escaping unseen in that direction, they fought until they were broken; and it was the cause of their holding out so long to assail the Christians, as they could, with safety to themselves.

CHAPTER XXII.

How the Governor went from Quizquiz, and thence to the River Grande.

THREE days having gone by since some maize had been sought after, and but little found in comparison with the great want there was of it, the Governor became obliged to move at once, notwithstanding the wounded had need of repose, to where there should be abundance. He accordingly set out for Quizquiz, and marched seven days through a wilderness, having many pondy places, with thick forests, fordable, however, on horseback, all to some basins or lakes that were swum. He arrived at a town of Quizquiz without being descried, and seized all the people before they could come out of their houses. Among them was the mother of the Cacique; and the Governor sent word to him, by one of the captives, to come and receive her, with the rest he had taken. The answer he returned was, that if his lordship would order them to be loosed and sent, he would come to visit and do him service.

The Governor, since his men arrived weary, and likewise weak, for want of maize, and the horses were also lean, determined to yield to the requirement and try to have peace; so the mother and the rest were ordered to

14

be set free, and with words of kindness were dismissed. The next day, while he was hoping to see the Chief, many Indians came, with bows and arrows, to set upon the Christians, when he commanded that all the armed horsemen should be mounted and in readiness. Finding them prepared, the Indians stopped at the distance of a crossbow-shot from where the Governor was, near a river-bank, where, after remaining quietly half an hour, six chiefs arrived at the camp, stating that they had come to find out what people it might be; for that they had knowledge from their ancestors that they were to be subdued by a white race; they consequently desired to return to the Cacique, to tell him that he should come presently to obey and serve the Governor. After presenting six or seven skins and shawls brought with them, they took their leave, and returned with the others who were waiting for them by the shore. The Cacique came not, nor sent another message.

There was little maize in the place, and the Governor moved to another town, half a league from the great river, where it was found in sufficiency. He went to look at the river, and saw that near it there was much timber of which piraguas might be made, and a good situation in which the camp might be placed. He directly moved, built houses, and settled on a plain a crossbow-shot from the water, bringing together there all the maize of the towns behind, that at once they might go to work and cut down trees for sawing out planks to build barges. The Indians soon came from up the stream, jumped on shore, and told the Governor that they were the vassals of a great lord, named Aquixo, who was the suzerain of many towns and people on the other shore; and they made known from him, that he would come the day after, with all his people, to hear what his lordship would command him.

The next day the Cacique arrived, with two hundred canoes filled with men, having weapons. They were painted with ochre, wearing great bunches of white and other plumes of many colours, having feathered shields in their hands, with which they sheltered the oarsmen on either side, the warriors standing erect from bow to stern, holding bows and arrows. The barge in which the Cacique came had an awning at the poop, under which he sate; and the like had the barges of the other chiefs: and there, from under the canopy, where the chief man was, the course was directed and orders issued to the rest. All came down together, and arrived within a stone's cast of the ravine, whence the Cacique said to the Governor, who was walking along the river-bank, with others who bore him company, that he had come to visit, serve, and obey him; for he had heard that he was the greatest of lords, the most powerful on all the earth, and that he must see what he would have him do. The Governor expressed his pleasure, and besought him to land, that they might the better confer; but the Chief gave no reply, ordering three barges to draw near, wherein was great quantity of fish, and loaves like bricks, made of the pulp of ameixas, which Soto receiving, gave him thanks and again entreated him to land.

Making the gift had been a pretext, to discover if any

harm might be done; but, finding the Governor and his people on their guard, the Cacique began to draw off from the shore, when the crossbow-men, who were in readiness, with loud cries shot at the Indians, and struck down five or six of them. They retired with great order, not one leaving the oar, even though the one next to him might have fallen, and covering themselves, they withdrew. Afterward they came many times and landed: when approached, they would go back to their barges. These were fine-looking men, very large and well formed; and what with the awnings, the plumes, and the shields, the pennons, and the number of people in the fleet, it appeared like a famous armada of galleys.

During the thirty days that were passed there, four piraguas were built, into three of which, one morning, three hours before daybreak, the Governor ordered twelve cavalry to enter, four in each, men in whom he had confidence that they would gain the land, notwithstanding the Indians, and secure the passage, or die: he also sent some crossbow-men of foot with them, and in the other piragua, oarsmen, to take them to the opposite shore. He ordered Juan de Guzman to cross with the infantry, of which he had remained Captain in the place of Francisco Maldonado: and because the current was stiff, they went up along the side of the river a quarter of a league, and in passing over they were carried down, so as to land opposite the camp; but, before arriving there, at twice the distance of a stone's cast, the horsemen rode out from the piraguas to an open area of hard and even ground, where they all reached without accident.

So soon as they had come to shore the piraguas returned; and when the sun was up two hours high, the people had all got over. The distance was near half a league: a man standing on the shore could not be told, whether he were a man or something else, from the other side. The stream was swift, and very deep; the water always flowing turbidly, brought along from above many trees and much timber, driven onward by its for There were many fish of several sorts, the greater differing from those of the fresh waters of Spain, as be told hereafter.

t
if
jd
pe

CHAPTER XXIII.

How the Governor went from Aquixo to Casqui, and thence to Pacaha; and how this Country differs from the other.

The Rio Grande being crossed, the Governor marched a league and a half, to a large town of Aquixo, which was abandoned before his arrival. Over a plain thirty Indians were seen to draw nigh, sent by the Cacique, to discover what the Christians intended to do, but who fled directly as they saw them. The cavalry pursued, killed ten, and captured fifteen. As the town toward which the Governor marched was near the river, he sent a captain, with the force he thought sufficient, to take the piraguas up the stream. These, as they frequently wound about through the country, having to go round the bays that swell out of the river, the Indians had opportunity to attack those in the piraguas, placing them in great peril, being shot at with bows from the ravines, while they dared not leave the shore, because of the swiftness of the current; so that, as soon as the Governor got to the town, he directly sent cross-bow-men to them down the stream, for their protection. When the piraguas arrived, he ordered them to be taken to pieces, and the spikes kept for making others, when they should be needed.

The Governor slept at the town one night, and the day following he went in quest of a province called Pacaha, which he had been informed was nigh Chisca, where the Indians said there was gold. He passed through large towns in Aquixo, which the people had left for fear of the Christians. From some Indians that were taken, he heard that three days' journey thence resided a great Cacique, called Casqui. He came to a small river, over which a bridge was made, whereby he crossed. All that day, until sunset, he marched through water, in places coming to the knees; in others, as high as the waist. They were greatly rejoiced on reaching the dry land; because it had appeared to them that they should travel about, lost, all night in the water. At midday they came to the first town of Casqui, where they found the Indians off their guard, never having heard of them. Many men and women were taken, much clothing, blankets, and skins; such they likewise took in another town in sight of the first, half a league off in the field, whither the horsemen had run.

This land is higher, drier, and more level than any other along the river that had been seen until then. In the fields were many walnut-trees, bearing tender-shelled nuts in the shape of acorns, many being found stored in the houses. The tree did not differ in any thing from that of Spain, nor from the one seen before, except the leaf was smaller. There were many mulberry-trees, and trees of amexeas, having fruit of vermilion hue, like one of Spain, while others were gray, differing, but far better. All the trees, the year round, were as green as if they stood in orchards, and the woods were open.

The Governor marched two days through the country of Casqui, before coming to the town where the Cacique was, the greater part of the way lying through fields thickly set with great towns, two or three of them to be seen from one. He sent word by an Indian to the Cacique, that he was coming to obtain his friendship and to consider him as a brother; to which he received for answer, that he would be welcomed; that he would be received with special good-will, and all that his lordship required of him should be done; and the Chief sent him on the road a present of skins, shawls, and fish. After these gifts were made, all the towns into which the Governor came were found occupied; and the inhabitants awaited him in peace, offering him skins, shawls, and fish.

Accompanied by many persons, the Cacique came half a league on the road from the town where he dwelt to receive the Governor, and, drawing nigh to him, thus spoke :—

VERY HIGH, POWERFUL, AND RENOWNED MASTER :—

I greet your coming. So soon as I had notice of you, your power and perfections, although you entered my territory capturing and killing the dwellers upon it, who are my vassals, I determined to conform my wishes to your will, and hold as right all that you might do, believing that it should be so for a good reason, providing against some future event, to you perceptible but from me concealed; since an evil may well be permitted to avoid another greater, that good can arise, which I trust will be so; for from so excellent a prince, no bad motive is to be suspected. My ability is so small to serve you, according to your great merit, that though you should consider even my abundant will and humility in proffering you all manner of services, I must still deserve little in your sight. If this ability can with reason be valued, I pray you receive it, and with it my country and my vassals, of me and them disposing at your pleasure; for though you were lord of the earth, with no more goodwill would you be received, served, and obeyed.

The Governor responded appropriately in a few words which satisfied the Chief. Directly they fell to making each other great proffers, using much courtesy, the Cacique inviting the Governor to go and take lodging in his houses. He excused himself, the better to preserve peace, saying that he wished to lie in the field; and, because the heat was excessive, he pitched the camp among some trees, quarter of a league from the town. The Cacique went to his town, and returned with many Indians singing, who, when they had come to where the Governor was, all prostrated themselves. Among them were two blind men. The Cacique made an address, of which, as it was long, I will give the substance in a few words. He said, that inasmuch as the Governor was son of the Sun, he begged him to restore sight to those Indians: whereupon the blind men arose, and they very earnestly entreated him to do so. Soto answered them, that in the heavens above there was One who had the power to make them whole, and do whatever they could ask of Him, whose servant he was; that this great Lord made the sky and the earth, and man after His image; that He had suffered on the tree of the true cross to save the human race, and risen from the grave on the third day,—what of man there was of Him dying, what of divinity being immortal; and that, having ascended into heaven, He was

15

there with open arms to receive all that would be con-
verted to Him. He then directed a lofty cross of wood to
be made and set up in the highest part of the town,
declaring to the Cacique that the Christians worshipped
that, in the form and memory of the one on which Christ
suffered. He placed himself with his people before it, on
their knees, which the Indians did likewise; and he told
them that from that time thenceforth they should thus
worship the Lord, of whom he had spoken to them, that
was in the skies, asking Him for whatsoever they stood in
need.

The Chief being asked what was the distance to
Pacaha, he answered that it was one day's journey, and
said that on the extreme of his territory there was a lake,
like an estuary, that entered into the Rio Grande, to which
he would send persons in advance to build a bridge, whereby they might pass over it. The night of the day the
Governor left, he slept at a town of Casqui; and the next
day he passed in sight of two other towns, and arrived
at the lake, which was half a crossbow-shot over, of great
depth and swiftness of current. The Indians had just
got done the bridge as he came up. It was built of wood,
in the manner of timber thrown across from tree to tree;
on one side there being a rail of poles, higher than the
rest, as a support for those who should pass. The Cacique of Casqui having come with his people, the Governor sent word by an Indian to the Cacique of Pacaha,
that though he might be at enmity with him of Casqui,
and that Chief be present, he should receive neither
injury nor insult, provided that he attended in peace

and desired his friendship, for as a brother would he treat him. The Indian went as he was bid, and returned, stating that the Cacique took no notice of the message, but that he fled out of the town, from the back part, with all his people. Then the Governor entered there, and with the cavalry charged in the direction the Indians were running, and at another town, a quarter of a league off, many were taken. As fast as they were captured, the horsemen delivered them to the Indians of Casqui, who, from being their enemies, brought them with great heed and pleasure to the town where the Christians were, greatly regretting that they had not the liberty to kill them. Many shawls, deer-skins, lion and bear skins, and many cat-skins were found in the town. Numbers who had been a long time badly covered, there clothed themselves. Of the shawls they made mantles and cassocks; some made gowns and lined them with cat-skins, as they also did the cassocks. Of the deer-skins were made jerkins, shirts, stockings, and shoes; and from the bear-skins they made very good cloaks, such as no water could get through. They found shields of raw cow-hide out of which armour was made for the horses.

CHAPTER XXIIII.

Of how the Cacique of Pacaha came in Peace, and he of Casqui, having absented himself, returned to excuse his Conduct; and how the Governor made Friendship between the Chiefs.

On Wednesday, the nineteenth day of June, the Governor entered Pacaha, and took quarters in the town where the Cacique was accustomed to reside. It was enclosed and very large. In the towers and the palisade were many loopholes. There was much dry maize, and the new was in great quantity, throughout the fields. At the distance of half a league to a league off were large towns, all of them surrounded with stockades.

Where the Governor stayed was a great lake, near to the enclosure; and the water entered a ditch that well-nigh went round the town. From the River Grande to the lake was a canal, through which the fish came into it, and where the Chief kept them for his eating and pastime. With nets that were found in the place, as many were taken as need required; and however much might be the casting, there was never any lack of them. In the many other lakes about were also many fish, though the flesh was soft, and none of it so good as that which came from the river. The greater number differ from those in the fresh water of Spain. There was a fish

called bagre, the third part of which was head, with gills
from end to end, and along the sides were great spines,
like very sharp awls. Those of this sort that lived in the
lake were as big as pike; in the river were some that
weighed from one hundred to one hundred and fifty
pounds. Many were taken with the hook. There was
one in the shape of barbel; another like bream, with the
head of a hake, having a colour between red and brown,
and was the most esteemed. There was likewise a kind
called peel-fish, the snout a cubit in length, the upper
lip being shaped like a shovel. Another fish was like a
shad. Except the bagres and the peel, they were all
of scale. There was one, called pereo, the Indians sometimes brought, the size of a hog, and had rows of teeth
above and below.

The Cacique of Casqui many times sent large presents
of fish, shawls, and skins. Having told the Governor
that he would deliver into his hands the Cacique of
Pacaha, he went to Casqui, and ordered many canoes to
ascend the river, while he should march by land, taking
many of his warriors. The Governor, with forty cavalry
and sixty infantry, was conducted by him up stream; and
the Indians who were in the canoes discovered the
Cacique of Pacaha on an islet between two arms of the
river. Five Christians entered a canoe, of whom was
Don Antonio Osorio, to go in advance and see what
number of people the Cacique had with him. There
were five or six thousand souls, who, directly as they saw
the people, taking the Indians who went in the canoes to
be Christians also, the Cacique, and as many as could

get into three canoes that were there, fled to the opposite
bank; the greater part of the rest, in terror and confusion, plunging into the river to swim, many, mostly
women and infants, got drowned. Then the Governor,
who was on land, without knowing what was passing
with Don Antonio and those who accompanied him,
ordered the Christians, in all haste, to enter the canoes
with the Indians of Casqui, and they directly joining
Don Antonio on the islet, many men and women were
taken, and much clothing.

Many clothes, which the Indians had in cane hurdles
and on rafts to carry over, floated down stream, the people
of Casqui filling their canoes with them; and, in fear
that the Christians might take these away, their Chief
went off with them down the river to his territory, without taking leave. At this the Governor became indignant,
and directly returning to Pacaha, two leagues on the road,
he overran the country of Casqui, capturing twenty or
thirty of its men. The horses being tired, and there remaining no time that day to go farther, he went on to
Pacaha, with the intention of marching in three or four
days upon Casqui, directly letting loose a man of Pacaha,
sending word by him to its Chief, that should he desire
his friendship to come to him, and together they would
go to carry war upon Casqui: and immediately there
arrived many people of Pacaha, bringing as the chief an
Indian, who was exposed by a prisoner, brother of the
Cacique. The Governor told them that their lord must
come; that he well knew that Indian was not he; for that
nothing could be done without its being known to him

before they so much as thought of it. The Cacique came the next day, followed by many Indians, with a large gift of fish, skins, and shawls. He made a speech, that all were glad to hear, and concluded by saying, that although his lordship had causelessly inflicted injury on his country and his subjects, he did not any the less cease to be his, and was always at his command. The Governor ordered his brother to be let go, and some principal men he held captives. That day a messenger arrived from Casqui, saying that his master would come early on the morrow to excuse the error he had committed in going away without his license; to which the Governor bade him say, in return, to the Cacique, that if he did not come himself in person he would go after him, and inflict the punishment he deserved.

The Chief of Casqui came the next day, and after presenting many shawls, skins, and fish, he gave the Governor a daughter, saying that his greatest desire was to unite his blood with that of so great a lord as he was, begging that he would take her to wife. He made a long and discreet oration, full of praise of Soto; and concluded by asking his forgiveness, for the love of that cross he had left, for having gone off without his permission; that he had done so because of the shame he felt for what his people had done without his consent. The Governor said that he had taken a good sponsor; that he had himself determined, if the Cacique had not come to apologize, to go after him and burn his towns, kill him and his people, and lay waste his country. To this the Chief replied :—

MASTER:—

I and mine belong to you; and my territory is yours, so that you will destroy it, if you will, as your own, and your people you will slay. All that falls from your hand I shall receive as from my lord's, and as merited chastisement. Know, that the service you have done me in leaving that cross has been signal, and more than I have deserved; for, you know, of great droughts the maize in our fields was perishing, and no sooner had I and mine thrown ourselves on our knees before it, asking for water, than the want was supplied.

The Governor made friendship between the Chiefs of Casqui and Pacaha, and placed them at the table, that they should eat with him. They had a difficulty as to who should sit at his right hand, which the Governor quieted by telling them that among the Christians the one seat was as good as the other; that they should so consider it, and while with him no one should understand otherwise, each taking the seat he first came to. Thence he sent thirty horsemen and fifty footmen to the Province of Caluça, to see if in that direction they could turn back towards Chisca, where the Indians said there was a foundry of gold and copper. They travelled seven days through desert, and returned in great extremity, eating green amexeas and maize-stalks, which they had found in a poor town of seven or eight houses. The Indians stated that thence towards the north, the country, being very cold, was very thinly populated; that cattle were in such plenty, no maize-field could be protected from them, and the inhabitants lived upon the meat. Seeing that the country was so poor off for maize that there could be no support, the Governor asked the Indians in what

direction there were most inhabitants; and they said that
they had knowledge of a large province and a country of
great abundance, called Quiguate, that lay in the southern direction.

16

CHAPTER XXV.

How the Governor went from Pacaha to Aquiguate and to Coligoa, and came to Cayas.

THE Governor rested in Pacaha forty days, during which time the two Caciques made him presents of fish, shawls, and skins, in great quantity, each striving to outdo the other in the magnitude of the gifts. At the time of his departure, the Chief of Pacaha bestowed on him two of his sisters, telling him that they were tokens of love, for his remembrance, to be his wives. The name of one was Macanoche, that of the other Mochila. They were symmetrical, tall, and full: Macanoche bore a pleasant expression; in her manners and features appeared the lady; the other was robust. The Cacique of Casqui ordered the bridge to be repaired; and the Governor, returning through his territory, lodged in the field near his town. He brought there much fish, exchanged two women for as many shirts with two of the Christians, and furnished a guide and tamemes. The Governor marched to one of his towns, and slept, and the next night came to another that was near a river, where he ordered him to bring canoes, that he might cross over. There taking his leave, the Chief went back.

The Governor travelled towards Aquiguate, and on

the fourth day of August came to the residence of the
Cacique, who, although he had sent him a present, on
the road, of many shawls and skins, abandoned the
place through fear on his arrival. That town was the
largest seen in Florida: one-half of it was occupied by
the Governor and his people; and, after a few days,
discovering that the Indians were dealing in falsehoods,
he ordered the other part to be burned, that it might
not afford them cover should they attack him at night,
nor be an embarrassment to his cavalry in a movement
to repel them. An Indian having come, attended by a
multitude, declaring himself to be the Cacique, the
Governor delivered him over to be looked after by his
body-guard. Many of the Indians went off, and returned
with shawls and skins; but, finding small opportunity
for carrying out their evil plan, one day the pretended
Cacique, walking out of the house with the Governor,
ran away with such swiftness that not one of the Christians could overtake him; and plunging into the river, at
the distance of a crossbow-shot from the town, he made
for the other shore, where many Indians, giving loud
shouts, began to make use of their arrows. The Governor directly crossed over to attack them with horse and
foot; but they dared not await him: following them up,
he came to a town that was abandoned, before which
there was a lake the horses could not pass over, and on
the other side were many females. The footmen having
crossed, capturing many of them, took much clothing.
Returning to the camp early in the night, the sentinels
seized a spy, who assenting to the request to lead to

where the Cacique was, the Governor directly set out
with twenty cavalry and fifty infantry in quest of him.
After travelling a day and a half, they found him in a
thick wood; and a soldier, ignorant of who he was, having struck him on the head with a cutlass, he called
out not to kill him, that he was the Chief; so he was
captured, and with him one hundred and forty of his
people.

The Governor, returning to Quiguate, directed him
to tell his people to come and serve the Christians; but,
after waiting some days, in the hope of their arrival, and
finding that they did not come, he sent two captains,
each on an opposite side of the river, with infantry and
cavalry, whereby many of both sexes were made prisoners. The Indians, seeing the harm that they received
for their rebellious conduct, waited on the Governor to
take his commands, coming and going often, bringing
with them presents of fish. The Cacique and two of his
wives being at their liberty in the quarters of the Governor, which were guarded by his halberdiers, he asked
them what part of the country was most inhabited; to
which they replied, that to the south, or down the river,
where were large towns, and the Caciques governed wide
territories, with numerous people; and that to the northwest was a province, near some mountains, called
Coligoa. He, with the others, deemed it well to go
thither first; saying that the mountains, perhaps, would
make a difference in the soil, and that silver and gold
might afterward follow.

The country of Aquiguate, like that of Casqui and

Pacaha, was level and fertile, having rich river margins, on which the Indians made extensive fields. From Tascaluça to the River Grande may be three hundred leagues; a region very low, having many lakes: from Pacaha to Quiguate there may be one hundred and ten leagues. There he left the Cacique in his own town; and an Indian guided them through an immense pathless thicket of desert for seven days, where they slept continually in ponds and shallow puddles. Fish were so plentiful in them that they were killed with blows of cudgels; and as the Indians travelled in chains, they disturbed the mud at the bottom, by which the fish, becoming stupefied, would swim to the surface, when as many were taken as were desired.

The inhabitants of Coligoa had never heard of the Christians, and when these got so near their town as to be seen, they fled up stream along a river that passed near by there; some throwing themselves into the water, whence they were taken by their pursuers, who, on either bank, captured many of both sexes, and the Cacique with the rest. Three days from that time came many Indians, by his order, with offerings of shawls, deer-skins, and two cowhides: they stated that at the distance of five or six leagues towards the north were many cattle, where the country, being cold, was thinly inhabited; and that, to the best of their knowledge, the province that was better provisioned than any other, and more populous, was one to the south, called Cayas.

About forty leagues from Quiguate stood Coligoa, at the foot of a mountain, in the vale of a river of medium

size, like the Caya, a stream that passes through **Estre-**
madura. The soil was rich, yielding maize in such pro-
fusion that the old was thrown out of store to make room
for the new grain. Beans and pumpkins were likewise
in great plenty: both were larger and better than those
of Spain: the pumpkins, when roasted, have nearly the
taste of chestnuts. The Cacique continued behind in his
own town, having given a guide for the way to Cayas.

We travelled five days, and came to the Province of
Palisema. The house of the Cacique was canopied with
coloured deer-skins, having designs drawn on them, and
the ground was likewise covered in the same manner, as
if with carpets. He had left it in that state for the use
of the Governor, a token of peace, and of a desire for
friendship, though still he did not dare to await his
coming. The Governor, finding that he had gone away,
sent a captain with horse and foot to look after him; and
though many persons were seen, because of the roughness
of the country, only a few men and boys were secured.
The houses were few and scattered: only a little maize
was found.

Directly the Governor set forward and came to Tata-
licoya, whence he took the Cacique, who guided him to
Cayas, a distance of four days' journey from that town.
When he arrived and saw the scattered houses, he
thought, from the information he had received of the
great populousness of the country, that the Cacique was
lying to him—that it was not the province; and he menaced him, bidding him tell where he was. The Chief, as
likewise the other Indians taken near by, declared that to

be in Cayas, the best town in all the province; and that although the houses were far apart, the country occupied being extensive, it had numerous people and many maize-fields. The town was called Tanico. The camp was placed in the best part of it, nigh a river. On the day of arrival, the Governor, with some mounted men, went a league farther, but found no one, and only some skins, which the Cacique had put on the road to be taken, a sign of peace, by the usage of the country.

CHAPTER XXVI.

How the Governor went to visit the Province of Tulla, and what happened to him.

The Governor tarried a month in the Province of Cayas. In this time the horses fattened and throve more than they had done at other places in a longer time, in consequence of the large quantity of maize there. The blade of it, I think, is the best fodder that grows. The beasts drank so copiously from the very warm and brackish lake, that they came having their bellies swollen with the leaf when they were brought back from watering. To that spot the Christians had wanted salt: they now made a quantity and took it with them. The Indians carry it into other parts, to exchange for skins and shawls.

The salt is made along by a river, which, when the water goes down, leaves it upon the sand. As they cannot gather the salt without a large mixture of sand, it is thrown together into certain baskets they have for their purpose, made large at the mouth and small at the bottom. These are set in the air on a ridge-pole; and water being thrown on, vessels are placed under them wherein it may fall; then, being strained and placed on the fire, it is boiled away, leaving salt at the bottom.

The lands on the shores of the river were fields, and

maize was in plenty. The Indians dared not cross the river to where we were. Some appearing, were called to by the soldiers who saw them, and having come over were conducted by them before the Governor. On being asked for the Cacique, they said that he was peaceful but afraid to show himself. The Governor directly sent them back to tell him to come, and, if he desired his friendship, to bring an interpreter and a guide for the travel before them; that if he did not do so he would go in pursuit, when it would be the worse for him. The Governor waited three days, and finding that the Cacique did not come, he went in pursuit and brought him there a captive, with one hundred and fifty of his people. He asked him if he had knowledge of any great cacique, and in what direction the country was most inhabited. The Indian stated, that the largest population about there was that of a province lying to the southward, thence a day and a half's travel, called Tulla; that he could give him a guide, but no interpreter; that the tongue of that country was different from his, and that he and his ancestors had ever been at war with its chiefs, so that they neither conversed together nor understood each other.

Then the Governor, with cavalry and fifty infantry, directly set out for Tulla, to see if it were such a land as he might pass through with his troops. So soon as it became known that he had reached there, the inhabitants were summoned; and as they gathered by fifteen and twenty at a time, they would come to attack the Christians. Finding that they were sharply handled, and that in running the horses would overtake them, they got

17

upon the house-tops, where they endeavoured to defend themselves with their bows and arrows. When beaten off from one roof, they would get up on to another; and the Christians while going after some, others would attack them from an opposite direction. The struggle lasted so long that the steeds, becoming tired, could not be made to run. One horse was killed and others were wounded. Of the Indians fifteen were slain, and forty women and boys made prisoners; for to no one who could draw a bow and could be reached was his life spared him.

The Governor determined at once to go back, before the inhabitants should have time to come together. That afternoon he set out, and travelling into the night, he slept on the road to avoid Tulla, and arrived the next day at Cayas. Three days later he marched to Tulla, bringing with him the Cacique, among whose Indians he was unable to find one who spoke the language of that place. He was three days on the way, and at his arrival found the town abandoned, the inhabitants not venturing to remain for him. But no sooner did they know that he was in the town, than, at four o'clock on the morning of the first night, they came upon him in two squadrons, from different directions, with bows and arrows and with long staves like pikes. So soon as they were felt, both cavalry and infantry turned out. Some Christians and some horses were injured. Many of the Indians were killed.

Of those made captive, the Governor sent six to the Cacique, their right hands and their noses cut off, with the message, that, if he did not come to him to apologize and render obedience, he would go in pursuit, and to him, and as many of his as he might find, would he do as he had done to those he sent. He allowed him three days in which to appear, making himself understood by signs, in the best manner possible, for want of an interpreter. At the end of that time an Indian, bearing a back-load of cow-skins from the Cacique, arrived, weeping with great sobs, and coming to where the Governor was, threw himself at his feet. Soto raised him up, and the man made a speech, but there was none to understand him. The Governor, by signs, told him to return and say to the Cacique, that he must send him some one who could speak with the people of Cayas. Three Indians came the next day with loads of cow-skins, and three days afterward came twenty others. Among them was one who understood those of Cayas. After a long oration from him, of apologies for the Cacique and in praise of the Governor, he concluded by saying, that he with the others had come, in behalf of the Chief, to inquire what his lordship would command, for that he was ready to serve him.

At hearing these words the Governor and the rest were all rejoiced; for in no way could they go on without a guide. He ordered the man to be safely kept, and told him to tell the Indians who came with him to go back to the Cacique and say, that he forgave him the past and greatly thanked him for the interpreter and the presents; that he should be pleased to see him, and to come the next day, that they might talk together. He came at the end of three days, and with him eighty Indians. As he and his men entered the camp they wept,—the token of obedience and the repentance of a past error, according

to the usage of that country. He brought a present of
many cow-skins, which were found very useful; the country being cold, they were taken for bed-covers, as they
were very soft and the wool like that of sheep. Near by,
to the northward, are many cattle. The Christians did
not see them, nor go where they were, because it was a
country thinly populated, having little maize. The Cacique of Tulla made an address to the Governor, in which
he apologized and offered him his country, his vassals, and
his person.. The speech of this Cacique—like those of
the other chiefs, and all the messengers in their behalf
who came before the Governor—no orator could more
elegantly phrase.

CHAPTER XXVII.

How the Governor went from Tulla to Autiamque, where he passed the Winter.

The Governor informed himself of the country in every direction. He ascertained that toward the west there was a thin population, and to the southeast were great towns, principally in a province, abundant of maize, called Autiamque, at the distance of about eighty leagues, ten days' journey from Tulla. The winter was already come. The cold, rain, and snow did not permit the people to travel for two or three months in the year, and the Governor feared to remain among that sparse population, lest his force could not be subsisted for that length of time. Moreover, the Indians said that near Autiamque was a great water, which, from their account, appeared to him to be an arm of the sea. Hence, he determined to winter in that province, and in the following summer to go to the sea-side, where he would build two brigantines,—one to send to Cuba, the other to New Spain, that the arrival of either might bear tidings of him. Three years had elapsed since he had been heard of by Doña Ysabel, or by any person in a civilized community. Two hundred and fifty of his men were dead, likewise one hundred and fifty horses. He desired to

recruit from Cuba of man and beast, calculating, out of
his property there, to refit and again go back to advance,
to discover and to conquer farther on towards the west,
where he had not reached, and whither Cabeça de Vaca
had wandered.

Having dismissed the Caciques of Tulla and Cayas,
the Governor took up his course, marching five days
over very sharp mountains, and arrived in a peopled
district called Quipana. Not a native could be captured,
because of the roughness of the country, and the town
was among ridges. At night an ambuscade was set,
in which two men were taken, who said that Autiamque
was six days' journey distant, and that there was another
province toward the south, eight days' travel off, called
Guahate, very abundant in maize and very populous.
However, as Autiamque was nearer, and most of the
Indians spoke of it, the Governor continued on his journey thither.

At the end of three days he came to a town
called Anoixi. Having sent a captain in advance, with
thirty horse and fifty foot, they came suddenly upon
the inhabitants, taking many of both sexes. On the
second day afterwards, the Governor arrived at another
town, called Catamaya, and slept in the adjacent fields.
Two Indians coming to him from the Cacique, with the
pretext of a message, in order to ascertain his business,
he told them to say to their master, that he wished to
speak with him; but they came no more, nor was other
word returned. The next day the Christians went to the
town, which was without people, and having taken what

maize they needed, that night they reached a wood to rest, and the day following arrived at Autiamque.

They found in store much maize, also beans, walnuts, and dried ameixas in large quantities. Some Indians were taken while gathering up their clothing, having already carried away their wives. The country was level and very populous. The Governor lodged in the best portion of the town, and ordered a fence immediately to be put up about the encampment, away from the houses, that the Indians without might do no injury with fire. Measuring off the ground by pacing, he allotted to each his part to build, according to the Indians he possessed; and the timber being soon brought by them, in three days it was finished, made of very high trees sunk deep in the ground, and traversed by many pieces.

Near by passed a river of Cayas, the shores of it well peopled, both above and below the town. Indians appeared on the part of the Cacique with a present of shawls and skins, and a lame Chief, the lord of a town called Tietiquaquo, subject to the Cacique of Autiamque, came frequently to visit the Governor, and brought him gifts of the things he possessed. The Cacique sent to the Governor to inquire what length of time he would remain in his territory; and hearing that he was to be there more than three days, he sent no more messages nor Indians, but treated with the lame Chief to insurge. Numerous inroads were made, in which many persons of both sexes were taken, and among the rest that Chief, whom the Governor, having reprehended and admonished, set at liberty, in consideration of the presents he had made, giving him two Indians to bear him away on their shoulders.

The Cacique of Autiamque, desiring to drive the strangers out of his territory, ordered spies to be set about them. An Indian, coming at night to the entrance of the palisade, was noticed by a soldier on guard, who, putting himself behind the door as he entered, struck him down with a cutlass. When taken before the Governor, he was asked why he came, but fell dead without utterance. The next night the Governor sent a soldier to beat the alarm, and cry out that he saw Indians, in order to ascertain how fast the men would hasten to the call. This was done also in other places, at times when it appeared to him they were careless, that he might reprove those who were late in coming; so that for danger, as well as for doing his duty, each one on such occasion would strive to be the first.

The Christians stayed three months in Autiamque, enjoying the greatest plenty of maize, beans, walnuts, and dried ameixas; also conies, which they had never had ingenuity enough to ensnare until the Indians there taught them. The contrivance is a strong spring, that lifts the animal off its feet, a noose being made of a stiff cord to run about the neck, passing through rings of cane, that it may not be gnawed. Many of them were taken in the maize-fields, usually when it was freezing or snowing. The Christians were there a month in snow, when they did not go out of town, save to a wood, at the distance of two crossbow-shots, to which, whenever fuel was wanted, a road was opened, the Governor and others, on horseback, going to and returning from it many times, when it was brought from there by those of foot. In this time many conies were killed with arrows by the Indians, who were now allowed to go at large in their shackles. The animal is of two sorts; one of them like that of Spain, the other of the colour, form, and size of the great hare, though longer even, and having bigger loins.

18

CHAPTER XXVIII.

How the Governor went from Autiamque to Nilco, and thence to Guachoya.

On Monday, the sixth day of March, of the year 1542 of the Christian era, the Governor set out from Autiamque to seek Nilco, which the Indians said was nigh the River Grande, with the purpose, by going to the sea, to recruit his forces. He had not over three hundred efficient men, nor more than forty horses. Some of the beasts were lame, and useful only in making out the show of a troop of cavalry; and, from the lack of iron, they had all gone a year without shoes, though, from the circumstance of travelling in a smooth country, they had little need of them.

Juan Ortiz died in Autiamque, a loss the Governor greatly regretted; for, without an interpreter, not knowing whither he was travelling, Soto feared to enter the country, lest he might get lost. Thenceforth a lad, taken in Cutifachiqui, who had learned somewhat of the language of the Christians, served as the interpreter. The death was so great a hindrance to our going, whether on discovery or out of the country, that to learn of the Indians what would have been rendered in four words, it became necessary now to have the whole day: and

oftener than otherwise the very opposite was understood
of what was asked; so that many times it happened the
road that we travelled one day, or sometimes two or
three days, would have to be returned over, wandering
up and down, lost in thickets.

The Governor went to a province called Ayays,
arriving at a town near the river that passed by Cayas,
and by Autiamque, from which he had been ten days in
coming. He ordered a piragua to be built, in which he
crossed; and, having arrived on the other shore, there set
in such weather that marching was impossible for four
days, because of snow. When that ceased to fall, he
travelled three days through desert, a region so low, so
full of lakes and bad passages, that at one time, for the
whole day, the travel lay through water up to the knees
at places, in others to the stirrups; and occasionally, for
the distance of a few paces, there was swimming. And
he came to Tutelpinco, a town untenanted, and found to
be without maize, seated near a lake that flowed copiously into the river, with a violent current. Five Christians, in charge of a captain, in attempting to cross, by
order of the Governor, were upset; when some seized
hold of the canoe they had employed, others of trees that
grew in the water, while one, a worthy man, Francisco
Bastian, a native of Villanueva de Barcarota, became
drowned. The Governor travelled all one day along the
margin of the lake, seeking for a ford, but could discover
none, nor any way to get over.

Returning to Tutelpinco at night, the Governor
found two friendly natives, who were willing to show

him the crossing, and the road he was to take. From the reeds and timber of the houses, rafts and causeways were made, on which the river was crossed. After three days' marching, at Tianto, in the territory of Nilco, thirty Indians were taken, among whom were two Chiefs of the town. A captain, with infantry and cavalry, was directly dispatched to Nilco, that the inhabitants might not have time to carry off their provisions. In going through three or four large towns, at the one where the Cacique resided, two leagues from where the Governor stayed, many Indians were found to be in readiness, with bows and arrows, who, surrounding the place, appeared to invite an onset; but so soon as they saw the Christians drawing nigh to them without faltering, they approached the dwelling of the Cacique, setting fire to it, and, by a pond near the town, through which the horses could not go, they fled.

The following day, Wednesday, the twenty-ninth of March, the Governor arrived at Nilco. making his quarters, and those of his people, in the town of the Cacique, which was in an open field, that for a quarter of a league over was all inhabited; and at the distance of from half a league to a league off were many other large towns, in which was a good quantity of maize, beans, walnuts, and dried ameixas. This was the most populous of any country that was seen in Florida, and the most abundant in maize, excepting Coça and Apalache. An Indian, attended by a party, arrived at the camp, and, presenting the Governor with a cloak of marten-skins and a string of pearls, he received some

margaridetas (a kind of bead much esteemed in Peru),
and other trinkets, with which he was well pleased. At
leaving, he promised to be back in two days, but did not
return. In the night-time, however, the Indians came in
canoes, and carrying away all the maize they could take,
set up their huts on the other side of the river, among
the thickest bushes. The Governor, finding that the
Indian did not arrive within the time promised, ordered
an ambuscade to be placed at some cribs, near the lake,
to which the Indians came for maize. Two of them
were taken, who told him that the person who had come
to visit him was not the Cacique, but one sent by him,
pretending to be he, in order to observe what might be
the vigilance of the Christians, and whether it was
their purpose to remain in that country, or to go farther.
Directly a captain, with men on horseback and foot, were
sent over to the other shore; but, as their crossing was
observed only ten or a dozen Indians, of both sexes,
could be taken; and with these the Christians returned
to camp.

This river, passing by Anilco, is the same that
flows by Cayas and Autiamque, and falls into the
River Grande, which flows by Pacaha and Aquixo,
near the Province of Guachoya, the lord of which
ascended in canoes to carry war upon him of Nilco.
In his behalf a messenger came to the Governor, saying
that the Cacique was his servant, desiring to be so considered, and that in two days from that time he would
come to make his salutation. He arrived in season,
accompanied by some of his principal men, and with

great proffers and courtesy, he presented many shawls and deer-skins. The Governor gave him some articles of barter, showing him much attention, and inquired what towns there might be on the river below. He replied that he knew of none other than his own; that opposite was the Province of a Cacique called Quigaltam; then, taking his leave, returned to his town.

The Governor determined to go to Guachoya within a few days, to learn if the sea were near, or if there were any inhabited territory nigh it, where he might find subsistence whilst those brigantines were building, that he desired to send to a country of Christians. As he crossed the River of Nilco, there came up Indians in canoes from Guachoya, who, when they saw him, thinking that he was in their pursuit, to do them harm, they returned down the river, and informed the Cacique, when he took away from the town whatsoever his people could carry, and passed over with them, all that night, to the other bank of the River Grande. The Governor sent a captain with fifty men, in six canoes, down the river to Guachoya; while he, with the rest, marched by land, arriving there on Sunday, the seventeenth day of April. He took up his quarters in the town of the Cacique, which was palisaded, seated a crossbow-shot from the stream, that is there called the River Tamaliseu, Tapatu at Nilco, Mico at Coça, and at its entrance is known as The River.

CHAPTER XXIX.

THE MESSAGE SENT TO QUIGALTAM, AND THE ANSWER BROUGHT BACK TO THE GOVERNOR, AND WHAT OCCURRED THE WHILE.

So soon as the Governor arrived in Guachoya, he ordered Juan de Añasco, with as many people as could go in the canoes, to ascend the river; for while they were coming from Anilco they saw some cabins newly built on the opposite shore. The Comptroller went, and brought back the boats laded with maize, beans, dried ameixas, and the pulp of them made into many loaves. The same day an Indian arrived from Guachoya, and said that the Cacique would come on the morrow. The next day, many canoes were seen ascending the river; and the people in them remained for an hour on the opposite side of the River Grande, in consultation, as to whether they should come to us or not; but finally they concluded to come, and crossed the river, among them being the Cacique of Guachoya with many Indians, bringing much fish, many dogs, skins, and blankets. So soon as they had landed, they went to the lodging of the Governor in the town, and having presented him with the offerings, the Cacique thus spoke:—

POTENT AND EXCELLENT MASTER:—

I entreat you to forgive me the error I committed in going away from this town, and not waiting to greet and to obey you; since the occasion should have been for me, and is, one of pride: but I dreaded what I should not have feared, and did consequently what was out of reason; for error comes of haste, and I left without proper thought. So soon as I had reflected, I resolved not to follow the inclination of the foolish, which is to persist in his course, but to take that of the discreet and the wise: thus have I changed my purpose, coming to see in what it is you will bid me serve you, within the farthermost limits of my control.

The Governor received him with much pleasure, thanking him for the proffers and gift. Being asked if he had any information of the sea, he said, none, nor of any other inhabited country below on that side of the river, except a town two leagues distant, belonging to a chief subject to him; nor on the other shore, save three leagues down, the Province of Quigaltam, the lord of which was the greatest of that country. The Governor, suspecting that the Cacique spoke untruthfully, to rid his towns of him, sent Juan de Añasco with eight of cavalry down the river, to discover what population might be there, and get what knowledge there was of the sea. He was gone eight days, and stated, when he got back, that in all that time he could not travel more than fourteen or fifteen leagues, on account of the great bogs that came out of the river, the cane-brakes and thick scrubs there were along the margin, and that he had found no inhabited spot.

The Governor sank into a deep despondency at sight of the difficulties that presented themselves to his reaching the sea; and, what was worse, from the way in which the men and horses were diminishing in numbers, he could not sustain himself in the country without succour. Of that reflection he pined: but, before he took to his pallet, he sent a messenger to the Cacique of Quigaltam, to say that he was the child of the Sun, and whence he came all obeyed him, rendering their tribute; that he besought him to value his friendship, and to come where he was; that he would be rejoiced to see him; and in token of love and his obedience, he must bring him something from his country that was in most esteem there. By the same Indian the Chief returned this answer:—

As to what you say of your being the son of the Sun, if you will cause him to dry up the great river, I will believe you: as to the rest, it is not my custom to visit any one, but rather all, of whom I have ever heard, have come to visit me, to serve and obey me, and pay me tribute, either voluntarily or by force: if you desire to see me, come where I am; if for peace, I will receive you with special good-will; if for war, I will await you in my town; but neither for you, nor for any man, will I set back one foot.

When the messenger returned, the Governor was already low, being very ill of fevers. He grieved that he was not in a state to cross the river at once, and go in quest of the Cacique, to see if he could not abate that pride; though the stream was already flowing very powerfully, was nearly half a league broad, sixteen fathoms in height, rushing by in furious torrent, and on either shore were many Indians; nor was his power any longer so great that he might disregard advantages, relying on his strength alone.

Every day the Indians of Guachoya brought fish, until they came to be in such plenty that the town was covered with them.

19

The Governor having been told by the Cacique, that on a certain night the Chief of Quigaltam would come to give him battle, he suspected it to be a fiction of his devising to get him out of his country, and he ordered him to be put under guard, and from that night forth the watch to be well kept. When asked why the Chief did not come, he said that he had, but that, finding the Governor in readiness, he dared not adventure; and he greatly importuned him to send the captains over the river, offering to supply many men to go upon Quigaltam; to which the Governor said, that so soon as he got well he would himself go to seek that Cacique. Observing how many Indians came every day to the town, and how populous was that country, the Governor fearing that they would plot together, and practise on him some perfidy, he permitted the gates in use, and some gaps in the palisade that had not yet been closed up, to remain open, that the Indians might not suppose he stood in fear, ordering the cavalry to be distributed there; and the night long they made the round, from each squadron going mounted men in couples to visit the scouts, outside the town, at points in the roads, and to the crossbow-men that guarded the canoes in the river.

That the Indians might stand in terror of them, the Governor determined to send a captain to Nilco, which the people of Guachoya had told him was inhabited, and, treating the inhabitants there severely, neither town would dare to attack him: so he commanded Captain Nuño de Tobar to march thither with fifteen horsemen, and Captain Juan de Guzman, with his company of foot, to ascend the river by water in canoes. The Cacique of Guachoya ordered canoes to be brought, and many warriors to come, who went with the Christians. Two leagues from Nilco, the cavalry, having first arrived, waited for the foot, and thence together they crossed the river in the night. At dawn, in sight of the town, they came upon a scout, who, directly as he saw the Christians, set up loud yells, and fled to carry the news to those in the place. Nuño de Tobar, and those with him, hastened on so rapidly, that they were upon the inhabitants before they could all get out of the town. The ground was open field; the part of it covered by the houses, which might be a quarter of a league in extent, contained five or six thousand souls. Coming out of them, the Indians ran from one to another habitation, numbers collecting in all parts, so that there was not a man on horseback who did not find himself amidst many; and when the Captain ordered that the life of no male should be spared, the surprise was such, that there was not a man among them in readiness to draw a bow. The cries of the women and children were such as to deafen those who pursued them. About one hundred men were slain; many were allowed to get away badly wounded, that they might strike terror into those who were absent.

Some persons were so cruel and butcher-like that they killed all before them, young and old, not one having resisted little nor much; while those who felt it their duty to be wherever there might be resistance, and were esteemed brave, broke through the crowds of Indians, bearing down many with their stirrups and the breasts of their horses, giving some a thrust and letting them go, but encountering a child or a woman would take and deliver it over to the footmen. To the ferocious and the bloodthirsty, God permitted that their sin should rise up against them in the presence of all—when there was occasion for fighting showing extreme cowardice, and in the end paying for it with their lives.

Eighty women and children were captured at Nilco, and much clothing. The Indians of Guachoya, before arriving at the town, had come to a stop, and from without watched the success of the Christians over the inhabitants; and when they saw that these were scattered, that the cavalry were following and lancing them, they went to the houses for plunder, filling the canoes with clothing; and lest the Christians might take away what they got, they returned to Guachoya, where they came greatly astonished at what they had seen done to the people of Nilco, which they, in great fear, recounted circumstantially to their Cacique.

CHAPTER XXX.

The Death of the Adelantado, Don Hernando de Soto, and how Luys Moscoso de Alvarado was chosen Governor.

The Governor, conscious that the hour approached in which he should depart this life, commanded that all the King's officers should be called before him, the captains and the principal personages, to whom he made a speech. He said that he was about to go into the presence of God, to give account of all his past life; and since He had been pleased to take him away at such a time, and when he could recognize the moment of his death, he, His most unworthy servant, rendered Him hearty thanks. He confessed his deep obligations to them all, whether present or absent, for their great qualities, their love and loyalty to his person, well tried in the sufferance of hardship, which he ever wished to honour, and had designed to reward, when the Almighty should be pleased to give him repose from labour with greater prosperity to his fortune. He begged that they would pray for him, that through mercy he might be pardoned his sins, and his soul be received in glory: he asked that they would relieve him of the charge he held over them, as well of the indebtedness he was

under to them all, as to forgive him any wrongs they
might have received at his hands.   To prevent any
divisions that might arise, as to who should command,
he asked that they would be pleased to elect a principal
and able person to be governor, one with whom they
should all be satisfied, and, being chosen, they would
swear before him to obey: that this would greatly satisfy
him, abate somewhat the pains he suffered, and moderate the anxiety of leaving them in a country, they knew
not where.

Baltasar de Gallegos responded in behalf of all,
consoling him with remarks on the shortness of the
life of this world, attended as it was by so many toils
and afflictions, saying that whom God earliest called
away, He showed particular favour; with many other
things appropriate to such an occasion: And finally,
since it pleased the Almighty to take him to Himself,
amid the deep sorrow they not unreasonably felt, it was
necessary and becoming in him, as in them, to conform
to the Divine Will: that as respected the election of a
governor, which he ordered, whomsoever his Excellency
should name to the command, him would they obey.
Thereupon the Governor nominated Luys Moscoso de
Alvarado to be his Captain-General; when by all those
present was he straightway chosen and sworn Governor.

The next day, the twenty-first of May, departed this
life the magnanimous, the virtuous, the intrepid Captain,
Don Hernando de Soto, Governor of Cuba and Adelantado of Florida.   He was advanced by fortune, in the
way she is wont to lead others, that he might fall the

greater depth: he died in a land, and at a time, that could afford him little comfort in his illness, when the danger of being no more heard from stared his companions in the face, each one himself having need of sympathy, which was the cause why they neither gave him their companionship nor visited him, as otherwise they would have done.

Luys de Moscoso determined to conceal what had happened from the Indians; for Soto had given them to understand that the Christians were immortal; besides, they held him to be vigilant, sagacious, brave; and, although they were at peace, should they know him to be dead, they, being of their nature inconstant, might venture on making an attack; and they were credulous of all that he had told them, who made them believe that some things which went on among them privately, and he had come at without their being able to see how, or by what means, that the figure which appeared in a mirror he showed, told him whatsoever they might be about, or desired to do; whence neither by word nor deed did they dare undertake any thing to his injury.

So soon as the death had taken place, Luys de Moscoso directed the body to be put secretly into a house, where it remained three days; and thence it was taken at night, by his order, to a gate of the town, and buried within. The Indians, who had seen him ill, finding him no longer, suspected the reason; and passing by where he lay, they observed the ground loose, and, looking about, talked among themselves. This coming to the knowledge of Luys de Moscoso, he ordered the corpse to be taken up at night, and among the shawls that enshrouded it having cast abundance of sand, it was taken out in a canoe and committed to the middle of the stream. The Cacique of Guachoya asked for him, saying: "What has been done with my brother and lord, the Governor?" Luys de Moscoso told him that he had ascended into the skies, as he had done on other many occasions; but as he would have to be detained there some time, he had left him in his stead. The Chief, thinking within himself that he was dead, ordered two well-proportioned young men to be brought, saying, that it was the usage of the country, when any lord died, to kill some persons, who should accompany and serve him on the way, on which account they were brought; and he told him to command their heads to be struck off, that they might go accordingly to attend his friend and master. Luys de Moscoso replied to him, that the Governor was not dead, but only gone into the heavens, having taken with him of his soldiers sufficient number for his need, and he besought him to let those Indians go, and from that time forward not to follow so evil a practice. They were presently ordered to be let loose, that they might return to their houses; but one of them refused to leave, alleging that he did not wish to remain in the power of one who, without cause, condemned him to die, and that he who had saved his life he desired to serve so long as he should live.

Luys de Moscoso ordered the property of the Governor to be sold at public outcry. It consisted of two male and three female slaves, three horses, and seven hundred swine. For each slave, or horse, was given two or three hundred cruzados, to be paid at the first melting up of gold or silver, or division of vassals and territory, with the obligation that should there be nothing found in the country, the payment should be made at the end of a year, those having no property to pledge to give their bond. A hog brought in the same way, trusted, two hundred cruzados. Those who had left any thing at home bought more sparingly, and took less than others. From that time forward most of the people owned and raised hogs; they lived on pork, observed Fridays and Saturdays, and the vespers of holidays, which they had not done before; for, at times, they had passed two or three months without tasting any meat, and on the day they got any, it had been their custom to eat it.

20

CHAPTER XXXI.

How the Governor Luys de Moscoso left Guachoya and went to Chaguate, and from thence
to Aguacay.

Some were glad of the death of Don Hernando de
Soto, holding it certain that Luys de Moscoso, who was
given to leading a gay life, preferred to see himself at
ease in a land of Christians, rather than continue the
toils of war, discovering and subduing, which the people had come to hate, finding the little recompense that
followed. The Governor ordered that the captains and
principal personages should come together, to consult
and determine upon what they would do; and, informed
of the population there was on all sides, he found that
towards the west the country was most inhabited, and
that descending the stream, after passing Quigaltam, it
was desert and had little subsistence. He besought them
all to give him their opinion in writing, signed with
their names, that, having the views of every one, he
might determine whether to follow down the river or
enter the land.

To every one it appeared well to march westwardly,
because in that direction was New Spain, the voyage by
sea being held more hazardous and of doubtful accom-

plishment, as a vessel of sufficient strength to weather a storm could not be built, nor was there captain nor pilot, needle nor chart, nor was it known how distant might be the sea; neither had they any tidings of it, or if the river did not take some great turn through the land, or might not have some fall over rocks where they might be lost. Some, who had seen the sea-card, found that by the shore, from the place where they were to New Spain, there should be about five hundred leagues; and they said that by land, though they might have to go round-about sometimes, in looking for a peopled country, unless some great impassable wilderness should intervene, they could not be hindered from going forward that summer; and, finding provision for support in some peopled coun-try where they might stop, the following summer they should arrive in a land of Christians; and that, going by land, it might be they should discover some rich country which would avail them. Moscoso, although it was his desire to get out of the land of Florida in the shortest time, seeing the difficulties that lay before him in a voy-age by sea, determined to undertake that which should appear to be the best to all.

Monday, the fifth of June, the Governor left Gua-choya, receiving a guide from the Cacique who remained in his town. They passed through a province called Catalte; and, going through a desert six days' journey in extent, on the twentieth of the month they came to Chaguate. The Cacique of the province had been to visit the Governor, Don Hernando de Soto, at Autiam-que, where he took him presents of shawls, skins, and

salt. The day before Luys de Moscoso arrived, a sick
Christian becoming missed, whom the Indians were suspected to have killed, he sent word to the Cacique to
look for and return him—that in so doing he would continue to be his friend ; if otherwise, the Cacique should
not hide from him anywhere, nor he nor his, and that he
would leave his country in ashes. The Chief directly
came, and, bringing the Christian, with a large gift of
shawls and skins, he made this speech :—

EXCELLENT MASTER :—

I would not deserve that opinion you have of me for all the
wealth of the world. Who impelled me to visit and serve that excellent lord, the Governor, your father, in Autiamque, which you
should have remembered, where I offered myself, with all loyalty,
truth, and love, to serve and obey his lifetime : or what could have
been my purpose, having received favours of him, and without
either of you having done me any injury, that I should be moved to
do that which I should not ? Believe me, no outrage, nor worldly
interest, could have been equal to making me act thus, or could
have so blinded me. Since, however, in this life, the natural course
is, after one pleasure should succeed many pains, fortune has been
pleased with your indignation to moderate the joy I felt in my heart
at your coming, and have failed where I aimed to hit, in pleasing
this Christian, who remained behind lost, treating him in a manner
of which he shall himself speak, thinking that in this I should do
you service, and intending to come with and deliver him to you at
Chaguate, serving you in all things, to the extent possible in my
power. If for this I deserve punishment from your hand, I shall
receive it as coming from my master's, as though it were favour.

The Governor answered, that because he had not
found him in Chaguate he was incensed, supposing that he
had kept away, as others had done ; but that, as he now
knew his loyalty and love, he would ever consider him a
brother, and would favour him in all matters. The Ca-

cique went with him to the town where he resided, the distance of a day's journey. They passed through a small town where was a lake, and the Indians made salt: the Christians made some on the day they rested there, from water that rose near by from springs in pools. The Governor was six days in Chaguate, where he informed himself of the people there were to the west. He heard that three days' journey distant, was a province called Aguacay.

On leaving Chaguate, a Christian remained behind, named Francisco de Guzman, bastard son of a gentleman of Sevilla, who, in fear of being made to pay for gaming debts in the person of an Indian girl, his concubine, he took her away with him; and the Governor, having marched two days before he was missed, sent word to the Cacique to seek for and send him to Aguacay, whither he was marching, but the Chief never did. Before arriving at this province they received five Indians, coming with a gift of skins, fish, and roasted venison, sent on the part of the Cacique. The Governor reached his town on Wednesday, the fourth day of July, and finding it unoccupied, lodged there. He remained in it a while, making some inroads, in which many Indians of both sexes were captured. There they heard of the South Sea. Much salt was got out of the sand, gathered in a vein of earth like slate, and was made as they make it in Cayas.

CHAPTER XXXII.

How the Governor went from Aguacay to Naguatex, and what happened to him.

The day the Governor left Aguacay he went to sleep near a small town, subject to the lord of that province. He set the encampment very nigh a salt lake, and that afternoon some salt was made. He marched the next day, and slept between two mountains, in an open grove; the next after, he arrived at a small town called Pato; and on the fourth day of his departure from Aguacay he came to the first inhabited place, in a province called Amaye. There they took an Indian, who said that thence to Naguatex was a day and a half's journey, all the way lying through an inhabited region.

Having passed out of Amaye, on Saturday, the twentieth of July, between that place and Naguatex, at mid-day, along a clump of luxuriant woods, the camp was seated. From thence Indians being seen, who had come to espy them, those on horseback went in their pursuit, killed six, and captured two. The prisoners being asked by the Governor why they had come, they said, to discover the numbers he had, and their condition, having been sent by their lord, the Chief of Naguatex; and that he, with other caciques, who came in his company and his cause, had determined on giving him battle that day.

While thus conferring, many Indians advanced, formed in two squadrons, who, so soon as they saw that they were descried, giving whoops, they assailed the Christians with great fury, each on a different quarter; but finding how firm was the resistance, they turned, and fleeing, many lost their lives; the greater part of the cavalry pursuing them, forgetful of the camp, when those that remained were attacked by other two squadrons, that had lain in concealment, who, in their turn, having been withstood, paid the penalty that the first had done.

When the Christians came together, after the Indians fled, they heard loud shouting, at the distance of a cross-bow-shot from where they were; and the Governor sent twelve cavalry to see what might be the cause. Six Christians were found amidst numerous Indians, two, that were mounted, defending four on foot, with great difficulty; and they, as well as those who went to their succour, finally ended by-killing many. They had got lost from those who followed after the first squadrons, and, in returning to the camp, fell among them with whom they were found fighting. One Indian, brought back alive, being asked by the Governor who they were that had come to give him battle, said the Cacique of Naguatex, the one of Maye, and another of a province called Hacanac, lord of great territories and numerous vassals, he of Naguatex being in command. The Governor, having ordered his right arm to be cut off, and his nose, sent him to the Cacique, with word that he would march the next day into his territory to destroy it, and that if he wished to dispute his entrance to await him.

The Governor stopped there that night, and the following day he came to the habitations of Naguatex, which were much scattered, and having asked for the town of the Cacique, he was told that it stood on the opposite side of a river near by. He marched thitherward; and coming to the river, on the other bank he saw many Indians awaiting him, set in order to defend the passage; but, as he did not know whether it might be forded or not, nor whereabouts it could be crossed, and having some wounded men and horses, he determined to repose for some time in the town where he was, until they should be healed.

In consequence of the great heats that prevailed, he pitched his camp a quarter of a league from the river, in a fine open grove of high trees, near a brook, close to the town. Some Indians taken there, having been asked if the river were fordable, said yes, at times it was, in certain places; on the tenth day he sent two captains, each with fifteen cavalry, one up and the other down the stream, with guides to show where they might get over, to see what towns were to be found on the opposite side. They were both opposed by the Indians, who defended the passages the best they could; but these being taken notwithstanding, on the other shore they found many habitations, with much subsistence; and having seen this, the detachments went back to the camp.

CHAPTER XXXIII.

How the Cacique of Naguatex came to visit the Governor, and how the Governor went thence, and arrived at Nondacao.

From Naguatex, where the Governor was, he sent a message to the Cacique, that, should he come to serve and obey him, he would pardon the past; and if he did not, he would go to look after him, and would inflict the chastisement he deserved for what he had done. At the end of two days the Indian got back, bringing word that to-morrow the Cacique would come. The day before his arrival, the Chief sent many Indians in advance of him, among whom were some principal men, to discover in what mood the Governor was, and determine whether he would himself come or not. They went back directly as they had announced his approach, the Cacique arriving in a couple of hours afterward, well attended by his people. They came one before another, in double file, leaving an opening through the midst, where he walked. They arrived in the Governor's presence weeping, after the usage of Tula (thence to the eastward not very distant), when the Chief, making his proper obeisance, thus spoke :—

Very High and Powerful Lord, whom all the Earth should serve and obey :—

I venture to appear before you, after having been guilty of so

21

great and bad an act, that, for only having thought of it, I merit punishment. Trusting in your greatness, although I do not deserve pardon, yet for your own dignity you will show me mercy, having regard to my inferiority in comparison with you, forgetting my weakness, which to my sorrow, and for my greater good, I have come to know.

I believe that you and yours must be immortal; that you are master of the things of nature; since you subject them all, and they obey you, even the very hearts of men. Witnessing the slaughter and destruction of my men in battle, which came of my ignorance, and the counsel of a brother of mine, who fell in the action, from my heart did I repent the error that I committed, and directly I desired to serve and obey you: wherefore have I come, that you may chastise and command me as your own.

The Governor replied, that the past would be forgiven; and that, should he thenceforward do his duty, he would be his friend, favouring him in all matters.

At the end of four days Luys de Moscoso set forward, and arrived at a river he could not pass, it ran so full, which to him appeared wonderful at the time, more than a month having gone by since there had been rain. The Indians said, that it often increased in that manner, without there being rain anywhere, in all the country. It was supposed to be caused by the sea entering in; but he learned that the water always flowed from above, and that the Indians nowhere had any information of the sea.

The Governor returned back to where he had been the last days; and, at the end of eight more, understanding that the river might then be crossed, he left, and passed over to the other bank, where he found houses, but no people. He lodged out in the fields, and sent word to the Cacique to come where he was, and to give him a guide to go on with. After some days, finding that the Cacique did not come, nor send any one, he dispatched two captains, each of them in a different direction, to set fire to the towns, and seize the people that might be found. They burned much provision, and captured many Indians. The Cacique, seeing the damage his territories were receiving, sent five principal men to Moscoso, with three guides, who understood the language farther on, whither he would go.

Directly the Governor set out from Naguatex, arriving, on the third day, at a hamlet of four or five houses, belonging to the Cacique of the poor province named Nissohone, a thinly peopled country, having little maize. Two days' journey on the way, the Indians who guided the Governor, in place of taking him to the west, would lead him to the east, and at times they went through heavy thickets, out of the road: in consequence, he ordered that they should be hanged upon a tree. A woman, taken in Nissohone, served as the guide, who went back to find the road.

In two days' time the Governor came to another miserable country, called Lacane. An Indian was taken, who said the land of Nondacao was very populous, the houses much scattered, as in mountainous regions, and there was plenty of maize. The Cacique came with his Indians, weeping, as those of Naguatex had done, which is, according to their custom, significant of obedience; and he made a present of much fish, offering to do whatsoever might be required of him. He took his departure, leaving a guide for the Province of Soacatino.

CHAPTER XXXIIII.

How the Governor marched from Nondacao to Soacatino and Guasco, passing through a Wilderness,
whence, for want of a Guide and Interpreter, he
retired to Nilco.

The Governor set out from Nondacao for Soacatino,
and on the fifth day came to a province called Aays.
The inhabitants had never heard of the Christians. So
soon as they observed them entering the territory the
people were called out, who, as fast as they could get
together, came by fifties and hundreds on the road, to
give battle. While some encountered us, others fell
upon our rear; and when we followed up those, these
pursued us. The attack continued during the greater
part of the day, until we arrived at their town. Some
men were injured, and some horses, but nothing so as to
hinder travel, there being not one dangerous wound
among all. The Indians suffered great slaughter.

The day on which the Governor departed, the guide
told him he had heard it said in Nondacao, that the
Indians of Soacatino had seen other Christians; at which
we were all delighted, thinking it might be true, and that
they could have come by way of New Spain; for if it
were so, finding nothing in Florida of value, we should
be able to go out of it, there being fear we might perish

in some wilderness. The Governor, having been led for
two days out of the way, ordered the Indian to be put to
the torture, when he confessed that his master, the Cacique of Nondacao, had ordered him to take them in
that manner, we being his enemies, and he, as his vassal,
was bound to obey him. He was commanded to be cast
to the dogs, and another Indian guided us to Soacatino,
where we came the following day.

The country was very poor, and the want of maize
was greatly felt. The natives being asked if they had
any knowledge of other Christians, said they had heard
that near there, towards the south, such men were moving
about. For twenty days the march was through a very
thinly peopled country, where great privation and toil
were endured; the little maize there was, the Indians
having buried in the scrub, where the Christians, at the
close of the day's march, when they were well weary,
went trailing, to seek for what they had need of it to eat.

Arrived at a province called Guasco, they found
maize, with which they loaded the horses and the Indians; thence they went to another settlement, called
Naquiscoça, the inhabitants of which said that they had
no knowledge of any other Christians. The Governor ordered them put to torture, when they stated that farther
on, in the territories of another chief, called Naçacahoz,
the Christians had arrived, and gone back toward the
west, whence they came. He reached there in two days,
and took some women, among whom was one who said
that she had seen Christians, and, having been in their
hands, had made her escape from them. The Governor

sent a captain with fifteen cavalry to where she said they were seen, to discover if there were any marks of horses, or signs of any Christians having been there; and after travelling three or four leagues, she who was the guide declared that all she had said was false; and so it was deemed of every thing else the Indians had told of having seen Christians in Florida.

As the region thereabout was scarce of maize, and no information could be got of any inhabited country to the west, the Governor went back to Guasco. The residents stated, that ten days' journey from there, toward the sunset, was a river called Daycao, whither they sometimes went to drive and kill deer, and whence they had seen persons on the other bank, but without knowing what people they were. The Christians took as much maize as they could find, to carry with them; and journeying ten days through a wilderness, they arrived at the river of which the Indians had spoken. Ten horsemen sent in advance by the Governor had crossed; and, following a road leading up from the bank, they came upon an encampment of Indians living in very small huts, who, directly as they saw the Christians, took to flight, leaving what they had, indications only of poverty and misery. So wretched was the country, that what was found everywhere, put together, was not half an alqueire of maize. Taking two natives, they went back to the river, where the Governor waited; and on coming to question the captives, to ascertain what towns there might be to the west, no Indian was found in the camp who knew their language.

The Governor commanded the captains and principal personages to be called together, that he might determine now by their opinions what was best to do. The majority declared it their judgment to return to the River Grande of Guachoya, because in Anilco and thereabout was much maize; that during the winter they would build brigantines, and the following spring go down the river in them in quest of the sea, where having arrived, they would follow the coast thence along to New Spain,—an enterprise which, although it appeared to be one difficult to accomplish, yet from their experience it offered the only course to be pursued. They could not travel by land, for want of an interpreter; and they considered the country farther on, beyond the River Daycao, on which they were, to be that which Cabeca de Vaca had said in his narrative should have to be traversed, where the Indians wandered like Arabs, having no settled place of residence, living on prickly pears, the roots of plants, and game; and that if this should be so, and they, entering upon that tract, found no provision for sustenance during winter, they must inevitably perish, it being already the beginning of October; and if they remained any longer where they were, what with rains and snow, they should neither be able to fall back, nor, in a land so poor as that, to subsist.

The Governor, who longed to be again where he could get his full measure of sleep, rather than govern and go conquering a country so beset for him with hardships, directly returned, getting back from whence he came.

CHAPTER XXXV.

How the Christians returned to Nilco, and thence went to Minoya, where they prepared to build Vessels in which to leave Florida.

When what had been determined on was proclaimed in the camp, many were greatly disheartened. They considered the voyage by sea to be very hazardous, because of their poor subsistence, and as perilous as was the journey by land, whereon they had looked to find a rich country, before coming to the soil of Christians. This was according to what Cabeça de Vaca told the Emperor, that after seeing cotton cloth, would be found gold, silver, and stones of much value, and they were not yet come to where he had wandered; for before arriving there, he had always travelled along the coast, and they were marching far within the land; hence by keeping toward the west they must unavoidably come to where he had been, as he said that he had gone about in a certain region a long time, and marched northward into the interior. Now, in Guasco, they had already found some turkoises, and shawls of cotton, which the Indians gave them to understand, by signs, were brought from the direction of the sunset; so that they who should take that course must approach the country of Christians.

There was likewise much other discontent. Many grieved to go back, and would rather have continued to run the peril of their lives than leave Florida poor. They were not equal, however, to changing what was resolved on, as the persons of importance agreed with the Governor. There was one, nevertheless, who said afterwards that he would willingly pluck out an eye, to put out another for Luys de Moscoso, so greatly would he grieve to see him prosper; with such bitterness did he inveigh against him and some of his friends, which he would not have dared to do, only he knew that in a couple of days from that time the government would have to be relinquished.

From Daycao, where they were, to the Rio Grande, was a distance of one hundred and fifty leagues, towards which they had marched always westwardly; and, as they returned over the way, with great difficulty could they find maize to eat; for, wheresoever they had passed, the country lay devastated, and the little that was left, the Indians had now hidden. The towns they had burned in Naguatex, of which they had repented, they found already rebuilt, and the houses full of maize. That country is populous and abundant. Pottery is made there of clay, little differing from that of Estremoz or Montemor.

To Chaguete, by command of the Cacique, the Indians came in peace, and said, that the Christian who had remained there would not come. The Governor wrote to him, sending ink and paper, that he might answer. The purport of the letter stated his determination to leave Florida, reminded him of his being a Christian,

22

and that he was unwilling to leave him among heathen; that he would pardon the error he had committed in going to the Indians, should he return; and that if they should wish to detain him, to let the Governor know by writing. The Indian who took the letter came back, bringing no other response than the name and rubric of the person written on the back, to signify that he was alive. The Governor sent twelve mounted men after him; but, having his watchers, he so hid himself that he could not be found. For want of maize the Governor could not tarry longer to look for him; so he left Chaguete, crossed the river at Aays, and following it down, he discovered a town which they had not seen before, called Chilano.

They came to Nilco, where the Governor found so little maize, that there was not enough to last while they made the vessels; for during seed-time, while the Christians were in Guachoya, the Indians, in fear of them, had not dared to come and plant the grounds; and no other land about there was known to have maize, that being the most fertile region of the vicinity, and where they had the most hope of finding sustenance. Everybody was confounded.

Many thought it bad counsel to have come back from the Daycao, and not to have taken the risk of continuing in the way they were going by land; as it seemed impossible they should escape by sea, unless a miracle might be wrought for them; for there was neither pilot nor sea-chart; they knew not where the river entered the sea, nor of the sea could they get any information; they had

nothing out of which to make sails, nor for rope a sufficiency of enequen (a grass growing there, which is like
hemp), and what they did find was saved for calk;
nor was there wherewith to pitch them. Neither could
they build vessels of such strength that any accident
might not put them in jeopardy of life ; and they greatly
feared what befell Narvaez, who was lost on the coast,
might happen to them also. But the most of all they
feared was the want of maize; for without that they
could not support themselves, or do any thing they would.
All were in great dismay.

The Christians chose to commend themselves to God
for relief, and beseech Him to point them out a way by
which they might be saved. By His goodness He was
pleased that the people of Anilco should come peacefully, and state that two days' journey thence, near the
River Grande, were two towns of which the Christians
had not heard, in a fertile country named Aminoya; but
whether it then contained maize or not, they were unable
to tell, as they were at war with those places ; they would
nevertheless be greatly pleased to go and destroy them, with
the aid of the Christians. The Governor sent a captain
thither, with horsemen and footmen, and the Indians
of Anilco. Arriving at Aminoya, he found two large
towns in a level, open field, half a league apart, in sight
of each other, where he captured many persons, and
found a large quantity of maize. He took lodging in
one of the towns, and directly sent a message to the Governor concerning what he had found, with which all were
well content. They set out from Anilco in the beginning

of December, and on that march, as well as before coming there from Chilano, they underwent great exposure;
for they passed through much water, and rain fell many
times, bringing a north wind, with severe cold, so that
when in the field they had the water both above and
below them; and if at the end of a day's journey they
found dry ground to lie upon, they had occasion to be
thankful. In these hardships nearly all the Indians in
service died, and also many Christians, after coming to
Aminoya; the greater number being sick of severe and
dangerous diseases, marked with inclination to lethargy.
André de Vasconcelos died there, and two Portuguese
brothers of Elvas, near of kin to him, by the name of
Soti.

The Christians chose for their quarters what appeared
to be the best town: it was stockaded, and stood a quarter of a league distant from the Rio Grande. The maize
that lay in the other town was brought there, and when
together the quantity was estimated to be six thousand
fanegas. For the building of ships better timber was
found than had been seen elsewhere in all Florida; on
which account, all rendered many thanks to God for so
signal mercy, encouraging the hope in them, that they
should be successful in their wish to reach a shore of
Christians.

CHAPTER XXXVI.

How Seven Brigantines were built, and the Christians took their Departure from Aminoya.

So soon as the Christians arrived in Aminoya, the Governor commanded the chains to be collected which every one brought along for Indians, the iron in shot, and what was in the camp. He ordered a furnace to be set up for making spikes, and likewise timber to be cut down for the brigantines. A Portuguese, of Ceuta, had learned to saw lumber while a captive in Fez; and saws had been brought for that purpose, with which he taught others, who assisted him. A Genoese, whom God had been pleased to spare (as without him we could not have gone away, there being not another person who knew how to construct vessels), built the brigantines with the help of four or five Biscayan carpenters, who hewed the plank and ribs for him; and two calkers, one a Genoese, the other a Sardinian, closed them up with the oakum, got from a plant like hemp, called enequen, of which I have before spoken; but from its scarcity the flax of the country was likewise used, as well as the ravellings of shawls. The cooper sickened to the point of death, and there was not another workman; but God was pleased to give him health, and notwith-

standing he was very thin, and unfit to labour, fifteen
days before the vessels sailed, he had made for each of
them two of the half-hogsheads sailors call quartos, four
of them holding a pipe of water.

The Indians of a province called Tagoanate, two
days' journey up the river, likewise those of Anilco and
Guachoya, and other neighbouring people, seeing the
vessels were building, thought, as their places of concealment were by the water's side, that it was the purpose to
come in quest of them; and because the Governor had
asked for shawls, as necessary out of which to make sails,
they came often, and brought many, as likewise a great
deal of fish.

Of a verity, it did appear that God chose to favour the
Christians in their extreme need, disposing the Indians
to bring the garments; otherwise, there had been no way
but to go and fetch them. Then the town where they
were, as soon as the winter should set in, would become
so surrounded by water, and isolated, that no one could
travel from it by land farther than a league, or a league
and a half, when the horses could no longer be used.
Without them we were unable to contend, the Indians
being so numerous; besides, man to man on foot, whether
in the water or on dry ground, they were superior, being
more skilful and active, and the conditions of the country
more favourable to the practice of their warfare.

They also brought us ropes; and the cables needed
were made from the bark of mulberry-trees. Anchors
were made of stirrups, for which others of wood were
substituted. In March, more than a month having

passed since rain fell, the river became so enlarged that it reached Nilco, nine leagues off; and the Indians said, that on the opposite side it also extended an equal distance over the country.

The ground whereon the town stood was higher, and where the going was best, the water reached to the stirrups. Rafts were made of trees, upon which were placed many boughs, whereon the horses stood; and in the houses were like arrangements; yet, even this not proving sufficient, the people ascended into the lofts; and when they went out of the houses it was in canoes, or, if on horseback, they went in places where the earth was highest.

Such was our situation for two months, in which time the river did not fall, and no work could be done. The natives, coming in canoes, did not cease to visit the brigantines. The Governor, fearing they would attack him in that time, ordered one of those coming to the town to be secretly seized, and kept until the rest were gone; which being done, he directed that the prisoner should be tortured, in order to draw out from him any plotting of treason that might exist. The captive said, that the Caciques of Nilco, Guachoya, Taguanate, and others, in all some twenty, had determined to come upon him, with a great body of people. Three days before they should do so, the better to veil their evil purpose and perfidy, they were to send a present of fish; and on the day itself, another present was to be sent in advance of them, by some Indians, who, with others in the conspiracy, that were serving, should set fire to the houses, after getting possession of the lances placed near the doors of the dwellings, when the Caciques, with all their people, being concealed in the thicket nigh the town, on seeing the flame, should hasten to make an end of them.

The Governor ordered the Indian to be put in a chain; and on the day that was stated, thirty men having come with fish, he commanded their right hands to be cut off, sending word by them to the Cacique of Guachoya, whose they were, that he and his might come when they pleased, he desired nothing better, but they should learn that they could not think of a thing that he did not know their thought before them. At this they were all greatly terrified; the Caciques of Nilco and Taguanate came to make excuses, and a few days after came the Cacique of Guachoya, with a principal Indian, his vassal, stating that he had certain information of an agreement between the Caciques of Nilco and Taguanate to come and give the Christians battle.

So soon as some Indians arrived from Nilco, the Governor questioned them, and they confirming what was said, he delivered them at once to the principal Indian of Guachoya, who took them out of the town and killed them. The next day came others from Taguanate, who likewise having confessed, the Governor commanded that their right hands and their noses should be cut off, and he sent them to the Cacique. With this procedure the people of Guachoya were well satisfied, and often came with presents of shawls and fish, and of hogs, which were the breeding of some sows lost there the year

before. Having persuaded the Governor to send people
to Taguanate, so soon as the waters fell, they brought
canoes, in which infantry went down the river, and a
captain proceeded by land with cavalry; and having
guided them until they came to Taguanate, the Christians assaulted the town, took many men and women,
and shawls, which, with what they had already, sufficed
for their want.

In the month of June the brigantines were finished,
and the Indians having stated that the river rose but
once in the year, which was with the melting of snow,
that had already passed, it being now summer, and a
long time since rain had fallen, God was pleased that the
water should come up to the town, where the vessels
were, whence they floated into the river; for had they
been taken over ground, there would have been danger of
tearing open the bottoms, thereby entirely wrecking
them, the planks being thin, and the spikes made short
for the lack of iron.

In the time that the Christians were there, the people
of Aminoya came to offer their service, being compelled
by hunger to beg some ears of that corn which had been
taken from them. As the country was fertile, they were
accustomed to subsist on maize; and as all that they
possessed had been seized, and the population was
numerous, they could not exist. Those who came to the
town were weak, and so lean that they had not flesh on
their bones, and many died near by, of clear hunger and
debility. The Governor ordered, under pain of heavy
punishments, that maize should not be given to them;

23

still, when it was seen that they were willing to work, and that the hogs had a plenty, the men, pitying their misery and destitution, would share their grain with them; so that when the time arrived for departure, there was not enough left to answer for what was needed. That which remained was put into the brigantines and the great canoes, which were tied together in couples. Twenty-two horses were taken on board, being the best there were in the camp; the flesh of the rest was jerked, as was also that of the hogs that remained. On the second day of July, of the year one thousand five hundred and forty-three, we took our departure from Aminoya.

CHAPTER XXXVII.

How the Christians, on their Voyage, were attacked in the River, by the Indians of Quigualtam, and what happened.

The day before the Christians left Aminoya, it was
determined to dismiss the men and women that were
serving, with the exception of some hundred slaves, more
or less, put on board by the Governor, and by those he
favoured. As there were many persons of condition,
whom he could not refuse what he allowed to others, he
made use of an artifice, saying, that while they should be
going down the river they might have the use of them;
but on coming to the sea they would have to be left,
because of the necessity for water, and there were but few
casks; while he secretly told his friends to take the slaves,
that they would carry them to New Spain. All those
to whom he bore ill-will, the greater number, not suspecting his concealment from them, which after a while
appeared, thought it inhuman for so short service, in
return for so much as the natives had done, to take them
away, to be left captives out of their territories, in the
hands of other Indians, abandoning five hundred males
and females, among whom were many boys and girls
who understood and spoke Spanish. The most of

them wept, which caused great compassion, as they were all Christians of their own free will, and were now to remain lost.

In seven brigantines went three hundred and twenty-two Spaniards from Aminoya. The vessels were of good build, except that the planks were thin, on account of the shortness of the spikes; and they were not pitched, nor had they decks to shed the water that might enter them, but planks were placed instead, upon which the mariners might run to fasten the sails, and the people accommodate themselves above and below.

The Governor appointed his captains, giving to each of them his brigantine, taking their word and oath to obey him until they should come to the land of Christians. He chose for himself the brigantine he liked best. On the day of his departure they passed by Guachoya, where the Indians, in canoes, were waiting for them in the river, having made a great arbour on the shore, to which they invited him, but he made excuse, and passed along. They accompanied him until arriving where an arm of the river extends to the right, near which they said was Quigualtam; and they importuned him to go and make war upon it, offering their assistance. As they had told him there were three days' journey down the river to that province, suspecting they had arranged some perfidy, he dismissed them there; then, submitting himself to where lay the full strength of the stream, went his voyage, driven on rapidly by the power of the current and aid of oars.

On the first day they came to land in a clump of trees,

by the left bank, and at dark they retired to the vessels. The following day they came to a town, where they went on shore, but the occupants dared not tarry for them. A woman who was captured, being questioned, said the town was that of a chief named Huhasene, a subject of Quigualtam, who, with a great many people, was waiting for them. Mounted men went down the river, and finding some houses, in which was much maize, immediately the rest followed. They tarried there a day, in which they shelled and got ready as much maize as was needed. In this time many Indians came up the river in canoes; and, on the opposite side, in front, somewhat carelessly put themselves in order of battle. The Governor sent after them the crossbow-men he had with him, in two canoes, and as many other persons as they could hold, when the Indians fled; but, seeing the Spaniards were unable to overtake them, returning, they took courage, and, coming nearer, menaced them with loud yells. So soon as the Christians retired, they were followed by some in canoes, and others on land, along the river; and, getting before them, arrived at a town near the river's bluff, where they united, as if to make a stand. Into each canoe, for every brigantine was towing one at the stern for its service, directly entered some men, who, causing the Indians to take flight, burned the town. Soon after, on the same day, they went on shore in a large open field, where the Indians dared not await their arrival.

The next day a hundred canoes came together, having from sixty to seventy persons in them, those of the

principal men having awnings, and themselves wearing
white and coloured plumes, for distinction. They came
within two crossbow-shot of the brigantines, and sent a
message in a small canoe, by three Indians, to the intent
of learning the character of the vessels, and the weapons
that we use. Arriving at the brigantine of the Governor,
one of the messengers got in, and said that he had been
sent by the Cacique of Quigaltam, their lord, to commend
him, and to make known that whatever the Indians of
Guachoya had spoken of him was falsely said, they being
his enemies; that the Chief was his servant, and wished
to be so considered. The Governor told him that he believed all that he had stated to be true; to say so to
him, and that he greatly esteemed him for his friendship.

With this the messengers went to where the others,
in the canoes, were waiting for them; and thence they all
came down yelling, and approached the Spaniards with
threats. The Governor sent Juan de Guzman, captain of
foot, in the canoes, with twenty-five men in armour, to
drive them out of the way. So soon as they were seen
coming, the Indians, formed in two parts, remained
quietly until they were come up with, when, closing, they
took Juan de Guzman, and those who came ahead with
him, in their midst, and, with great fury, closed hand to
hand with them. Their canoes were larger than his, and
many leaped into the water—some to support them, others
to lay hold of the canoes of the Spaniards, to cause them
to capsize; which was presently accomplished, the Christians falling into the water, and, by the weight of their
armour, going to the bottom; or when one by swimming,

or clinging to a canoe, could sustain himself, they with paddles and clubs, striking him on the head, would send him below.

When those in the brigantines who witnessed the defeat desired to render succour, the force of the stream would not allow them to return. One brigantine, which was that nighest to the canoes, saved four men, who were all of those that went after the Indians who escaped. Eleven lost their lives; among whom was Juan de Guzman and a son of Don Carlos, named Juan de Vargas. The greater number of the others were also men of consideration and of courage. Those who escaped by swimming said, that they saw the Indians get into the stern of one of their canoes with Juan de Guzman, but whether he was carried away dead or alive, no one could state.

CHAPTER XXXVIII.

How the Christians were Pursued by the Indians.

The natives, finding they had gained a victory, took so great encouragement that they proceeded to attack the brigantines, which they had not dared to do before. They first came up with one in the rear-guard, commanded by Calderon, and at the first volley of arrows twenty-five men were wounded. There were only four on board in armour, who went to the side of the vessel for its defence. Those unprotected, finding how they were getting hurt, left the oars, placing themselves below under the cover; and the brigantine, beginning to swing about, was going where the current of water chanced to take her, when one of the men in armour, seeing this, without waiting the Captain's order, made one of the infantry take the oar and steer, while he stood before to cover him with his shield. The Indians afterwards came no nearer than bow-shot, whence they could assail without being assaulted, or receiving injury, there being in each brigantine only a single crossbow much out of order; so that the Christians had little else to do than to stand as objects to be shot at, watching for the shafts. The natives, having left this brigantine, went to another, against which they fought for half an hour: and, one after another, in this way they ran through with them all.

The Christians had mats with them to lie upon of two thicknesses, very close and strong, so that no arrow could pierce them, that, when safety required, were hung up; and the Indians, finding that these could not be traversed, directed their shafts upward, that, exhausted, fell on board, inflicting some wounds. Not satisfied with this, they strove to get at the men with the horses; but the brigantines were brought about the canoes in which they were, to give them protection, and in this position conducted them along. The Christians, finding themselves thus severely tried, and so worn out that they could bear up no longer, determined to continue their journey in the dark, thinking that they should be left alone on getting through the region of Quigualtam. While they proceeded and were least watchful, supposing themselves to be left, they would be roused with deafening yells near by: and thus were they annoyed through the night and until noon, when they got into another country, to the people of which they were recommended for a like treatment, and received it.

Those Indians having gone back to their country, these followed the Christians in fifty canoes, fighting them all one day and night. They sprang on board a brigantine of the rear-guard, by the canoe that floated at the stern, whence they took out an Indian woman, and wounded from thence some men in the brigantines. The men with the horses in the canoes, becoming weary with rowing day and night, at times got left behind, when

24

the Indians would directly set upon them, and those in
the brigantines would wait until they should come up :
so that in consequence of the slow way that was made,
because of the beasts, the Governor determined to go on
shore and slaughter them.   So soon as any befitting
ground for it was seen, a landing was made, the animals
were butchered, and the meat cured and brought on board.
Four or five horses having been let go alive, the Indians,
after the Spaniards had embarked, went up to them, to
whom being unused, they were alarmed, running up and
down, neighing in such way that the Indians took fright,
plunging into the water; and thence entering their
canoes, they went after the brigantines, shooting at the
people without mercy, following them that evening and
the night ensuing, until ten o'clock the next day, when
they returned up stream.

From a small town near the bank, there came out
seven canoes that pursued the Christians a short distance,
shooting at them; but finding, as they were few, that
little harm was done, they went back.   From that time
forth the voyage, until near the end, was unattended by
any misadventure; the Christians in seventeen days going
down a distance of two hundred and fifty leagues, a little
more or less, by the river.   When near the sea, it becomes divided into two arms, each of which may be a
league and a half broad.

CHAPTER XXXIX.

How the Christians came to the Sea, what occurred then, and what befell them on the
Voyage.

Half a league before coming to the sea, the Christians cast anchor, in order to take rest for a time, as they
were weary from rowing. They were disheartened also,
many days having gone by since they had eaten other
thing than maize, parched and then boiled, given out in
daily rations of a casque by strake to a mess of three.

While riding at anchor, seven canoes of natives came
to attack those we had brought in the canoes along with
us. The Governor ordered men to enter ours in armour,
to go after the Indians and drive them away. There
also came some by land, through thicket and bog, with
staves, having very sharp heads of fish-bone, who fought
valiantly those of us who went out to meet them. Such
as were in the canoes, awaited with their arrows the
approach of those sent against them; and presently,
on the engaging of these, as well as those on land, they
wounded some on our side in both contests. When we
on shore drew nigh to them they would turn their backs,
running like fleet steeds before infantry, making some
turns without ever getting much beyond the flight of an

arrow, and, returning again, they would shoot without
receiving any injury from us, who, though we had some
bows, were not skilled to use them; while the Indians on
the water, finding their pursuers unable to do them harm,
though straining at the oars to overtake them, leisurely
kept within a circle, their canoes pausing and returning, as in a skirmish. The men discovered that the
more successful their effort to approach, the greater was
their own injury; so, when they succeeded simply in
driving them off, they went back to the brigantines.

After remaining two days, the Christians went to
where that branch of the river enters the sea; and having sounded there, they found forty fathoms depth of
water. Pausing then, the Governor required that each
should give his opinion respecting the voyage, whether
they should sail to New Spain direct, by the high sea, or
go thither keeping along from shore to shore. There
were different opinions upon this, in which Juan de
Añasco, who was very presumptuous, valuing himself
much upon his knowledge of navigation, with other
matters of the sea of which he had little experience,
influenced the Governor; and his opinion, like that of
some others, was, that it would be much better to put
out to sea, and cross the Gulf by a passage three-fourths
less far, than going from shore to shore, which was very
circuitous, because of the bend made by the land. He
said that he had seen the sea-chart; that whence they
were the coast ran west to the River of Palmas, and
thence south to New Spain; consequently, that keeping in sight of land, there would be wide compassing,

with long detention, and risk of being overtaken by the winter before coming to the country of Christians; while, with a fair wind, in ten or twelve days' time they should arrive there, by keeping a straight course.

The majority were not of that way of thinking, and said there was more safety in going along the coast, though it might take longer; the vessels being frail, and without decks, a light storm might suffice to wreck them; and in consequence of the little room they had for water, if calm or head wind should occur, or adverse weather, they would also run great hazard; but even were the vessels so substantial that they might venture in them, there being neither pilot nor sea-card to show the way, it was not wise to traverse the sea. This, the opinion of the greater number, was approved; and it was decided to go along from one to another shore.

When they were about to depart, the brigantine of the Governor parted her cable, the anchor attached to it remaining in the river; and, notwithstanding she was near the shore, the depth was so great that, although it was industriously sought for by divers, it could not be found. This gave much anxiety to the Governor and the others on board. With a stone for crushing maize, and the bridles that remained, belonging to some of the fidalgos and gentlemen who rode, they made a weight that took the place of the anchor.

On the eighteenth day of July the vessels got under weigh, with fair weather, and wind favourable for the voyage. The Governor, with Juan de Añasco, put to sea in their brigantines, and were followed by all the

rest, who, at two or three leagues out, having come
up with the two, the Captains asked the Governor why
he did not keep the land; and told him that if he
meant to leave it he should say so, though he ought not
to do that without having the consent of the rest,
otherwise they would not follow his lead, but each would
do as he thought best.   The Governor replied that he
would do nothing without consulting them; he desired
to get away from the shore to sail the better, and with the
greater safety at night; that in the morning, when time
served, he would return.   With a favourable wind they
sailed all that day in fresh water, the next night, and the
day following until vespers, at which they were greatly
amazed; for they were very distant from the shore, and
so great was the strength of the current of the river, the
coast so shallow and gentle, that the fresh water entered
far into the sea.

That afternoon, on the starboard bow, they saw
some kays, whither they went, and where they reposed at
night.   There Juan de Añasco, with his reasoning, concluded by getting all to consent, and deem it good, that
they should go to sea, declaring, as he had before said,
that it would be a great gain, and shorten their voyage.
They navigated two days, and when they desired to get
back in sight of land they could not, because the wind
came off from it: and on the fourth day, finding that the
water was giving out, fearing extremity and peril, they
all complained of Juan de Añasco, and of the Governor,
who had listened to his advice: and all the Captains

declared they would run no farther out, and that the Governor might go as he chose.

It pleased God that the wind should change a little; and, at the end of four days from the time of their having gone out to sea, by strength of arm they arrived, in want of fresh water, in sight of the coast, and with great labour gained it on an open beach. That afternoon the wind came round from the south, which on that coast is a side wind, and so stiff that it threw the brigantines on to the land, the anchors bending of their slenderness, and dragging. The Governor ordered all to leap into the water, on the larboard side, to hold them, and when each wave had passed they would launch the brigantines to seaward, sustaining them in this manner until the wind went down.

CHAPTER XL.

How the Brigantines lost Sight of each other in a
Storm, and afterwards came together at a Kay.

The tempest having passed off from the beach where
the brigantines were riding, the people went on shore.
With mattocks they dug holes there, into which the water
having flowed, they thence filled their pipkins. The
next day they left; and sailing two days, they entered a
basin, like a cove, which afforded shelter against a high
wind that blew from the south. There they tarried, unable to leave, until the fourth day, when the sea subsided
and they went out by rowing. They sailed until near
evening; the wind then freshened, driving them in such
manner upon the land, that they regretted having left the
harbour; for no sooner was it nightfall than the storm
began to rise on the sea, and with its approach the wind
gradually increased. The brigantines separated. The
two that were farthest out entered an arm of the sea, a
couple of leagues beyond the place where the others
found themselves at dark. The five that were astern
remained from half a league to a league apart, along an
exposed beach, upon which the winds and waves were
casting them, without one vessel's knowing the fate of
another. The anchors having yielded, the vessels were

dragging them: the oars, at each of which seven and eight were pulling seaward, could not hold the vessels; the rest of the men, leaping into the water, with the utmost diligence, after the wave had passed that drove them to the shore, would launch the brigantine; while those on board, before another wave could come, baled out with bowls the water that came in upon them.

While thus engaged, in great fear of being lost, from midnight forward they suffered the intolerable torment of a myriad of mosquitos. The flesh is directly inflamed from their sting, as though it had received venom. Towards morning the wind lulled, and the sea went down; but the insects continued none the less. The sails, which were white, appeared black with them at daylight; while the men could not pull at the oars without assistance to drive away the insects. Fear having passed off with the danger of the storm, the people observing the swollen condition of each other's faces, and the marks of the blows they had given and received to rid them of the mosquitos, they could but laugh. The vessels came together in a creek, where lay the two brigantines that preceded them. Finding a scum the sea casts up, called copee, which is like pitch, and used instead on shipping, where that is not to be had, they payed the bottoms of their vessels with it.

After remaining two days they resumed their voyage; and having run likewise two days, they entered an arm of the sea and landed. Spending there a couple of days, they left; six men on the last day having gone up the bay in a canoe without finding its head. The brigantines

25

went out in a head-wind blowing from the south, which being light, and the people having a strong desire to hasten the voyage, they pulled out by strength of arm to sea with great toil, and making little headway for two days, they entered by an arm of the sea behind an islet which it encircles, where followed such bad weather, that they were not unmindful to give thanks for that good shelter. Fish abounded there. They were taken in nets and with the line. A man having thrown out a cord made fast to his arm, a fish caught at the hook and drew him into the water up to the neck, when, remembering a knife that he had providentially kept, he cut himself loose.

At the close of the fourteenth day of their stay, the Almighty having thought proper to send fair weather, the Christians very devoutly formed a procession for the return of thanks, in which, moving along the beach, they supplicated Him that He would take them to a land in which they might better do Him service.

CHAPTER XLI.

How the Christians arrived at the River Panico.

Wheresoever the people dug along the shore they found fresh water. The jars being filled, and the procession concluded, they embarked; and, going ever in sight of land, they navigated for six days. Juan de Añasco said it would be well to stand directly out to sea; for that he had seen the card, and remembered that, from the Rio de Palmas onward, the coast ran south, and up to that time they had gone westwardly. According to his opinion, by the reckoning he kept, the river could not be distant from where they were.

That night they ran out, and in the morning they saw palm-trees rising above the water, the coast trending southwardly; and from midday forward great mountains appeared, which had nowhere been seen until then; for to that place, from the port of Espiritu Santo, where they had entered Florida, was a low, level shore, not discoverable at sea until very near. From what they observed, they thought that during the night they had passed the Rio de Palmas, sixty leagues distant from Panico, in New Spain. So they consulted together.

Some were of opinion that it would not be well to sail in the dark, lest they should overrun the Rio de

Panico; others, that they could not be so near as to run
by it that night, and that it would not be well to lose a
favourable wind; so they agreed to spread half the sails
and keep on their way. Two of the brigantines, which
ran with all sail up, at daylight passed the river without
seeing it: of the five that remained behind, the first that
arrived was the one Calderon commanded, from which,
when a quarter of a league off, and before the entrance
had been discovered, the water was observed to be thick
and found to be fresh. Coming opposite the river, they
saw where the waves broke upon a shoal, at the entrance
into the sea; and, not any one knowing the place, they
were in doubt whether they should go in there or pass
by; but finally, having agreed to enter, they approached
the shore without getting into the current, and went in
the port, where no sooner had they come, than they saw
Indians of both sexes in the apparel of Spain. Asking in
what country they were, they received the answer in their
own language, that it was the Rio de Panico, and that
the town of the Christians was fifteen leagues inland.
The pleasure that all received at this news cannot be sufficiently expressed: they felt as though a life had been
newly given them. Many, leaping on shore, kissed the
ground; and all, on bended knees, with hands raised
above them, and their eyes to heaven, remained untiring
in giving thanks to God.

Those who were coming astern, when they saw that
Calderon with his brigantine had anchored in the river,
directly steered to enter the port. The other two, which
had gone by, tried to run to sea, that they might put

about to join the rest, but could not, the wind being adverse and the sea fretful ; so, fearing that they might be lost, they came nigh the land and cast anchor. A storm came up, and finding that they could not sustain themselves there, much less at sea, they determined to run on shore; and as the brigantines were small, drawing but little water, and the beach sandy, the force of the wind on the sails carried them up dry, without injury to any one.

If those who gained the haven at that time were made happy, these were oppressed by a double weight of gloom, not knowing what had happened to their companions, nor in what country they were, fearing likewise that it might be one of a hostile people. They had come upon the coast two leagues below the port. So soon as they found themselves clear of the sea, each took on the back what he could carry of his things, and, travelling inland, they found Indians, who told whence they were, and changed what was sorrow into joy. The Christians rendered many thanks to God for having rescued them from those numberless perils.

CHAPTER XLII.

How the Christians came to Panico, and of their Reception by the Inhabitants.

From the time the Christians left the River Grande, to come by sea from Florida to the River of Panico, were fifty-two days. On the tenth day of September, of the year 1543, they entered the Panico, going up with the brigantines. In the many windings taken by the stream, the light wind was often unfavourable, and the vessels in many places made slow headway, having to be towed with much labour against a strong current; so that, after having sailed four days, the people, discovering themselves greatly retarded in the desire to get among Christians, and of taking part in the divine offices, which for a long season had not been listened to by them, they gave up the brigantines to the sailors, and went on by land to Panico.

Just as the Christians arrived at the town, in their clothing of deer-skin, dressed and dyed black, consisting of frock, hose, and shoes, they all went directly to the church, to pray and return thanks for their miraculous preservation. The townspeople, having already been informed of their coming by the Indians, and now knew of the arrival, invited some to their houses, and entertained them for acquaintance' sake, or for having heard of them, or because they came from the same parts of country with themselves. The Alcalde-Mayor took the Governor home with him: the rest, as they came up, he directed to be lodged by sixes and tens, according to the means of individuals, who provided their guests with abundance of fowls and maizen-bread, and with the fruits of the country, which are like those of Cuba, already described.

The town of Panico might contain some seventy housekeepers. The dwellings were chiefly of stone and mortar; some were of poles, and all of them thatched with grass. The country is poor. No gold or silver is to be found. Residents have the fullest supply both of food and servants. The most wealthy have not an income above five hundred cruzados annually, which is tribute paid by their Indian vassals, in cotton clothing, fowls, and maize.

Of the persons who got back from Florida, there landed at that port three hundred and eleven Christians. The Alcalde-Mayor directly sent a townsman by post to inform the Viceroy, who resided in Mexico, of the arrival of three hundred of the men who had gone with Don Hernando de Soto in the discovery and conquest of Florida; and, for their being in the service of the King, that he would make provision for their support. Don Antonio de Mendoza was greatly amazed at this news, as were all others of that city; for the people having entered far into Florida, they had been considered lost, nothing being heard from them in a long while; and it appeared to him to be a thing impossible, that without a fortress to which they might betake themselves, or support of any sort, they should have sustained themselves for such a length of time among the heathen. He immediately gave an order, directing that subsistence should be given them wheresoever it might be needed, and the Indians found requisite for carrying their burdens; and, should there be refusal, to take by force, without incurring any penalty, whatsoever should be necessary. The mandate was so well obeyed, that on the road, before the people had arrived at the towns, the inhabitants went out to receive them, bringing fowls and provisions.

CHAPTER XLIII.

THE FAVOUR THE PEOPLE FOUND IN THE VICEROY AND RESIDENTS OF MEXICO.

FROM Panico to the great city of Mestitam, Mexico, there are sixty leagues, and as many leagues from each to the port of Vera Cruz, which is where the embarka-tions take place for Spain, and where those who go hence to New Spain arrive. These three towns, equi-distant, are inhabited by Spaniards, and form a triangle: Vera Cruz on the south, Panico on the east, and Mexico, which is inland, on the west. The country is so popu-lous, that the Indian towns farthest apart are not more than half a league to a league from each other.

Some of the people who came from Florida remained in Panico, reposing a month, others fifteen days, or such time as each pleased; for no one turned a grudging face to his guest, but, on the contrary, gave him of every thing he had, and appeared sad at his leave-taking; which may well enough be believed, for the provisions the natives brought in payment of their tribute more than sufficed for consumption, so that there was no one in that town to buy or to sell, and few Spaniards being there, the inhabitants were glad of company. All the clothing in the custody of the Alcalde-Mayor, paid to

26

him there as the Emperor's tax, he divided among those
that would go to receive any.

He who had a coat of mail was happy, since for it a
horse might be had in exchange. Some got mounted,
and those not able to get beasts, who were the greater
number, took up the journey on foot. They were well
received by the Indians, and better served than they
could have been at their own homes, particularly in
respect of every thing to eat; for, if an Indian was asked
for a fowl, he would bring four; and if for any sort of
fruit, though it might be a league off, some one would
run to fetch it; and were a Christian ill, the people
would carry him, in a chair, from their own to the next
town. Wheresoever they came, the Cacique of the place,
through an Indian who bears a rod of justice in his hand
they call tapile (which is equivalent to saying meirinho),
ordered provisions to be brought, and men for the loads
of such things as there were, and the others necessary to
carry the invalids.

The Viceroy sent a Portuguese to them, twenty
leagues from Mexico, with quantity of confections, raisins, pomegranates, and other matters proper for the sick,
should they need them; and, in advance, ordered that all
should be clothed at the royal charge. The news of
their approach being known to the citizens, they went
out on the highway to receive them, and with great
courtesy entreated for their companionship as favour, each
one taking to his house as many as he dared, giving
them for raiment all the best he could, the least well
dressed wearing clothes worth thirty cruzados and up-

ward. Clothing was given to those who chose to go for
it to the residence of the Viceroy, and the persons of
condition ate at his board: at his house was a table for
all those of less rank that would eat there. Directly he
informed himself of the quality of each one, that he
might show him the consideration that was his due.
Some of the Conquistadores placed them all down to
table together, fidalgos and boors, oftentimes seating the
servant and his master shoulder to shoulder; which was
done mostly by artisans and men of mean condition,
those better bred asking who each one was, and making
a difference in persons.

Nevertheless, all did the best they could with good
will, telling those they had under their roofs that they
could bring no impoverishment, nor should they hesitate
to receive whatsoever they offered; since they had found
themselves in like condition when others had assisted
them, such being the fortunes of the country. God
reward them: and those whom He saw fit should escape, coming out of Florida to tread the soil of Christians, be He pleased that they live to serve Him; and
to the dead, and to all those who believe in Him, and
confess that in Him is their faith, grant, through His
compassion, the glory of paradise. Amen.

CHAPTER XLIIII.

WHICH SETS FORTH SOME OF THE DIVERSITIES AND PECU-
LIARITIES OF FLORIDA; AND THE FRUIT, BIRDS, AND
BEASTS OF THE COUNTRY.

FROM the port of Espiritu Santo, where the Christians
went on shore, to the Province of Ocute, which may be a
distance of four hundred leagues, a little more or less, the
country is very level, having many ponds, dense thickets,
and, in places, tall pine-trees: the soil is light, and there
is not in it a mountain nor a hill.

The land of Ocute is more strong and fertile than the
rest, the forest more open; and it has very good fields
along the margins of the rivers. From there to Cutifachiqui are about one hundred and thirty leagues, of
which eighty leagues are of desert and pine forests,
through which run great rivers. From Cutifachiqui to
Xuala there may be two hundred and fifty leagues, and
all a country of mountains: the places themselves are
on high level ground, and have good fields upon the
streams.

Thence onward, through Chiaha, Coça, and Talise,
the country of which is flat, dry, and strong, yielding
abundance of maize, to Tascaluça, may be two hundred
and fifty leagues; and thence to Rio Grande, a distance of

about three hundred leagues, the land is low, abounding in lakes. The country afterward is higher, more open, and more populous than any other in Florida; and along the River Grande, from Aquixo to Pacaha and Coligoa, a distance of one hundred and fifty leagues, the land is level, the forest open, and in places the fields very fertile and inviting.

From Coligoa to Autiamque may be two hundred and fifty leagues of mountainous country; thence to Guacay may be two hundred and thirty leagues of level ground; and the region to Daycao, a distance of one hundred and twenty leagues, is continuously of mountainous lands.

From the port of Espiritu Santo to Apalache they marched west and northeast; from Cutifachiqui to Xuala, north; to Coça, westwardly; and thence to Tascaluça and the River Grande, as far as the Provinces of Quizquiz and Aquixo, to the westward; from thence to Pacaha northwardly, to Tula westwardly, to Autiamque southwardly, as far as the Province of Guachoya and Daycao.

The bread that is eaten all through Florida is made of maize, which is like coarse millet; and in all the islands and Indias belonging to Castilla, beginning with the Antillas, grows this grain. There are in the country many walnuts likewise, and amexeas, mulberries, and grapes. The maize is planted and picked in, each person having his own field; fruit is common for all, because it grows abundantly in the woods, without any necessity of setting out trees or pruning them. Where there are mountains the chestnut is found, the fruit of which is somewhat smaller than the one of Spain. Westward of the Rio Grande the walnut differs from that which is found before coming there, being of tenderer shell, and in form like an acorn; while that behind, from the river back to the port of Espiritu Santo, is generally rather hard, the tree and the nut being in their appearance like those of Spain. There is everywhere in the country a fruit, the produce of a plant like ligoacam, that is propagated by the Indians, having the appearance of the royal pear, with an agreeable smell and taste; and likewise another plant, to be seen in the fields, bearing a fruit like strawberry, near to the ground, and is very agreeable. The amexeas are of two sorts, vermilion and gray, of the form and size of walnuts, having three or four stones in them. They are better than any plums that are raised in Spain, and make much better prunes. The grapes appear only to need dressing; for, although large, they have great stones: the other fruits are all in great perfection, and are less unhealthy than those of Spain.

There are many lions and bears in Florida, wolves, deer, jackals, cats, and conies; numerous wild fowl, as large as pea-fowl; small partridges, like those of Africa, and cranes, ducks, pigeons, thrushes, and sparrows. There are blackbirds larger than sparrows and smaller than stares; hawks, goss-hawks, falcons, and all the birds of rapine to be found in Spain.

The Indians are well proportioned: those of the level country are taller and better shaped of form than those of the mountains; those of the interior enjoy a greater abundance of maize and clothing than those of the coast, where the land is poor and thin, and the people along it more warlike.

The direction from the port of Espiritu Santo to Apalache, and thence to Rio de las Palmas, is from east to west; from that river towards New Spain, it is south-wardly; the sea-coast being gentle, having many shoals and high sand-hills.

Deo Gratias.

This Relation of the Discovery of Florida was impressed in the house of Andree de Burgos, Printer and Cavalleiro of the house of Senhor Cardinal iffante.

It was finished the tenth day of February, of the year one thousand five hundred and fifty-seven, in the noble and ever loyal city of Evora.

INDEX

OF THE CHAPTERS CONTAINED IN THE

DISCOVERY OF FLORIDA.

27

225

CHAPTER VI.

CHAPTER VII.

CHAPTER VIII.

CHAPTER IX.

CHAPTER X.

CHAPTER XI.

CHAPTER XII.

CHAPTER XIII.

227

CHAPTER XXII.

CHAPTER XXIII.

CHAPTER XXIIII.

CHAPTER XXV.

CHAPTER XXVI.

CHAPTER XXVII.

CHAPTER XXVIII.

CHAPTER XXIX.

ANNOTATIONS

MADE BY THE TRANSLATOR TO MATTERS IN THE RELAÇAM.

ERRATA.—A gentleman who has carefully scrutinized the text makes some suggestions of error. Where the difference of time is but a day—and the instances of such in the original are many—it has not been annotated. It may be well to name, for the purposes of investigation, the days of the week on which several years begin: Wednesday in 1539, Thursday, leap year, in 1540, Saturday in 1541, Sunday in 1542, and Monday in 1543.

The following are the more important errors:—at page 39, the year 1540 should be 1539; at page 52, line 8, the 21st of the month was on *Sunday*, not Wednesday; at page 69, the 5th day of July should be that day in *June;* at page 75, the 16th of July should be the 26th; at page 91, Sunday, the 18th of November, came on Thursday, and, as the stay at Mauvilla was twenty-eight days from the 18th of October, probably *Sunday* the 14th is the right date; at page 98, there is a typographical blunder, one or more, also error in the date on the first line of the section, which might correctly read *Tuesday* the 15th; at page 112, the 19th day of June came on *Sunday*—the 29th was Wednesday. At page 154, the 22d of July came on *Saturday.*

At page 73, the 7th day of July is a misprint for the 2d; and at page 56, Tuesday the 12th should be *Monday*—both errors in the translation.

CHAPTER I.

THESE items of accounts, selected from two early manuscripts, to show the value of moneys mentioned in different parts of the text, give some idea, likewise,. of the decreased value of the precious metals from their dates to the present time. In an appraisement made " in the usual money of Castilla," at Cadiz, of personal property given in dower, by Catalina de Prado, with her daughter, Maria Gomez, to Alonso Velez, in the year 1529, are these among other estimates :—

	Maravedis.	
One negress slave, named Ynés, sixteen years of age, little more or less, valued at fifty ducados . .	xviiiM	diil
One jewel with three pearls and a garnet, at six thousand mrs.	viM	
One cross ✠ of lignum vitæ of Indias, set in gold with three pearls, at two castellanos . . .	Mdiiii	lxx
One pair house table-cloths, at six reales . .	Mii	iiii

Items of ship's expenses, presented in a suit between the *Oidores* Matienzo and Villalobos, in the Island of Española, before the *escribano* Pedro Ledesma, in the year 1526, concerning the right to a discovery, made in 1520, of a shore and river on the eastern coast of North America, in latitude 33° 30′.

First—four arrobas of olive oil, cost eighteen reales and a half, come to four pesos and five tomines in gold	IIIIpº Vtᵉ
Also—bought in Baracoa three hundred and forty-two cargas of bread, at four and a half reales each, come to ninety-six pesos one tomine and six granos	XCVIpº Itᵉ VIgº
Two linen shirts, one ducado	pº VItᵉ

These show the *grano* to have been one 96th in the 100 parts of the *peso;* the *tomine*, one 8th of the *peso;* the *real*, one 16th; the *maravedi*, one 544th part, or 34 parts to the real; the *castellano*, 89 parts of the *peso;* and the *ducado*, 69 parts, although in Cuba it appears to have been rated at 75 parts. The *cruzado*, a Portuguese coin, according to numerous authorities, is the same as the *ducado*. It is so stated in the "Florida of the Inca;" and Garibay, in treating of the events of the year 1521, says: "The cruzado is of equal value with the Castilian ducado." The *peso* is considered to be an ounce of pure silver, of the weight of sixteen ounces to the Castilian pound.

In the apportionment of treasure arising from spoil and the ransom of Atahualpa, which took place at Caxamalca, the 17th day of June, 1533, the name of Soto stands third in importance on the roll, with the share of $23,000. The gross sum of metal amounted to 1,326,539 pesos in gold and 408,952 pesos of silver, the *peso* being the value of an ounce of silver—sixteen to the pound. The statement is made from the official records.

	Marks of silver.	Pesos in gold.
To the Church	90	2,220
The Adelantado Francisco Pizarro, himself, inter-		
preters, and a horse	2,350	57,220
Hernando Pizarro	1,267	31,080
Hernando de Soto	724	17,740
Father Ino. de Sosa, Vicar of the Army . .	310—6	7,770
Juan Pizarro	407—2	11,100
Pedro de Candia	407—2	9,909
Gonzalo Pizarro	384—5	9,909

Then follow the names of fifty-seven others of cavalry and one hundred and five of infantry.

AMONG the papers in the noted suit brought by Doña Ysabel de Bobadilla against Hernan Ponçe de Leon, existing in the *Archivo Real de Indias*, at Sevilla, is an instrument of writing made at Cuzco, the 27th day of June, in the year 1535, which shows that Soto and Ponçe held their property in common, each with the other, in whatsoever either might possess, or should in any way acquire, or of whatsoever nature; and that they had been thus associated for eighteen or nineteen years. Directly upon its execution, as appears from testimony, Soto went to Nombre de Dios, where he embarked for Spain.

Another instrument, made by the same parties at Havana, the 13th day of May, 1539, ratifying the first, declares the amount taken by the Adelantado to Spain, and registered, to be fifty thousand dollars in gold and three thousand marks of silver; and it further states, that he had received seven thousand castellanos as the dower of his wife, although this, from the relinquishment of a paternal bequest by the mother of Ysabel, printed in the Appendix, appears to have been specifically a stock-farm in Panamá, with the breeding mares, cattle, and the slaves tending them. Besides these amounts, from the evidence afforded by a letter of instructions, preserved in the *Biblioteca Nacional* of Madrid,

28

addressed probably by Soto while in Spain, seemingly to his agent at Court, the property of the partners in lands, houses, and Indians, in Peru, appears likewise to have been large.

YSABEL DE BOBADILLA was the third daughter of Pedro Árias Dávila, *el Galán*, conqueror of Nicaragua, the second of the house and estate of Puñonrostro, by Ysabel de Bobadilla, granddaughter of Francisco Fernandez de Bobadilla and Maria Peñalosa, residents of Segovia. Doña Maria Peñalosa, the second daughter, named after her maternal grandmother, became the wife of Rodrigo de Contreras, Governor of Nicaragua, by the appointment of his father-in-law; and the eldest daughter, Doña Elvira, became the wife of Urban de Arellano. A son, Árias Gonçalo Dávila, succeeded to the name and estates.

The marriage of Ysabel and Soto was childless; the descendants of her sister Elvira continue in Spain; those of Maria are perpetuated in America in the name of Contreras.

The title of Count of Puñonrostro began with Juan, brother of Pedro Árias, or Pedrárias, as he was usually called, who, having served Fernando and Ysabel in their wars, and afterwards Felipe, the husband of Juana, their daughter, held Toledo successfully against the *Comuneros* for the grandson, afterward the Emperor Charles V.; and, among other noted military actions of the time, relieved the fortress at Madrid. For his well-tried loyalty the Emperor conferred on him a title—the name of his town—of which a grandchild, Juan Portocarrero, became the next possessor, and whose son married Francisca, granddaughter of the first Marquis of Charcas, Francisco Pizarro, Conqueror of Peru; the title thence went to the line of Pedrárias, through his son Árias Gonzalo, to Pedro Árias de Bobadilla, who became the third count of Puñonrostro. The title has continued in the family to the Count, in the present Marquis of Casasola, by the name Árias Dávila Mathieu, who, in the year 1858, was Chief Equerry of Her Majesty Queen Ysabel II.

Pedrárias Dávila had the seigniory of Puñonrostro, but was never count: he was a great military disciplinarian, and in the year 1514 became governor of Tierra-firme.

THE PATENT issued to Hernando de Soto, dated at Valladolid, the 20th day of April, in the year 1537, a translation of which is given in the Appendix, confers on him military and political authority, the position of governor and captain-general over two hundred leagues of the coast he should select from that he shall discover, conquer, quiet, and colonize, within the Province of Rio de las Palmas, that of Florida, and those farther on, of Tierra Nueva, in the country given aforetime to Lucas Vazquez de Ayllón, with the office of alguazil-mayor in perpetuity over a dozen leagues square of land, in fee, to be apportioned to him, not to include any seaport or chief town of a Province, " with the jurisdiction and title that we shall designate at the time we direct the bestowal." The portion of the instrument quoted is probably to be understood as a promise to confer a title of nobility, and of the grade doubtless the Relacam states, which had precedents in the fortunate career of American adventure. That all the important aids attending the enterprise might be the better held in hand for success, the government of the Island of Cuba was also bestowed on him, to continue during the royal pleasure.

CHAPTER II.

THE fortunes attending the army of Pánfilo de Narvaez, in its attempt to conquer Florida, are told by Alvar Nuñez Cabeca de Vaca, one of four survivors of that enterprise. In 1557, the time at which the *Relaçam* came from the press, his narrative had already been made public many years, having been printed in 1542, at Zamora, with the title: *La relacion que dio Aluar nuñez cabeça de vaca de lo acaescido en las Indias en la armada donde yua por gouernador Pāphilo de narbaez, desde el año de veynte y siete hasta el año de treynta y seys que boluio a Seuilla con tres de su compañia.* Of this edition, only one copy—that in the possession of James Lenox, in this country—is known to be extant. In 1555 it was printed at Valladolid with the production styled *Commentarios*, after the return of Cabeça de Vaca from the government of the Province of La Plata, written by his secretary, Pero Hernandez, the works together bearing the title: *La relacion y comentarios del governador Aluar nuñez cabeça de vaca de lo acaescido en las dos jornadas que hizo a las Yndias*, the first book bearing the running title of *Naufragios*.

The *Relacion* of Cabeça de Vaca is a story of wild misadventure, from the Bay of Tampa to Yec'ora, or Village of Corazones, at the junction of the Mulatos with the eastern branch of the River Yakee, in Sonora, made in the long period of nearly eight years, from 1528 to 1536, during the early part of which the army was wasted and lost by privation, accidents, shipwreck, in conflicts with the natives, and civil broils. In this time, near the close of the journey, he saw traces of the precious metals, and cotton clothing worn by the Indians, who told him of the great houses towards the north—in Cíbola. The host of Soto, it will be seen in the twenty-seventh and thirty-fifth chapters, marked well the position the narrator indicated, and the reasons why he believed the country to have wealth.

GEIRA, in Portuguese, the quantity of arable land a pair of oxen may ordinarily plough in a day.

AMONG the records belonging to the marquisate of Astorga, which * * * * * Osorio, Count of Altamira, Duke of Montemar, represents, is the will of Don Pedro Alvarez Osorio, second Marquis of Astorga, father of the nobleman referred to in the text, dated at Astorga, the 7th day of July, in the year 1505, some passages of which doubtless refer to members of the family afterward in the army of Soto.

"Again: inasmuch as Don Diego and Doña Teresa, my legitimate children, and Don Alonso, and Don Juan, and Don Antonio, and Doña Ysabel, and Doña Catalina, my children, are not of age, it is my wish, and I desire, that they remain under tutelage and government until they are of an age to know how to take the management of their estates."

"Again: I order what I have taken from the Jews against their will, when they went out of the kingdom, movable as well as real, to be ascertained and returned to the owners or to their heirs."

"Again: I order that there be annually given to Don Antonio, my son, for his subsistence, one hundred thousand maravedises, until such time as the income of fifty thousand maravedises shall be given to him from the Church, to be paid in the best manner and form possible, with which duty I charge my son Don Alvaro, under pain of forfeiture of my benediction; and should that sum not be coming from the Church, let the hundred thousand be paid during lifetime."

"Again: to Galaor Osorio, other twenty thousand maravedis; and I strongly charge it upon Don Alvaro, my son, so to aid and favour him, that he may receive income from the Church, and to assist him with some benefices that may become vacant, to which he may have the presentation."

"Again: I order that there be given to his brother, Garcia Osorio, forty thousand maravedis: And likewise I order that they strive to bring back Villagomez, my servant (*criado*), to this House, and return to strive, for he is servant and kinsman, and that they give him what shall be proper."

Some particulars in the life of Garcia Osorio appear in one of the official papers printed in the Appendix.

THE BIEDMA spoken of is Luys, not Antonio. He wrote the account of the march of the army, *Relacion de la Isla de la Florida*, given in this volume. His title as *factor*, and that of Añasco as *contador*, of Gaytan as treasurer, and Gallegos as *alcaide-mayor*, are also added in translations made from the book of entries at Sevilla.

CHAPTER V.

The person mentioned as Governor of one of the Canary Islands was Guillén Peraza de Ayala, proprietor of Hierro and Gomera. His mother, Doña Beatriz de Bobadilla, was first cousin to the mother of Doña Ysabel, and a sister of the Marquesa de Moya, the associate of the Queen of Castilla from childhood, and her honored intimate through life. The father of these celebrated women was Mosen Pedro de Bobadilla, castellan of the Alcázares of Segovia.

Some highly interesting particulars in the life of Doña Beatriz are given in the " History of the Canaries," by Glas, translated, according to Viera y Clavijo, from a work on the subject of those Islands, in manuscript, by the Franciscan Juan de Galindo. Hernan Peraza, Conde de la Gomera, having been sent to Spain, on the complaint of the widow of Juan Rejon, charged with the murder of her husband, a pardon was granted him by Ysabel, through the intercession of influential friends, in consideration of his returning to serve, with some companies of troops, in the conquest of the Great Canary. At the same time, as the King was supposed to have a passion for one of the Ladies of Honour, Beatriz, and an opportunity for removing her creditably from Court presented itself, she was given in marriage by the Queen, with great ceremonial, to Hernan Peraza, who returned with her to the Islands.

In the course of time, the Count, becoming enamoured with a female of the country, was killed by one of the natives—a deed for which he, with many others, supposed accomplices, was punished with great cruelty by Pedro de Vera, the final subjugator of the people of that Group, after a protracted war of seventy-seven years. This is the grandsire of that Vera, the very opposite in character, who, with the maternal name of Cabeça de Vaca, wrote the story of the disasters he shared with Narvaez in attempting the conquest of Florida.

The widow of Peraza soon after married Alonso de Lugo, though not before she had, by arbitrary acts, caused two Spaniards to be hanged—one for treason to her government, the other for expressions cast on the purity of her womanly conduct. Coming to Spain afterward, against the advice of her husband, to answer for her administration, she was received with the most friendly feelings at Court. One morning, however, the beauteous Beatriz was found lying in her bed lifeless. The funeral, by order of the Queen, was one of magnificence.

Alonso de Lugo continued to administer the affairs of Gomera, until the youthful Count, assisted by his friends, obliged him to relinquish the station; and the step-father being taken from the Island, Guillén governed for the public content and welfare.

Garcilasso names the daughter of the Count of Gomera, Doña Leonor, and describes her as a beauty of seventeen summers, whom the Adelantado earnestly solicited of her father, that he might marry her to some one of high position in his prospective conquest. The lady, it may be seen, is mentioned in the will of Soto, with substantial remembrance both of her and her husband.

CHAPTER VI.

THE RIVER CÁUTO, misspelled Tanto in the text, is the largest river of Cuba, and runs its entire course westwardly a distance of sixty leagues.

AÑASCO, called Danhusco in the text, bore the royal license of exclusive privilege to trade with the inhabitants of Florida. The record of it exists in the archives of Indias at Seville, in the volume entitled *Libro de la Florida de Capitulaciones y Asientos desde el año* 1517, *hasta el de* 1578, a translation of which into English is given in the Appendix to this volume.

CHAPTER IX.

THE *ano paracusi* (according to the friar Francisco Pareja, in his Catechism in Spanish of the Timuquana tongue), with *holata yco*, or *olata aco*, or *utinama*, are principal caciques, having other chiefs subject to them. From this stock comes a counsellor, *ynihama*, "who leads the cacique by the hand," and from him descend other lines or stages in society. Perhaps the XIIII. plate in the *Brevis Narratio* of De Bry, Second Part, illustrates the rank and relation of these personages to each other.

CHAPTER XI.

VILLA HARTA (in the Portuguese, *Villa-farta*) is a small town of Spain, in the Province of Córdova, six leagues from the city, and twenty-eight from Sevilla, situated in a healthy climate, on the side of the elevated mountain of La Solana, having an uneven, stony, and fertile soil. It is strictly agricultural, and only commercial to the extent of sending away its superfluous productions of grain and wine, pork, and a little honey. The district is also very plentiful in game. Its insignificance could scarcely have permitted it to rise to the casualty of giving its name to another town; and the meaning of the word "harta," abundant, will be thought perhaps sufficient reason alone for its use, without seeking other explanation.

THE name of the Chief Uzachil is spelled, in Oviedo, *Uçahile ;* by Garcilasso, *Ochile ;* by Captain Biedma, *Veachile ;* in Herrera, *Osachile ;* and is perhaps that of the personage or dignitary spoken of by Cabeça de Vaca as met by the army of Narvaez, in about the same region of country, in the year 1528, whom he calls Dulchanchellin.

"Having learned this much, we left the next day, going ever in quest of that country which the Indians had told us of as Apalache, carrying for guides those of them we had taken. We travelled until the seventeenth day of June, without seeing any natives who would venture to await our coming up with them, when a chief approached, carried on the back of another Indian, and covered with a painted deer-skin, having a great many people walking in advance of him, playing on flutes of cane. In this manner he came up to where the Governor stood, and was with him an hour. By signs we gave him to understand that we were going to Apalache; and it appeared to us, by those he made, that he was an enemy to its people, and would go to assist us against them. We gave him beads and hawk-bells, with other articles of traffic, and he presented the Governor with the skin he wore, and then returned, we following him in the road he took.

"That night we came to a very wide and deep river, with current very rapid. As we could not venture to cross with rafts, we made a canoe for the purpose, and spent a day in getting over. If the Indians had desired to dispute our passage, they could well have done so; for, even with their help, we had great difficulty in effecting it. One of the horsemen, Juan Vazquez by name, a native of Cuellar, impatient of detention, having entered the river, the violence of the current cast him from his horse, when he grasped the reins of the bridle, and both were drowned. The people of that chief, whose name was Dulchanchellin, found the body of the beast, and told us where we should find the corpse in the river below. This death gave us much pain, for until then, not one had been missing."—NAUFRAGIOS.

29

CHAPTER XV.

In the account given of the march of Soto by his private secretary (see Oviedo), Guazule or Guazulle is spelled Guasili; and the writer says, because of the good fortune that attended the soldiers there, the Chief having given them many tamemes, much maize, and many little dogs, they would say at a favourable throw of dice, "The house of Guasuli!" in recollection of the luck that there befell them. The word is spelled, in all the other narratives, nearly in the same way as that more familiar to Spanish ears, Guazul or Gazul, the name borne by a tribe of *Berberiscos* of the coast of Africa, who had given it to a town of the Peninsula they once guarded—Alcalá de los Guazules (*al*, the; *calat*, castle), whence has come the word there *gandul*, vagabond, as a term of reproach, from the Arabic into the familiar language of the country.

BARBACOA, MAIZ, TAMEME, PETACA, are words used in this narrative derived from Indian tongues, and recognized in the Spanish. "Barbacoa," of which we have not the elements, is from the Yucayo, and in its simplest signification appears to mean scaffolding raised on posts, such an arrangement as was made for burning Ortiz, mentioned in Chapter IX.; or a crib, such as was used for storing the crop; or a staging put up in the fields, whereon the natives watched, that birds should not take the grain. From it, through the Spanish, comes the word into the English "barbacue," and, perhaps, the word "bucanier," through the French. "Maiz" belongs also to the same language, the one spoken by the natives of Cuba and Hayti. "Tameme," used by the descendants of the Spaniards in Mexico, is from *tlamama* or *tlameme* in the Mexican language proper, signifying porter, or carrier of loads on the back. "Petaca" is likewise from the Mexican, a corruption of *petla calli*, cane house, a word in general use all over Spanish America for cigar-case, or other box made of grass.

CHAPTER XVII.

The Ameijoa is the green gage, the Claudia of Spain, where it is produced in perfection and abundance. The shape of the plum is precisely that of the persimmon, the fruit undoubtedly that is referred to as growing without being planted, and wild in the woods. Moreover, as will be seen in the concluding chapter, which treats of the soil of Florida, its animal and vegetable life, this fruit is spoken of as of two kinds, the red and gray, and as being the size of a walnut, with three or four pits, and also as making a far better prune than the plum of Spain. They are the *Diospyros Virginiana* and the *D. Texana*.

CHAPTER XXIV.

With reference to the fishes that are mentioned in this chapter, we are indebted for the following observations to Professor Theodore Gill, of the Smithsonian Institution.

"I have carefully perused the account, and although there is little on which to base the identification of the species, I am disposed to believe that the following conjectures will at least closely approximate the truth. The historian enumerates five species, of which three have scales, while the others are naked. The scaleless species are the 'bagre' and the 'peel-fish.'

"The 'bagre' is undoubtedly the large 'cat-fish' of the West, known as *Ictalurus corulescens*, that being the only species that attains a weight of 'one hundred to one hundred and fifty pounds.' The head is large, as in all its congeners, but not as big as would be inferred from the text; the 'great spines, like very sharp awls,' along the side, are the spines of the pectoral fins. The species is very generally distributed in the hydrographical basin

of the Mississippi. The 'peel-fish,' with 'the snout a cubit in
length, the upper lip being shaped like a shovel,' is very clearly
the singular fish universally known throughout the West as the
'spoonbill-cat' or sturgeon, and 'paddle-fish.' It is related to
the ordinary sturgeons, but is distinguished by the peculiar
leaf-like expansion of the snout, the extension of the gill covers,
and the presence of minute teeth on the jaws in the young.
The species observed was the *Polyodon spatula*, occurring in
the Mississippi River and all its larger tributaries. The only
other species of the genus, besides the American, inhabit the
rivers of China and Japan.

"The scaly fishes are not so easily determinable. The one
shaped like a barbel was probably the *Cycleptus elongatus*, a
member of the family of 'suckers,' or *Catastomidæ*. That species
would probably be recognized by most or all casual observers as
having a greater superficial resemblance to the barbel of Europe
than any other of our fishes. The fish 'like a shad' was perhaps
the species which has been introduced into the ichthyological sys-
tem as *Pomolobus chrysochloris*, and which is very closely related
to the 'fall herring' or 'shad' of the Eastern fishermen. The
bream-like fish cannot be identified with any approach to certainty; but it is possible that it may have been the fish now known
in Louisiana and Mississippi as 'tarpon' or 'big scale,' and called
by naturalists *Megalops cyprinoides*. That species more nearly
fulfils the requisites as to form of head and excellence as food than
any of the species of the lower Mississippi basin known to me.
The 'perco' is probably referable to the genus *Haploidonotus*,
the species of which are generally called 'white perch' or 'drum'
by the inhabitants of the west. That type, at least, is the only
one that possesses the combination of scaly body, teeth in the
jaws, and size, referred to in the notice." RAFINESQUE writes:
"A remarkable peculiarity of this fish consists in the strange
grunting noise which it produces, and from which is derived
its specific name, *H. grunniens*. It is intermediate between the
dumb grunt of a hog, and the single croaking noise of the bull-
frog: that grunt is only repeated at intervals, and not in quick
succession."—*Ichthyologia Ohiensis*, 1820, p. 25.

POLYODON SPATULA.

HEAD AND SNOUT FROM ABOVE.

Drawn from specimens in the Smithsonian Institution, for THE BRADFORD CLUB.

"I will merely add that all the fishes mentioned, save the *Megalops*, ascend high up the Mississippi River and its larger tributary streams, while the *Megalops* enters the rivers of the Southern coast generally, and does not ascend far above tide-water."

In a note to the translation made by Hakluyt of this work, republished in London by the Hakluyt Society, and edited by William B. Rye, with good discretion and research, is this curious conjecture :—

"The words *pexe perco*, in the original Portuguese, are in all probability a misprint for *pexe*, or *peyxe*, fish, and *porco*, hog, the two words together meaning a porpoise, which English word, indeed, is derived from the corresponding Latin words, *porcus piscis*."

CHAPTER XXV.

The River Caya, a western limit of Spain, takes its rise in the adjoining kingdom of Portugal, among the mountains of San Manuel and La Rabona, flowing through the Province of Badajóz, and, at about a league from the city of the same name, empties itself into the River Guadiana. The stream, unspanned by bridges, is crossed during the season of floods in little boats.

CHAPTER XXXI.

The ocean, as surveyed from Biscay, was the North Sea, and that name, for the maritime people there, extended over the Atlantic : the discovery of another ocean, the Pacific, as seen from Panamá, became, in contradistinction for Spaniards, the South Sea.

CHAPTER XLI.

THE RIVER PÁNUCO, in the text misspelled Panico, has for its outlet the bar of Puerto Escondido. The town of Pánuco is about nine leagues distant from that entrance, situate on the south bank of the river, in 22° 4′ of northern latitude.

CHAPTER XLIII.

THE *topile* was an officer that the conquerors, *conquistadores*, found in the civil government of Mexico, with powers judicial and ministerial similar to those exercised by the *marino* or *alguazil* among themselves, and by the sheriff in England.

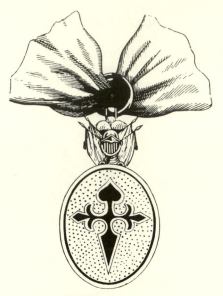

ORDER OF ST. JAGO.

SOTO.

ÁRIAS.

RELATION

OF THE

CONQUEST OF FLORIDA,

PRESENTED BY

LUYS HERNANDEZ DE BIEDMA

IN THE YEAR 1544

TO THE

KING OF SPAIN IN COUNCIL.

TRANSLATED FROM THE ORIGINAL DOCUMENT.

30

ACCOUNT

OF

THE ISLAND OF FLORIDA.

WE arrived at the port of Baya Honda, where we landed six hundred and twenty men and two hundred and twenty-three horses.   As soon as we went on shore, we found out, from some Indians taken, that there was a Christian in the country, one of the people who had come into it with Pánfilo de Narvaez, and we started in search of him.   He was in the possession of a chief, some eight leagues distant from the harbour.   We met him on the way, for the Cacique, hearing that we had left the ships, asked the Christian if it was his desire to go where we were;   who answered that it was, and he sent him off with nine Indians.   He came naked like them, with a bow and some arrows in his hands, his body wrought over like theirs.   They who discovered the natives thought they were come to spy out the condition of our people, and dashed after them.   The Indians fled towards a little wood near by, but the horsemen coming up with them, one Indian received a thrust from a lance, and the Christian, having nearly forgotten our language, himself would have been slain, had he not remembered to call upon the name of Our Lady, whereby he was recognized.   We brought him with great rejoicing before the Governor.

Twelve years had passed since the Christian had come among the Indians.   He knew their tongue, and, from the long habit of speaking that only, he was more than four days among us before he could connect an idea without putting to every word of Spanish four or five words of Indian, though he came after a while to recover our speech entirely.   His knowledge of the country was so limited that he could tell us of nothing twenty leagues off, neither from having seen it nor by hearsay; however, from first seeing us, he said there was no place at which to find gold.

We left Baya Honda to explore inland, taking with us all the people that had come on shore excepting twenty-six cavalry and sixty infantry, left in charge of the port until the Governor should be heard from, or should send orders for them to join him.   We took our way towards the west, then turned to the northwest, having information of a Cacique named Uurripacuxi, who lived about twenty leagues from the coast, to whom the Indians said they all paid tribute.· Thence we went, through swamps and over rivers, fifteen or twenty leagues, to a town which the Indians represented to us as very wonderful, and where the inhabitants, by shouting, caused birds on the wing to drop.   On arrival there we found it to be a small town, called Etocale. We got some maize, beans, and little dogs, which were no small relief to people who came perishing with hunger.

We remained seven or eight days, and in that time made several forays, to catch Indians for guides to the Province of Apalache, which had great fame wheresoever we went. Three or four men were taken, of whom the best informed knew nothing of the country two leagues in advance. We went on still in the direction of New Spain, keeping some ten or twelve leagues from the coast.

In four or five days' march we passed through several towns, and came to a moderately large one, called Aguacalecuen. The inhabitants were all found to have gone off affrighted into the woods. We remained six or seven days, to hunt some Indians for guides, and while engaged in the search we caught ten or twelve women, one of whom was declared to be the daughter of the Cacique. The consequence was, that her father came to us in peace. He promised we should have interpreters and guides; but, as he did not give them, we had to take him along with us. With the intent of wresting him from us, at the close of six or seven days' march there came upon us about three hundred and fifty warriors, with bows and arrows, of whom we killed some and captured the remainder. Among them were Indians who had knowledge of the country farther inland, yet they told us very false stories.

We crossed another river, in a Province called Veachile, and found towns on the farther bank which the inhabitants had left, though we did not fail, in consequence, to find some food in them, which we needed. We set out for another town, named Aguile,

which is on the confines of Apalache, a river dividing
the one from the other province. Across this stream we
made a bridge, by lashing many pines together, upon
which we went over with much danger, as there were
Indians on the opposite side who disputed our passage;
when they found, however, that we had landed, they
went to the nearest town, called Ivitachuco, and there
remained until we came in sight, when as we appeared
they set all the place on fire and took to flight.

There are many towns in this Province of Apalache,
and it is a land abundant in subsistence. They call all
that other country we were travelling through, the Province of Yustaga.

We went to another town, called Iniahico. There it
appeared to us to be time we should know of those who
remained at the port, and that they should hear from us;
for we proposed to travel so far inland that we might not
be able to hear of them again. The distance we had
now marched from them was one hundred and ten
leagues, and the Governor gave orders that they should
come to where we then were.

From that town we went to look for the sea, which
was about nine leagues off, and we found, on the shore,
where Pánfilo de Narvaez had built his boats. We found
the spot whereon the forge had stood, and many bones of
horses. The Indians told us, through the interpreter,
what others like us there had done. Juan de Añasco put
signals on some trees standing near the water, because he
was commanded to return to the port, and bid the people
there come on by the way we had marched, while he

should sail in the two brigantines and the boat that were left, and we would await his arrival, at the Province of Apalache.

Juan de Añasco sent the people on by land, while he came by sea, as the Governor had ordered, encountering much fatigue and danger; for he could not find the coast he had observed from the land before leaving, discovering no marks whatsoever from the sea, as these were in shallow inlets, that with the rise of tide had water in them, and with the ebb were bare. We made a piragua, which went out every day two leagues to sea, looking for the brigantines, to show them where to stop. I was thankful when the people arrived, not less for those that came by land than those by water.

On the arrival of the brigantines, the Governor directed that they should sail westwardly to discover a harbour, if one were near, whence to ascertain, by exploring the coast, if any thing could be found inland. Francisco Maldonado, a gentleman of Salamanca, had the command. He coasted along the country, and entered all the coves, creeks, and rivers he discovered, until he arrived at a river having a good entrance and harbour, with an Indian town on the seaboard. Some inhabitants approaching to traffic, he took one of them, and directly turned back with him to join us. On this voyage he was absent two months, which appeared to us all to be a thousand years, inasmuch as it detained us so long from advancing to what we understood was to be found in the interior.

After Maldonado got back, the Governor told him,

that, as we were about to set off in quest of the country
which that Indian stated to be on another sea, he must
return with the brigantines to Cuba, where the Doña
Ysabel de Bobadilla, his wife, remained; and if within
six months' time he should hear nothing of us, to come
with the brigantines, and run the shore as far as the
River Espiritu Santo, to which we should have to resort.
The vessels went to the Island, and we took our way
again northward, going to seek after what the Indian
had told us of.

We marched five days through an uninhabited country, when, coming to a great river, as we could not
build a bridge over it, because of the stiffness of the
current, we made a piragua. With this we reached the
opposite shore, where we found a Province called Acapa-
chiqui, very abundant in the food to which the Indians
are accustomed. We saw some towns, and others there
were we did not visit, because the country was one of
very large swamps. There was a change in the habitations, which were now in the earth, like caves: heretofore
they were covered with palm-leaves and with grass.
We continued on, and came to two other rivers, over
which we had to make bridges, in our usual manner,
by tying pine-trees together. Arrived at another Province, called Otoa, we found a town rather larger than
any we had seen to that time. We went thence to
towns of another province, which may be about two
days' march distant, where we took some persons not on
the look-out, they never having heard of us. The people
agreed to come and serve us peacefully for the return of

the captives, whom the Governor gave up, keeping only a part as interpreters and guides, for the use of the way.

We were five or six days in going through this Province, called Chisi, where we were well supplied by the Indians from their slender stores; and having marched three days more without seeing any large town, we came to the Province of Altapaha. Here we found a river that had a course not southwardly, like the rest we had passed, but eastward to the sea, where the Licentiate, Lucas de Ayllón, had come; whence we gave still more credit to what the Indian said, and we came to believe as true all the stories that he had told us. This province was thickly peopled, and the inhabitants all desired to serve us. The Governor inquired of them for that province, Cofitachyque, of which we came in pursuit; they said it was not possible to go thither, there being no road, and on the journey we should famish, there being no food. We went on to other caciques, of the names Ocuti and Cafaqui, who gave us of what they had to eat. They said if we were going to make war on the Lady of Cofitachique, they would give us all we should desire for the way; but we should understand there was no road over which to pass; that they had no intercourse, because of their enmity, except when they made war upon each other, which was carried on through obscure and intricate parts, out of which no one would be expected to issue, and that they were on the journey from twenty to twenty-two days, eating in the time only plants and the parched maize they took with them. Seeing our determination, they gave us eight hundred Indians to carry

31

our loads of clothing and provisions, and also others as guides.

We were taken directly to the eastward, and thus travelled three days. The Indian who deceitfully led us had said, that he would place us whither we were going in that time; and notwithstanding, towards the close, we began to discover his perfidy, the Governor did not desist from the course, but commanded that we should husband our provisions as much as possible, since he suspected we should find ourselves—which did actually come to pass—in embarrassment and want. We went on through this wilderness, and at the end of thirteen days arrived at some cottages. The Indians had now become so bewildered, that they knew not in what direction to turn. The road had given out, and the Governor went around to regain it, but, failing to find it, he came back to us desperate. He directed that the people should return some half a league to a great river, and there he began to give out rations of fresh pork from the hogs we drove with us, a pound to each man, which we ate boiled, without salt or other seasoning.

The Governor sent in two directions to find a path, or any mark indicating inhabitants—one person up the river to the north and northeast, and the other down along it to the south and southeast, and he allowed to each ten days in which to go and return. He that went to the south and southeastward came in, after being gone four days, with the news that he had come upon a little town having some provisions. He brought three or four people from it, who speaking with our perfidious Indian, he understood them. This was no little relief to us, because of the difficulty there is everywhere in the country of being understood; and once more the guide repeated the falsehoods he had before told us, which we believed, because we heard him talk the language with those Indians. We directly set out, with all our people, for that little village, to await there the return of those who had gone in other directions to seek for paths. We tarried four or five days, until all had come together. About fifty hanegas of maize were found in the place, and some parched meal; there were many mulberry-trees loaded with fruit, and likewise some other small fruits.

Thence we set out for the town of Cofitachique, two days' journey from the village, seated on the banks of a river, which we believed to be the Santa Elena, where the Licentiate Ayllón had been. Having arrived at the stream, the Lady of this town sent to us her niece, borne in a litter, the Indians showing her much respect, with the message that she was pleased we had arrived in her territory, and that she would give us of all she could or might possess. She likewise sent the Governor a necklace of five or six strings of pearls. We were furnished with canoes in which to pass over the river, and the Lady gave us one-half of the town; but after staying three or four days, she suddenly went off into the woods. The Governor caused her to be sought, and not finding her, he opened a mosque, in which were interred the bodies of the chief personages of that country. We took from it a quantity of pearls, of the weight of as many as six arrobas and a half, or seven, though they were injured from lying in the earth, and in the adipose substance of the dead. We found buried two wood axes, of Castilian make, a rosary of jet beads, and some false pearls, such as are taken from this country to traffic with the Indians, all of which we supposed they got in exchange, made with those who followed the Licentiate Ayllón. From the information given by the Indians, the sea should be about thirty leagues distant. We knew that the people who came with Ayllón hardly entered the country at all; that they remained continually on the coast, until his sickness and death. In strife for command, they then commenced to kill each other, while others of them died of hunger; for one, whose lot it was to have been among them, told us that of six hundred men who landed, only fifty-seven escaped—a loss caused, to a great extent, by the wreck of a big ship they had brought, laden with stores. Having remained in the town of this Lady some ten or eleven days, it became necessary that we should go thence in quest of a country which might furnish food, as the quantity where we were was sufficient only for the necessities of the Indians, and we, our horses and followers, consumed it very fast.

Again we took the direction of the north, and for eight days we travelled through a poor country, scarce of food, until arriving at one called Xuala, where we still found some Indian houses, though a thin population, for the country was broken. Among these ridges we discovered the source of the great river whence we had taken our departure, believed to be the Espiritu Santo. We went on to a town called Guasuli, where the inhabitants gave us a number of dogs, and some maize, of which they had but little. From there we marched four days, and arrived at a town called Chiha, which is very plentiful in food. It is secluded on an island of this river of Espiritu Santo, which, all the way from the place of its rise, forms very large islands. In this province, where we began to find the towns set about with fence, the Indians get a large quantity of oil from walnuts. We were detained twenty-six or twenty-seven days to refresh the horses, which arrived greatly fatigued, having worked hard and eaten little.

We left, following along the banks of the river, and came to another province, called Costehe, the towns of which are likewise on islands in the river, and thence we went to Coça, one of the finest countries we discovered in Florida. The Cacique came out in a hurdle to receive us, with great festivity and many people, he having numerous towns subject to him. The next morning we saw all the inhabitants, and having detained the Cacique, that he might give us persons to carry our loads, we tarried some days until we could get them. We found plums like those here in Castile, and great quantities of vines, on which were very good grapes. From this we went to the west and southwest, passing through the towns of the Cacique for five or six days, until we came to another province, called Italisi. The people being gone, we went to look for them. Some Indians came to us, by whom the Governor sent to call the Cacique, who, coming, brought to us a present of twenty-six or twenty-seven women, skins of deer, and whatever else they had.

From this point we went south, drawing towards the coast of New Spain, and passed through several towns, before coming to another province, called Taszaluza, of which an Indian of such size was chief that we all considered him a giant. He awaited us quietly at his town, and on our arrival we made much ado for him, with joust at reeds, and great running of horses, although he appeared to regard it all as small matter. Afterward we asked him for Indians to carry our burdens; he answered that he was not accustomed to serving any one, but it was rather for others all to serve *him*. The Governor ordered that he should not be allowed to return to his house, but be kept where he was. This detention among us he felt—whence sprang the ruin that he afterwards wrought us, and it was why he told us that he could there give us nothing, and that we must go to another town of his, called Mavila, where he would bestow on us whatever we might ask. We took up our march in that direction, and came to a river, a copious flood, which we considered to be that which empties into the Bay of Chuse. Here we got news of the manner in which the boats of Narvaez had arrived in want of water, and of a Christian, named Don Teodoro, who had stopped among these Indians, with a negro, and we were shown a dagger that he had worn. We were here two days, making rafts for crossing the river. In this time the Indians killed one of the guard of the

Governor, who thereupon, being angry, threatened the Cacique, and told him that he should burn him if he did not give up to him those who had slain the Christian. He replied that he would deliver them to us in that town of his, Mavila. The Cacique had many in attendance. An Indian was always behind him with a fly-brush of plumes, so large as to afford his person shelter from the sun.

At nine o'clock, one morning, we arrived at Mavila, a small town very strongly stockaded, situated on a plain. We found the Indians had demolished some habitations about it, to present a clear field. A number of the chiefs came out to receive us as soon as we were in sight, and they asked the Governor, through the interpreter, if he would like to stop on that plain, or preferred to enter the town, and said that in the evening they would give us the Indians to carry burdens. It appeared to our Chief better to go thither with them, and he commanded that all should enter the town, which we did.

Having come within the enclosure, we walked about, talking with the Indians, supposing them to be friendly, there being not over three or four hundred in sight, though full five thousand were in the town, whom we did not see, nor did they show themselves at all. Apparently rejoicing, they began their customary songs and dances; and some fifteen or twenty women having performed before us a little while, for dissimulation, the Cacique got up and withdrew into one of the houses. The Governor sent to tell him that he must come out, to which he answered that he would not; and the Captain of the body-guard entered the door to bring him forth, but seeing many Indians present, fully prepared for battle, he thought it best to withdraw and leave him. He reported that the houses were filled with men, ready with bows and arrows, bent on some mischief. The Governor called to an Indian passing by, who also refusing to come, a gentleman near took him by the arm to bring him, when, receiving a push, such as to make him let go his hold, he drew his sword and dealt a stroke in return that cleaved away an arm.

With the blow they all began to shoot arrows at us, some from within the houses, through the many loop-holes they had arranged, and some from without. As we were so wholly unprepared, having considered ourselves on a footing of peace, we were obliged, from the great injuries we were sustaining, to flee from the town, leaving behind all that the carriers had brought for us, as they had there set down their burdens. When the Indians saw that we had gone out, they closed the gates, and beating their drums, they raised flags, with great shout-ing; then, emptying our knapsacks and bundles, showed up above the palisades all we had brought, as much as to say that they had those things in possession. Directly as we retired, we bestrode our horses and completely en-circled the town, that none might thence anywhere escape. The Governor directed that sixty of us should dismount, and that eighty of the best accoutred should form in four parties, to assail the place on as many sides, and the first of us getting in should set fire to the houses, that no more harm should come to us: so we handed over

our horses to other soldiers who were not in armour, that
if any of the Indians should come running out of the
town they might overtake them.

We entered the town and set it on fire, whereby a
number of Indians were burned, and all that we had was
consumed, so that there remained not a thing. We
fought that day until nightfall, without a single Indian
having surrendered to us—they fighting bravely on like
lions. We killed them all, either with fire or the sword,
or, such of them as came out, with the lance, so that
when it was nearly dark there remained only three alive;
and these, taking the women that had been brought
to dance, placed the twenty in front, who, crossing their
hands, made signs to us that we should come for them.
The Christians advancing toward the women, these
turned aside, and the three men behind them shot their
arrows at us, when we killed two of them. The last
Indian, not to surrender, climbed a tree that was in the
fence, and taking the cord from his bow, tied it about
his neck, and from a limb hanged himself.

This day the Indians slew more than twenty of our
men, and those of us who escaped only hurt were two
hundred and fifty, bearing upon our bodies seven hundred and sixty injuries from their shafts. At night we
dressed our wounds with the fat of the dead Indians,
as there was no medicine left, all that belonged to us
having been burned. We tarried twenty-seven or twenty-
eight days to take care of ourselves, and God be praised
that we were all relieved. The women were divided as
servants among those who were suffering most. We

32

learned from the Indians that we were as many as forty leagues from the sea. It was much the desire that the Governor should go to the coast, for we had tidings of the brigantines; but he dared not venture thither, as it was already the middle of November, the season very cold; and he found it necessary to go in quest of a country where subsistence might be had for the winter; here there was none, the region being one of little food.

We resumed our direction to the northward, and travelled ten or twelve days, suffering greatly from the cold and rain, in which we marched afoot, until arriving at a fertile province, plentiful in provisions, where we could stop during the rigour of the season. The snows fall more heavily there than they do in Castile. Having reached the Province of Chicaza, the warriors came out to interrupt the passage of a river we had to cross. We were detained by them three days. Finally, we went over in a piragua we built, when the Indians fled to the woods. After seven or eight days, messengers from the Cacique arrived, saying that he and all his people desired to come and serve us. The Governor received the message well, and sent word to him to do so without fail, and that he would present him with many of the things he brought. The Cacique came, having with him a number of persons, who bore him upon their shoulders. He gave us some deer-skins and little dogs. The people returned, and every day Indians came and went, bringing us many hares, and whatever else the country supplied.

. In the night-time we captured some Indians, who, on a footing of peace, came to observe how we slept and guarded. We, unaware of the perfidy that was intended, told the Cacique that we desired the next day to continue our march, when he left, and that night fell upon us. As the enemy knew whereabout our sentinels were set, they got amongst us into the town, without being observed, by twos and fours, more than three hundred men, with fire which they brought in little pots, not to be seen. When the sentinels discovered that more were coming in troop, they beat to arms; but this was not done until the others had already set fire to the town. The Indians did us very great injury, killing fifty-seven horses, more than three hundred hogs, and thirteen or fourteen men; and it was a great mysterious providence of God, that, though we were not resisting them, nor giving them any cause to do so, they turned and fled; had they followed us up, not a man of all our number could have escaped. Directly we moved to a cottage about a mile off.

We knew that the Indians had agreed to return upon us that night; but, God be praised, in consequence of a light rain, they did not come; for we were in so bad condition, that, although some horses still remained, we had no saddles, lances, nor targets, all having been consumed. We hastened to make them, the best we could with the means at hand; and at the end of five days, the Indians, coming back upon us with their squadrons in order, attacked us with much concert at three points. As we were prepared, and, moreover, aware of their approach, we met them at the onset, beat them back, and did them some injury; so that, thank God, they returned no more. We remained here perhaps two months, getting ready what were necessary of saddles, lances, and targets, and then left, taking the direction to the northwest, toward a Province called Alibamo.

At this time befell us what is said never to have occurred in the Indias. In the highway over which we had to pass, without there being either women to protect or provisions to secure, and only to try our valour with theirs, the Indians put up a very strong stockade directly across the road, about three hundred of them standing behind it, resolute to die rather than give back. So soon as they observed our approach, some came out to shoot their arrows, threatening that not one of us should remain alive. When we had surveyed that work, thus defended by men, we supposed they guarded something—provision perhaps—of which we stood greatly in need; for we had calculated to cross a desert of twelve days' journey in its extent, where we could have nothing to eat but what we carried. We alighted, some forty or fifty men, and put ourselves on two sides, arranging that at the sound of the trumpet we should all enter the barricade at one time. We did accordingly, carrying it, although at some cost, losing on our side seven or eight men, and having twenty-five or twenty-six more wounded. We killed some Indians, and took others, from whom we learned that they had done this to measure themselves with us, and nothing else. We looked about for food, although at great hazard, that we might begin our journey in the wilderness.

We travelled eight days with great care, in tenderness of the wounded and the sick we carried. One mid-day we came upon a town called Quizquiz, and so suddenly to the inhabitants, that they were without any notice of us, the men being away at work in the maize-fields. We took more than three hundred women, and the few skins and shawls they had in their houses. There we first found a little walnut of the country, which is much better than that here in Spain. The town was near the banks of the River Espiritu Santo. They told us that it was, with many towns about there, tributary to a lord of Pacaha, famed throughout all the land. When the men heard that we had taken their women, they came to us peacefully, requesting the Governor to restore them. He did so, and asked them for canoes in which to pass that great river. These they promised, but never gave; on the contrary, they collected to give us battle, coming in sight of the town where we were; but in the end, not venturing to make an attack, they turned and retired.

We left that place and went to encamp by the river-side, to put ourselves in order for crossing. On the other shore we saw numbers of people collected to oppose our landing, who had many canoes. We set about building four large piraguas, each capable of taking sixty or seventy men and five or six horses. We were engaged in the work twenty-seven or twenty-eight days. During this time, the Indians every day, at three o'clock in the afternoon, would get into two hundred and fifty very large canoes they had, well shielded, and come near the shore on which we were; with loud cries they would exhaust their arrows upon us, and then return to the other bank. After they saw that our boats were at the point of readiness for crossing, they all went off, leaving the passage free. We crossed the river in concert, it being nearly a league in width, and nineteen or twenty fathoms deep. We found some good towns on the other side; and once more following up the stream, on the way to that Province of Pacaha, we came first to the province of another lord, called Icasqui, against whom he waged severe war. The Cacique came out peacefully to meet us, saying that he had heard of us for a long time, and that he knew we were men from heaven, whom their arrows could not harm; wherefore, he desired to have no strife, and wished only to serve us. The Governor received him very kindly, and permitting no one to enter the town, to avoid doing mischief, we encamped in sight, on a plain, where we lay two days.

On the day of our arrival, the Cacique said that inasmuch as he knew the Governor to be a man from the sky, who must necessarily have to go away, he besought him to leave a sign, of which he might ask support in his wars, and his people call upon for rain, of which their fields had great need, as their children were dying of hunger. The Governor commanded that a very tall cross be made of two pines, and told him to return the next day, when he would give him the sign from heaven for which he asked; but that the Chief must believe nothing could be needed if he had a true faith in the cross. He returned the next day, complaining much because we so long delayed giving him the sign he asked, and he had good-will to serve and follow us. Thereupon he set up a loud wailing because the compliance was not immediate, which caused us all to weep, witnessing such devotion and earnestness in his entreaties. The Governor told him to bring all his people back in the evening, and that we would go with them to his town and take thither the sign he had asked. He came in the afternoon with them, and we went in procession to the town, while they followed us. Arriving there, as it is the custom of the Caciques to have near their houses a high hill, made by hand, some having the houses placed thereon, we set up the cross on the summit of a mount, and we all went on bended knees, with great humility, to kiss the foot of that cross. The Indians did the same as they saw us do, nor more nor less; then directly they brought a great quantity of cane, making a fence about it; and we returned that night to our camp.

In the morning, we took up our course for Pacaha, which was by the river upward. We travelled two days, and then discovered the town on a plain, well fenced about, and surrounded by a water-ditch made by hand. Hastening on as fast as possible, we came near and halted, not daring to enter there; but going about on one side and the other, and discovering that many people were escaping, we assailed and entered the town, meeting no opposition. We took only a few people, for nearly all had fled, without, however, being able to carry off the little they possessed. While we yet halted in sight of the town, before venturing to enter it, we saw

coming behind us a large body of Indians, whom we supposed to be advancing to the assistance of the place; but
going to meet them, we found they were those we had left
behind, among whom we had raised the cross, and were
following to lend us their succour, should we need any.
We took the Cacique to the town, where he gave the
Governor many thanks for the sign we had left him,
telling us the rain had fallen heavily in his country the
day before, and his people were so glad of it that they
wished to follow and not leave us. The Governor put
him into the town, and gave him every thing found
there, which was great riches for those people—some
beads made of sea-snails, the skins of cats and of
deer, and a little maize. He returned home with them,
much gratified. We remained in this town twenty-
seven or twenty-eight days, to discover if we could take a
path to the northward, whereby to come out on the South
Sea.

Some incursions were made to capture Indians who
might give us the information; particularly was one un-
dertaken to the northwest, where we were told there were
large settlements, through which we might go. We went
in that direction eight days, through a wilderness which
had large pondy swamps, where we did not find even trees,
and only some wide plains, on which grew a plant so rank
and high, that even on horseback we could not break our
way through. Finally, we came to some collections of
huts, covered with rush sewed together. When the
owner of one moves away, he will roll up the entire
covering, and carry it, the wife taking the frame of

poles over which it is stretched; these they take down and put up so readily, that though they should move anew every hour, they conveniently enough carry their house on their backs. We learned from this people that there were some hamlets of the sort about the country, the inhabitants of which employed themselves in finding places for their dwellings wherever many deer were accustomed to range, and a swamp where were many fish; and that when they had frightened the game and the fish from one place, so that they took them there not so easily as at first, they would all move off with their dwellings for some other part, where the animals were not yet shy. This Province, called Caluç, had a people who cared little to plant, finding support in meat and fish.

We returned to Pacaha, where the Governor had remained, and found that the Cacique had come in peacefully, living with him in the town. In this time arrived the Cacique from the place behind, at which we had put up the cross. The efforts of these two chiefs, who were enemies, each to place himself on the right hand when the Governor commanded that they should sit at his sides, was a sight worth witnessing.

Finding that there was no way by which to march to the other sea, we returned towards the south, and went with the Cacique to where was the cross, and thence took the direction to the southwest, to another Province called Quiquate. This was the largest town we found in Florida, and was on an arm of the Rio Grande. We remained there eight or nine days, to find guides and

33

interpreters, still with the intention of coming out, if possible, on the other sea; for the Indians told us that eleven days' travel thence was a province where they subsisted on certain cattle, and there we could find interpreters for the whole distance to that sea.

We departed with guides for the Province called Coligua, without any road, going at night to the swamps, where we drank from the hand and found abundance of fish. We went over much even country and other of broken hills, coming straight upon the town, as much so as if we had been taken thither by a royal highway, instead of which not a man in all time had passed there before. The land is very plentiful of subsistence, and we found a large quantity of dressed cows' tails, and others already cured. We inquired of the inhabitants for a path in the direction we held, or a town on it, near or far. They could give us no sort of information, only that if we wished to go in the direction where there were people, we should have to return upon a west-south-western course.

We continued to pursue the course chosen by our guides, and went to some scattered settlements called Tatil Coya. Here we found a copious river, which we afterwards discovered empties into the Rio Grande, and we were told that up the stream was a great Province, called Cayas. We went thither, and found it to be a population that, though large, was entirely scattered. It is a very rough country of hills. Several incursions were made; in one of which the Cacique and a large number of people were taken. On asking him about the particulars of the country, he told us that in following up the river we should come upon a fertile Province, called Tula. The Governor, desiring to visit there, to see if it were a place in which he could winter the people, set off with twenty men on horseback, leaving the remainder in the Province at Cayas.

Before coming to the Province of Tula, we passed over some rough hills, and arrived at the town before the inhabitants had any notice of us. In attempting to seize some Indians, they began to yell and show us battle. They wounded of ours that day seven or eight men, and nine or ten horses; and such was their courage, that they came upon us in packs, by eights and tens, like worried dogs. We killed some thirty or forty of them. The Governor thought it not well to stay there that night with his small force, and returned on the way we had come, going through a bad passage of the ridge, where it was feared the natives would beset us, to a plain in a vale made by the river. The next day we got back to where the people lay; but there were no Indians of ours, nor could any in the province be found, to speak the language of these we brought.

Orders were given that all should make ready to go to that province. We marched thither at once. The next morning after our arrival, at daybreak, three very large squadrons of Indians came upon us by as many directions: we met them and beat them, doing some injury, so much that they returned upon us no more. In two or three days they sent us messengers of peace, although we did not understand a thing they said, for want of an interpreter. By signs we told them to bring persons in there who could understand the people living back of us; and they brought five or six Indians, who understood the interpreters we had. They asked who we were, and of what we were in search. We asked them for some great provinces where there should be much provision (for the cold of winter had begun to threaten us sharply), and they said that on the route we were taking they knew of no great town; but they pointed, that if we wished to return to the east and southeast, or go northwest, we should find large towns.

Discovering that we could not prevail against the difficulty, we returned to the southeast, and went to a Province that is called Quipana, at the base of some very steep ridges; whence we journeyed in a direction to the east, and, having crossed those mountains, went down upon some plains, where we found a population suited to our purpose, for there was a town nigh in which was much food, seated by a copious river emptying into the Rio Grande, from whence we came. The Province was called Viranque. We stopped in it to pass the winter. There was so much snow and cold, we thought to have perished. At this town the Christian died whom we had found in the country belonging to the people of Narvaez, and who was our interpreter. We went out thence in the beginning of March, when it appeared to us that the severity of the winter had passed; and we followed down the course of this river, whereon we found other provinces well peopled, having a quantity of food, to a Province called Anicoyanque, which appeared to us to be one of the best we had found in all the country. Here another Cacique, called Guachoyanque, came to us in peace. His town is upon the River Grande, and he is in continual war with the other chief with whom we were.

The Governor directly set out for the town of Guacho-yanque, and took its Cacique with him. The town was good, well and strongly fenced. It contained little pro-vision, the Indians having carried that off. Here the Governor, having before determined, if he should find the sea, to build brigantines by which to make it known in Cuba that we were alive, whence we might be sup-plied with some horses and things of which we stood in need, sent a Captain in the direction south, to see if some road could be discovered by which we might go to look for the sea; because, from the account given by the Indians, nothing could be learned of it; and he got back, reporting that he found no road, nor any way by which to pass the great bogs that extend out from the River Grande. The Governor, at seeing himself thus sur-rounded, and nothing coming about according to his expectations, sickened and died. He left us recommend-ing Luis de Moscoso to be our Governor.

Since we could find no way to the sea, we agreed to take our course to the west, on which we might come out by land to Mexico, should we be unable to find any thing, or a place whereon to settle. We travelled seven-teen days, until we came to the Province of Chavite, where the Indians made much salt; but we could learn noth-ing of them concerning the west: thence we went to another Province, called Aguacay, and were three days on the way, still going directly westward. After leaving this place, the Indians told us we should see no more settlements unless we went down in a southwest-and-by-south direction, where we should find large towns and food; that in the course we asked about, there were some large sandy wastes, without any people or subsistence whatsoever.

We were obliged to go where the Indians directed us, and went to a Province called Nisione, and to another called Nondacao, and another, Came; and at each remove we went through lands that became more sterile and afforded less subsistence. We continually asked for a province which they told us was large, called Xuacatino. The Cacique of Nondacao gave us an Indian purposely to put us somewhere whence we could never come out: the guide took us over a rough country, and off the road, until he told us at last he did not know where he was leading us; that his master had ordered him to take us where we should die of hunger. We took another guide, who led us to a Province called Hais, where, in seasons, some cattle are wont to herd; and as the Indians saw us entering their country, they began to cry out: "Kill the cows—they are coming;" when they sallied and shot their arrows at us, doing us some injury.

We went from this place and came to the Province of Xacatin, which was among some close forests, and was scant of food. Hence the Indians guided us eastward to other small towns, poorly off for food, having said that they would take us where there were other

Christians like us, which afterwards proved false; for they could have had no knowledge of any others than ourselves, although, as we made so many turns, it might be in some of them they had observed our passing. We turned to go southward, with the resolution of either reaching New Spain, or dying. We travelled about six days in a direction south and southwest, when we stopped.

Thence we sent ten men, on swift horses, to travel in eight or nine days as far as possible, and see if any town could be found where we might re-supply ourselves with maize, to enable us to pursue our journey. They went as far as they could go, and came upon some poor people without houses, having wretched huts, into which they withdrew; and they neither planted nor gathered any thing, but lived entirely upon flesh and fish. Three or four of them, whose tongue no one we could find understood, were brought back. Reflecting that we had lost our interpreter, that we found nothing to eat, that the maize we brought upon our backs was failing, and it seemed impossible that so many people should be able to cross a country so poor, we determined to return to the town where the Governor Soto died, as it appeared to us there was convenience for building vessels with which we might leave the country.

We returned by the same road we had taken, until we came to the town; but we did not discover so good outfit as we had thought to find. There were no provisions in the town, the Indians having taken them away, so we had to seek another town, where we might pass the winter and build the vessels. I thank God that we found two towns very much to our purpose, standing upon the Rio Grande, and which were fenced around, having also a large quantity of maize. Here we stopped, and with great labour built seven brigantines, which were finished at about the end of six months. We threw them out into the water, and it was a mystery that, calked as they were with the bark of mulberry-trees, and without any pitch, we should find them stanch and very safe. Going down the river, we took with us also some canoes, into which were put twenty-six horses, for the event of finding any large town on the shore of the sea that could sustain us with food, while we might send thence a couple of brigantines to the Viceroy of New Spain, with a message to provide us with vessels in which we could get away from the country.

The second day, descending the stream, there came out against us about forty or fifty very large and swift canoes, in some of which were as many as eighty warriors, who assailed us with their arrows, following and shooting at us. Some who were in the vessels thought it trifling not to attack them; so, taking four or five of the small canoes we brought along, they went after them. The Indians, seeing this, surrounded them, so that they could not get away, and upset the canoes, whereby twelve very worthy men were drowned, beyond the reach of our succour, because of the great power of the stream, and the oars in the vessels being few.

The Indians were encouraged by this success to follow us to the sea, which we were nineteen days in reaching, doing us much damage and wounding many people; for, as they found we had no arms that could reach them from a distance, not an arquebuse nor a crossbow having remained, but only some swords and targets, they lost their fears, and would draw very nigh to let drive at us their arrows.

We came out by the mouth of the river, and entering into a very large bay made by it, which was so extensive that we passed along it three days and three nights, with fair weather, in all the time not seeing land, so that it appeared to us we were at sea, although we found the water still so fresh that it could well be drunk, like that of the river. Some small islets were seen westward, to which we went: thenceforward we kept close along the coast, where we took shell-fish, and looked for other things to eat, until we entered the River of Pánuco, where we came and were well received by the Christians.

Luys Hernandez De Biedma.

34

APPENDIX.

TRANSLATIONS.

———•••———

CONVEYANCE OF DOWER BY THE WIDOW OF PE- DRÁRIAS DÁVILA TO HERNANDO DE SOTO, IN CON- SIDERATION OF THE ESPOUSAL OF HER DAUGHTER.

Be it known to all who shall see this writing, that I, Doña Ysabel de Bobadilla, wife that was of Pedrárias de Avila, deceased, —be he in glory—Governor that was of Tierra Firme, my lord and husband, declare, that inasmuch as, by the assistance of Our Lord and His Blessed Mother, espousals of marriage are concerted and contracted, by words of assent, between Doña Ysabel de Bobadilla, my legitimate daughter and of said Pedrárias, with you, Señor Captain Fernando de Soto, being at this Court of their Majesties, native and resident of the City of Badajóz, by these presents, hence- forth I promise and obligate myself to give you, and do henceforth give in dower and marriage with the said Doña Ysabel de Bobadilla, my daughter, for her and for her goods of dower, that you may keep and marry her with the consent and in the peace of the Holy Mother Church of Rome, that is to say, all the cattle with their young which the said Governor, my lord and husband, established and left at Panamá, in Tierra Firme, with all the cottage, the slaves who tend the cattle, the stud of horses with them in the fields, and every thing else that to said round cottage and stock is in all or in any wise belonging, with the increase of slaves, and whatever else is thereto pertinent, which the said Pedrárias de Avila, by a clause made of his will between living, in pure and perfect gift irrevocable in favour of said Doña Ysabel de Bobadilla, my daughter, that she thereby might the better and more honorably marry, as more fully

may be found in the clause referred to of said will, which I deem
here inserted and incorporated with the same force and vigour it
would have were it written out word for word; of the which I, for
what therein belongs to me and appertains, or that can appertain,
by reason of any right of dower, paraphernalia, and goods, acquired
during the matrimony existing between me and the said Pedrárias
Dávila, my lord and husband, as well in whatever other manner, I
consent publicly, and approve consent to the aforementioned dona-
tive made by Pedro Arias, and do so by good, lasting, and genuine
signature, for this and in all time of the world, for evermore . . .
Done at Valladolid, the 14th day of November, of the year 1536.

One of the witnesses to this release was Juan de Añasco.   The document exists in full
in the *Archivo de Indias.*

LETTER OF HERNANDO DE SOTO RESPECTING CON-CESSIONS HE DESIRES SHALL BE OBTAINED FOR HIM AT COURT.[1]

✚

VERY MAGNIFICENT SIR:

That which Your Worship is to favour me in is as follows:

Inasmuch as His Majesty has not ceded to Francisco Pizarro
more than two hundred and seventy-five leagues by Royal grant,
of the six hundred that the said Governor Pizarro holds from
Santiago, whence begins his government, to the mines of Callao,
which divide his territory from that of Don Diego de Almagro, as
will appear by an agreement made between them, must be taken off
from the beginning of his government to the town of San Miguel,
an extent may be of one hundred leagues, which region, from
said town to Panamá, supposing now His Majesty should be pleased
to grant it to me in government, is the most sterile and unprofitable of that country, although I am of opinion that by way of

---

[1] The original of these instructions, only the signature to which is in the hand-
writing of Soto, exists in the *Biblioteca Nacional*, at Madrid.   It was no doubt written
while he was in Spain, in the year 1536 or 1537.

Quito there is good opening into the interior, whereby to serve His Majesty in the Provinces through which I came.

Your Worship, not being able to get what I have set forth, will try then for the government of Guatemala, with permission to make discovery in the South Sea, and for the title of Adelantado, with concession from His Majesty of the tenth part of whatever I may at my own cost discover in the sea, and conquer, with patent, and to my successors.

What Your Worship will send to the Señor Comendador, to be negotiated with His Majesty, is as follows:

The mantle of Santiago for Fernan Ponçe de Leon, and also for me.

All the Indians of Apportionment which said Hernan Ponçe de Leon and I hold by schedule from His Majesty, with other property in lands and houses,[1] in fee simple, and if possible with a title.

Let the government that may be got for me be in perpetuity if possible, and if not, then for the longest term Your Worship may be enabled to secure: And when you shall have acted on these instructions, and discovered where is the best chance of success, you will let me know how I am to treat with these Lords of the Council in the business, and what I am to write to the Señor Comendador, and when.

---

[1] The words *se an de dar*, to be given, are here driven through with a pen.

CONCESSION MADE BY THE KING OF SPAIN TO HERNANDO DE SOTO OF THE GOVERNMENT OF CUBA AND CONQUEST OF FLORIDA, WITH THE TITLE OF ADELANTADO.

[Translation made from a copy in the *Archivo de Indias* at Sevilla, rubricated by the Secretary Samano.]

THE KING.

INASMUCH as you, Captain Hernando de Soto, set forth that you have served us in the conquest, pacification, and settlement of the Provinces of Nicaragua and Perú, and of other parts of our Indias; and that now, to serve us further, and to continue to enlarge our patrimony and the royal crown, you desire to return to those our Indias, to conquer and settle the Province of Rio de las Palmas to Florida, the government whereof was bestowed on Pánfilo de Narvaez, and the Provinces of Tierra-Nueva, the discovery and government of which was conferred on Lucas Vazquez de Ayllón; and that for the purpose you will take from these, our kingdoms and our said Indias, five hundred men, with the necessary arms, horses, munitions, and military stores; and that you will go hence, from these our kingdoms, to make the said conquest and settlement within a year first following, to be reckoned from the day of the date of these articles of authorization; and that when you shall leave the Island of Cuba to go upon that enterprise, you will take the necessary subsistence for all that people during eighteen months—rather over than under that time—entirely at your cost and charges, without our being obliged, or the kings who shall come after us, to pay you, nor satisfy the expenses incurred therefor, other than such as you in these articles may be authorized to make; and you pray that I bestow on you the conquest of those lands and provinces, and with it the government of the said Island of Cuba, that you may from there the better control and provide all the principal and important material for the conquest and settlement, whereupon I have ordered to be made with you the terms and contract following:

First, I give you, the said Captain Hernando de Soto, power and authority, for us and in our name, and in that of the royal crown of Castilla, to conquer, pacify, and populate the lands that there are from the Province of the Rio de las Palmas to Florida, the government of which was bestowed on Pánfilo de Narvaez; and, further, the Provinces of the said Tierra-Nueva, the government whereof was in like manner conferred on the said Licentiate Ayllón.

Also, purposing to comply in this with the service of God our Lord, and to do you honour, we engage to confer on you the dignity of Governor and Captain-General of two hundred leagues of coast, such as you shall designate, of what you discover, so that within four years, to be reckoned from the time you arrive in any part of the lands and provinces before mentioned, you shall choose and declare whence you would have the two hundred leagues begin; that from where you designate they shall be measured along the coast, for all the days of your life, with the annual salary of fifteen hundred ducats, and five hundred ducats gratuity, in all two thousand, which you shall receive from the day you set sail in the Port of San Lúcar, to go upon your voyage, to be paid to you from the duties and profits to us appertaining in those said lands and provinces which you so offer to conquer and colonize; and in that time should there be neither duties nor profits, we shall not be obliged to order that you be paid any thing.

Also, we will confer on you the title of our Adelantado over the said two hundred leagues which you shall thus select and make known for your government in the said lands and provinces you so discover and colonize, and will likewise bestow on you the office of High-Constable (Alguazil mayor) over those territories in perpetuity.

Also, we give permission, the judgment of our officers of said province being in accord, that you build there as many as three stone fortresses in the harbours and places most proper for them, they appearing to you and to our said officers to be necessary for the protection and pacification of that country; and we confer on you the Lieutenancy of them, and on one heir for life, or successor whom you shall name, with the annual salary to each of the fortresses of one hundred thousand maravedis, which you shall enjoy from the time they be severally built and finished and enclosed, in the opinion of our said officers; to be done at your own cost, without our being obliged, or any of the kings who shall come after us, to pay you what you may expend on those fortresses.

Again, inasmuch as you have petitioned us to bestow on you some portion of the land and vassals in said province you would conquer and populate, considering what you have served us, and the expenditure you will meet from this time in making said conquest and pacification, we receive the petitions favourably: hence we promise to bestow on you, and by these presents we do, twelve leagues of land in square in the said two hundred leagues you shall designate to hold in government in the said territories and provinces before declared, which we command our officers of the said province to assign, after you shall have designated the said two hundred leagues, to include no sea-port, nor the principal town, and that with the jurisdiction and title we shall confer at the time we give you the deeds.

Again, as has been said, you have petitioned us, that for the better governing and providing of all the principal and important matters for the conquest and settlement of said territories and provinces, I should order that there be given to you with them the government of the said Island of Cuba, which, to that end, we deem well, and is our pleasure, for the time it shall be our will, that you hold the government of said island; and for thus much we will order to be given you our provision by which you will be obliged to have a Chief-Justice, who shall be a lawyer, to whom we shall require you to pay yearly on that Island the salary of two hundred *pesos* of gold; and we give to you five hundred ducats annual gratuity for the government of said Island, while you hold the same, to be paid from the duties and profits we may have from the province you have thus to conquer, pacify, and hold in government; and if there be none there, we shall not be obliged to pay you that, nor any other thing more than the two hundred *pesos* of the said Chief-Justice.

Also, we give you liberty and right that you from these our kingdoms and lordships, or from the Kingdom of Portugal, or Islands of Cabo Verde, or Guinea, do and may pass, or whosoever may exercise your power, to the said Island of Cuba fifty negro slaves, not less than one-third of them to be females, free of the import duties that of right may belong to us at said island, upon paying the license of two ducats on each to Diego de la Haya, which sum by our order he is charged to collect.

Again, also, we promise that upon your arrival in that country of your government, which' you have thus to conquer and settle, we give liberty and right to whomsoever shall have your power, that you may take thither from these our said kingdoms, or from Portugal, or the Islands of Cabo Verde, other fifty negro slaves, the third part of them females, free from all duties.

Also, we concede to those who shall go to settle in that country within the six years first following, to be reckoned forward from the day of the date of these presents, that of the gold which may be taken from the mines shall be paid us the tenth, and the said six years being ended, shall pay us the ninth, and thus annually declining to the fifth part; but from the gold and other things that may be got by barter, or is spoil got by incursions, or in any other manner, shall be paid us thereupon one-fifth of all.

Also we give, free of import duty, to the inhabitants of that country for the said six years, and as much longer as shall be our will, all they may take for the furnishing and provision of their houses, the same not being to sell; and whatsoever they or any other, merchants or traffickers, sell, shall go free of duty for two years, and not longer.

Likewise, we promise that for the term of ten years, and until we command otherwise, we will not impose on the inhabitants of those countries any excise duty, or other tribute whatsoever. ·

Likewise, we grant that to said inhabitants may be given through you the lots and grounds proper to their conditions, as has been done, and is doing, in the Island of Española; and we also give you license, in our name, during the time of your government, that you take the bestowal of the Indians of that land, observing therein the instructions and provisions that will be given to you.

Again, we bestow on the hospital that may be built in that country, to assist the relief of the poor who may go thither, the

35

charity of one hundred thousand maravedis from the fines imposed by the tribunal of that country.

Again, also, according to your petition and consent, and of the settlers of that country, we promise to give to its hospital, and by these presents we do give, the duties of *escobilla* and *relabes*, existing in the foundries that may there be made; and, as respects that, we will order our provision to be issued to you in form.

Also, likewise we will order, and by the present command and defend, that from these our kingdoms do not pass into said country, nor go, any one of the persons prohibited from going into those parts, under the penalties contained in the laws and ordinances of our letters, upon which subject this by us and by the Catholic Kings are given, nor any counsellors nor attorneys to exercise their callings.

The which, all that is said, and each thing and part thereof, we concede to you, conditioned that you, the said Don Hernando de Soto, be held and obliged to go from these our realms in person to make the conquest within one year next following, to be reckoned from the day of the date of this charter.

Again, on condition that when you go out of these our said kingdoms, and arrive in said country, you will carry and have with you the officers of our exchequer, who may by us be named; and likewise also the persons, religious and ecclesiastical, who shall be appointed by us for the instruction of the natives of that Province in our Holy Catholic Faith, to whom you are to give and pay the passage, stores, and the other necessary subsistence for them, according to their condition, all at your cost, receiving nothing from them during the said entire voyage; with which matter we gravely charge you, that you do and comply with, as a thing for the service of God and our own, and any thing otherwise we shall deem contrary to our service.

Again, whensoever, according to right and the laws of our kingdoms, the people and captains of our armaments take prisoner any prince or lord of the countries where, by our command, they make war, the ransom of such lord or cacique belongs to us, with all the other things movable found or belonging to him; but, considering the great toils and perils that our subjects undergo in the conquest of the Indias, as some recompense, and to favour them, we make known and command, that if in your said conquest and government any cacique or principal lord be captured or seized, all the treasures, gold, silver, stones, and pearls that may be got from him by way of redemption, or in any other manner whatsoever, we award you the seventh part thereof, and the remainder shall be divided among the conquerors, first taking out our fifth; and in case the said cacique or lord should be slain in battle, or afterward by course of justice, or in any other manner whatsoever, in such case, of the treasures and goods aforesaid obtained of him justly we have the half, which, before any thing else, our officers shall take, after having first reserved our fifth.

Again, since our said officers of said Province might have some doubt in making the collection of our duties, especially on gold and silver, stones and pearls, as well those that may be found in sepulchres, and other places where they may be hidden, as those got by ransom and incursion, or other way, our pleasure and will is, that, until some change, the following order be observed.

First, we order that of the gold and silver, stones and pearls that may be won in battle, or on entering towns, or by barter with the Indians, should and must be paid us one-fifth of all.

Likewise, that all the gold and silver, stones, pearls, and other things that may be found and taken, as well in the graves, sepulchres, *ocues*, or temples of the Indians, as in other places where they were accustomed to offer sacrifices to their idols, or in other concealed religious precincts, or buried in house, or patrimonial soil, or in the ground, or in some other public place, whether belonging to the community or an individual, be his state or dignity what it may, of the whole, and of all other, of the character that may be and is found, whether finding it by accident or discovering it by search, shall pay us the half, without diminution of any sort, the other half remaining to the person who has found or made the discovery; and should any person or persons have gold, silver, stones, or pearls, taken or found, as well in the said graves, sepulchres, *ocues*, or Indian temples, as in the other places where they were accustomed to offer sacrifices, or other concealed religious places, or interred as before said, and do not make it known, that they may receive, in conformity with this chapter, what may belong to them, they have forfeited all the gold and silver, stones and pearls, besides the half of their goods, to our tribunal and exchequer.

And we, having been informed of the evils and disorders which occur in making discoveries and new settlements, for the redress thereof, and that we may be enabled to give you license to make them, with the accord of the members of our Council and of our consultation, a general provision of chapters is ordained and dispatched, respecting what you will have to observe in the said settlement and conquest, and we command it here to be incorporated in teno: as follows :[1]—

*   *   *   *   *   *

Hence, by these presents, you, the said Captain Hernando de Soto, doing as aforesaid at your cost, according to and in the manner before contained, observing and complying with the said provision here incorporated, and all the other instructions we shall henceforth command you to obey, and to give with regard to that country, and for the good treatment and conversion to our Holy Catholic Faith of the natives of it, we promise and declare that to you will be kept these terms, and whatever therein is contained, in and through all; and you doing otherwise, and not complying therewith, we shall not be obliged to keep with you and comply with the aforesaid, nor any matter of it; on the contrary, we will order that you be punished, and proceed against you as against one who keeps not nor complies with, but acts counter to, the commands of his natural king and lord.   In confirmation whereof we order that the present be given, signed by my name, and witnessed by my undersigned Secretary. Done at the town Valladolid, the twentieth day of the month of April, of the year one thousand five hundred and thirty-seven.

I The King.

---

[1] This Ordinance, first placed in the charter granted to Francisco Montejo for the conquest of Yucatan, dated the seventh day of December, of the year 1526, signed by the King, his Secretary, Francisco de los Cobos, Mercurinus cancellorius, fr. G. Epus. Oxomes, Dotor Caravajal, Epus. Canariensis, el Dotor Beltram, fr. G. Epus. Civitatem, was afterwards inserted in all like concessions, and is deemed to follow here.

ROYAL CEDULA PERMITTING JUAN DE AÑASCO TO TRAFFIC WITH THE INDIANS OF FLORIDA, SO LONG AS THERE ARE NO DUTIES ON IMPORTS IN THAT PROVINCE.

THE KING.

Inasmuch as thou on thy part, Juan de Añasco, our Comptroller of the Province of Florida, the government whereof I have conferred on the Captain Hernando de Soto, hast petitioned me to command that thou be permitted to traffic with the Indians of the Province, notwithstanding thou be our Comptroller there, or in such way allowed as might to us be deemed proper, we by this present do license and empower thee, so long as in that Province we shall not be paid the duties of almoxarifadgo, to bargain, contract, and traffic with the Indians thereof, alone or in company, as thou wilt, and shalt deem proper, as well in the things of these our kingdoms, as in those which in that country may be produced or may exist there; observing in respect thereof the ordinances that are or may be enacted by our Governor and officers of that Province, to the extent that neither thou nor the said company treat or contract with our exchequer, directly or indirectly, under penalty of forfeiture of our favour, and of your goods to the fiscal advantage of our Treasury. Dated at Valladolid, the fourth day of the month of May, of the year one thousand five hundred and thirty-seven.

I THE KING.

WILL OF HERNANDO DE SOTO.

In Dei Nomine, Amen.

KNOW ye who shall see this testamentary letter, that I, the Adelantado, Don Hernando de Soto, being of sound body and free mind, such as my Redeemer Jesus Christ has been pleased to bestow on me, believing firmly in what believes and holds the Holy Mother Church, in the most Holy Trinity, Father, Son, and Holy Ghost, three persons and one only true God, promising as a faithful Christian to live and die in His Holy Catholic faith, mindful of the blood that Jesus Christ shed for me as the price of my redemption, and endeavouring to repay and satisfy so great benefit, knowing that death is a natural thing, and that the more I shall be prepared for it the better will He be pleased, I declare that I commend my soul to God, who created it of nothing, and redeemed it with His most holy passion, that He place it among the number of the elect in His glory, and I order the body to the earth, of which it was made.

First, I command, should God take me from this present life on the sea, that my corpse be so disposed of, that it may be taken to the land wheresoever our Lord shall be pleased it shall come to port, and should a church be there, or should one there be built, that it be deposited therein until such time as there are arrangements for taking it to Spain, to the city of Xeréz, near Badajóz, where it be consigned to the sepulchre where lies my mother, in the Church of San Miguel; and in that church I order that of my goods a site and place be bought where a chapel be built that shall have for its invocation Our Lady of the Conception, in which edifice and work I desire there be expended two thousand ducats, one thousand five hundred in the structures and enclosure, and the five hundred in an altar-piece, representing the same Invocation of Our Lady of the Conception; and I order that vestments be made, with a chasuble, two dalmatics, an antependium and a cope, with three albs, and a chalice with its cover, both of silver, and two other chasubles for daily use, for which I direct there be paid of my goods other three hundred ducats; and I order that the mentioned vestments be of silk, of the color which to the patron and my executors, and to those of the said chapel, shall appear well; and I order that of my goods be bought a perpetual rent of twelve thousand maravedis, in good possession, which shall be given to a chaplain who shall say five masses each week for my soul, the souls of my parents, and that of Doña Ysabel de Bobadilla, my wife, and he shall be appointed by the patron of the chapel, with the understanding that should there be a clergyman of my line, who desires to be chaplain, it be given to him in preference to any other, and that he be the nearest of kin, should there be two or more.

Also, I order that if the body of my father or of my mother be in Badajóz, or in any other part whatsoever, not in that chapel, they be taken out and brought thence, and be entombed there where my body shall be, or should be placed, which is in the midst of the chapel, in such manner that the foot of the sepulchre adjoin the foot-stone of the altar; and thereon I order to be placed a tomb covered over by a fine black broadcloth, in the middle of which be put a red cross of the Commandery of the Order of the Knights of Saint Jago,[1] that shall be for use on week-days, and another pall of black velvet, with the same cross in the midst, with four escutcheons of brocade, bearing my arms; which escutcheons I wish and order to be likewise placed on the chapel, altar-piece, and railing, and vestments, in such manner as to the patron and executors shall appear most becoming.

Also, to the end that this chapel and chaplaincy be kept in repair and appointment, the chapel and the income alike, I order that Doña Ysabel de Bobadilla, my wife, be the patroness; and, after her, should God give me children, I desire the patron to be my eldest legitimate son, or my eldest legitimate daughter, should I have no male child, that they, or either of them, who shall be the patron, may buy the site for, and make the said chapel, and do all the foregoing appertaining to it, and buy the said twelve thousand maravedis, and appoint the chaplain. And should God not grant me legitimate sons or daughters, I order that after the lifetime of my wife, the patron be Juan Mendez de Soto, my brother, and after his life, his eldest son; and if he be without a male child, I order that the successor to that patronage be the eldest son of Catalina de Soto, my sister; and should she have no male child, let the successor thereto be the eldest son of Maria de Soto, my sister; and if it happen of the designated patrons there should be no issue male, I order the patronage to succeed to the next nearest of kin, being always male.

Also, in order that the chapel, and vestments, and rent for the chaplaincy, may always be available, and that in each year, on All Saints' Day, a mass be sung, and another on All Souls' Day, with its vigil, and offerings of bread and wine, there shall be a perpetual rent of five thousand maravedis, on good possessions, to be bought

[1] See page 228.

with my goods, and I order that they be used in no other way than for what is expressed.

Also, I order that on the day my body is interred, it be followed by the *curas* and clergy of the parishes, with their crosses, and by the orders there may be in the city aforesaid, and that there be paid them what is customary; and I require that each *cura*, with the clergy of their church, sing a mass on that day, and they be paid what is usual; and I order that on the same day thirty masses be said for me, and that there be paid therefor what is customary.

Also, I order that there be said twenty masses of *requiem* in the said chapel, for the soul of the Captain Compañon, and that what is usual be paid for them.

Also, that there be twenty masses of Our Lady of the Conception said in the chapel.

Also, I order that ten masses of the Holy Ghost be said in the chapel.

Also, I order that ten masses be said of All Saints in said chapel.

Also, I order that ten masses be said, five of them of the Passion, and five of the Wounds, in the aforesaid, my chapel.

Also, I order that sixty masses be said for souls in purgatory, in my said chapel; all which masses shall be said by whom my executors shall please.

Also, toward the completion of pious works, I order to each of them one real.

Also, I order for the redemption of captives, two reals.

Also, I order, that inasmuch as I gave Ysabel de Soto in espousal to Don Carlos Enrriquez, and it was understood should be given with her in marriage and for dowry whatever I might think best, I order that of my goods there be given to him three thousand ducats, which are the dowry of marriage of the said Ysabel de Soto, my cousin.

I confess to have received in dowry with Doña Ysabel de Bobadilla, my legitimate wife, seven thousand castellanos, of which, at the time of making this my will, I have received two thousand castellanos, the same being within my control; in Spain are deposited other two thousand in the House of Contratacion, and the remaining three thousand are in the possession of the debtor to whom was sold certain cattle in which the dowry was assigned.

Also, I admit that at the time I married Ysabel de Bobadilla, I sent her in marriage pledge six thousand ducats, all which, the seven thousand castellanos of dowry, as well as the six thousand ducats of *arras*, I order that she have and inherit of my goods, as her sole undivided property, that should belong to her of my said estate.

Also, I command that of my goods be given to my nephew, Pedro de Soto, five hundred ducats.

Also, I order that to a boy, who they say is my son, called Andrés de Soto, be given four hundred ducats from my goods.

Also, I order that to a daughter I left in Nicaragua, called Doña Maria de Soto, married to Hernan Nieto, be given one thousand ducats from my goods.

Also, I order to be given to Alonso Ayala, my mayordomo, from my goods three hundred ducats.

Also, I order that to Rodrigo Rangel, my secretary, be given, for the good service he has rendered me, three hundred ducats of my goods; to Castro, my carver, I order fifty ducats from my goods.

Also, I order two thousand ducats for the marriage of the maids of Doña Ysabel, who are Maria Arias, and Catalina Ximenes, and Mexia, and Arellano, and Carreño, which will be divided among them by Doña Ysabel de Bobadilla, my wife, as shall appear well to her, and as they shall have served her.

Also, I order to Doña Leonor de Bobadilla, in marriage, one thousand ducats, for the service that she and Nuño de Tobár have rendered, of which I desire she have five hundred, and he five hundred, to avoid delicacy or doubts.

Also, I order to Leonor de Bolaños two hundred ducats for her services.

Also, I acknowledge and declare that I have made a writing of companionship with the Captain Hernan Ponçe de Leon, in which are contained many things, as will appear by it, which was executed before Domingo de la (*illegible*), public notary, resident in Lima, and of that city, in the Province of Peru, which was amended and reaffirmed, with some additions, by another writing, made and exe-

36

cuted before Francisco Sepero, and Francisco de Alcocer, notaries of His Majesty, in the town of San Christóbal, of the Havana, in the Island of Fernandina, named Cuba, which I have present: whence I say and declare, that of all the goods that to me belong, or can be mine, of which I have no exact knowledge, I admit that of the whole, one-half I possess are his; and of all goods whatsoever that he possesses and has, the half are mine, by reason of the partnership and brotherhood that we have formed, as contained in those writings.

Also, I declare that, in the event my body cannot be had for taking to Spain, for sepulture, as is set forth, it be no impediment or hindrance to the founding of that chapel and the chaplaincy aforesaid; but that all be done as in this my will is expressed and declared.

Also, I order, that this my will being executed in the manner set forth, of the remainder of my goods be purchased one hundred and fifty thousand maravedis of perpetual rents, in good possessions, which shall be joined with the other one hundred and fifty thousand maravedis of income which I have belonging to me of my share in the royal revenues from silk, in the city of Grenada, which, taken together, amounts to three hundred thousand maravedis, of which I wish and order to be made two parts, one, being one hundred and fifty thousand maravedis, Doña Ysabel de Bobadilla, my wife, to have and enjoy all her lifetime, and the other one hundred and fifty thousand maravedis be employed yearly in marrying three orphan damsels, daughters of some that be of my line, and to the fifth degree, the poorest that can be found; the which shall be employed by Doña Ysabel de Bobadilla, my wife, in their marriage, on whom I confer all my power complete to that full object, and they whom she shall elect and name, shall be elected and named as though I myself had done so; and if it happen that damsels shall not be found of my lineage to the fifth degree, I wish and order that they be any other damsels, orphans, daughters of nobility, of the poorest there may be in the city of Xeréz, near Badajóz, who likewise are to be selected and named by Doña Ysabel de Bobadilla, my wife; and I order that after her days the said rent of one hundred and fifty thousand maravedis I leave to her during life be united to the other hundred and fifty thousand maravedis, being three hundred thousand maravedis of rent employed in the marriage of six damsels yearly, in the same manner as hereinbefore declared of the three, to each of whom shall be given fifty thousand maravedis for their dowry—the half in money, the half in apparel and furniture; and for the better execution hereof, I leave for patrons and administrators of the three hundred thousand maravedis' rent, the very reverend fathers, the prior, or president, of the Convent of Santo Domingo, of the city of Badajóz, and the minister of the Convent of the Santisima Trinidad, of that city, and the prior of Sto. Agustin, of that city, and the guardian of San Francisco, which is within that city, who now are, or shall be, to whom I give my complete power to that end, and I order that the persons whom they name and designate stand named and designated as if by me; and I entreat them as favour, and charge their consciences, that this be done with all diligence, for it is in the service of Our Lord, mindful of all the foregoing contained above, that they be all six damsels of nobility of my line, the nearest of kin, and to the fifth degree, and should there be no relatives of my line within this grade, I desire they be daughters of nobility, orphan damsels, the poorest there are in the city of Xeréz, of Badajóz. And should there be no orphans that are of the poorest, I give such patrons the full power I have and possess, and of right belonging to me, to receive the said three hundred thousand maravedis, and have an administrator, that they may be collected, to whom shall be paid such salary for his trouble as they shall deem just; and, that there may be memory of this, I desire that each of these reverend fathers have one thousand maravedis of alms, which, with what will have to be given the administrator, shall be taken from the said three hundred thousand maravedis.

And in order to make compliance with and protect this my will, and the bequests in it contained, I leave as my executors Doña Ysabel de Bobadilla, my wife, Captain Hernan Ponçe de Leon, Juan Mendez de Soto, my brother, and Gutierrez Garay de Cardeñosa, and, in default of him, his son Hernan Gutierrez Cardeñosa, to whom and to each I give *in solidum* all my complete power, with general administration, and all its incidences and dependences, accidences, annexes and connexes, so much, in such case as may be requisite, that without authority of judge or superior, but of their own inherent, they may enter upon those my said goods, and take of them all that may be necessary, and sell them at public outcry, or otherwise, at very low, or bad price, to comply with all the requirements of this my will, according as they are therein contained, discharging them conformably to law.

Made in the town of San Christóbal of the Havana, on the tenth day of the month of May, in the year of the birth of Our Redeemer Jesus Christ one thousand five hundred and thirty-nine.

EL ADELANTADO DON HERNANDO DE SOTO.

All in this will contained is correct, and was set forth in the presence of Señor Fray Juan de Gallegos, and Señor Fray Francisco de la Rocha.

FRAY JUAN DE GALLEGOS.
FRAY FRANCISCO DE LA ROCHA.

Besides this, and over what is set forth, I order that all the debts that it shall appear at any time I owe, by information or truth spoken, be paid from my goods; and inasmuch as I caused some soldiers to be quartered of my armament in the city of Santiago, and the other towns of this Island, the inhabitants of which gave them subsistence, if any thing because of this should be asked, let there be paid of my goods whatsoever shall appear I am indebted in this behalf.

Made on the said day of May, one thousand five hundred and thirty-nine years.

EL ADELANTADO DON HERNANDO DE SOTO.

Witnesses: { FR. JUAN DE GALLEGOS.
{ FR. FRANCISCO DE ROCHA.

Translated from a copy in the Lonja, at Sevilla, among the papers existing in the action of Ysabel de Bobadilla, widow, against Hernan Ponçe de Leon.

The name Maria de Soto seems not to be well transcribed from the original instrument, since the mention of Doña Mencia, as the sister of Hernando, is observed to occur several times among the voluminous papers in the suit, which is in conformity with what Salazar y Castro writes in his history of the House of Silva, that Maria Enriquez de Vargas brought with her in marriage the entailed estate of Manchada, with other lands from her parents, Don Alonzo Enriquez, Prefect of Badajóz, and Doña Mencia de Soto, sister of the Adelantado of Florida.

LETTER TO THE KING OF SPAIN FROM OFFICERS AT HAVANA IN THE ARMY OF SOTO.

[Original in the *Archivo General de Indias*, at Sevilla.]

On the envelope is written :—

✝

TO THE S. I. C. MAJESTY

OF THE EMPEROR AND KING OUR LORD.

H. I. C. Mᵞ.

WE gave relation to Your Majesty from Saint Jago de Cuba of the favourable beginning of our expedition, which, it appears, the Adelantado Don Hernando de Soto brought with his good fortune, wherewith to serve in the matter of which he comes in control. Suffice it to say, that he has thought best to look both into the state of the Island and the population, as Your Majesty is informed; but with great toil and cost to himself, as he wished to travel throughout, visiting the towns, which had much need of attention. As well has he been detained, at great expense with his soldiers, longer than he wished, while providing himself, without loss of time, in every particular useful for his conquest, managing aptly in all matters, and setting every thing in complete order.

We inform Your Majesty, that to-day, on the eve of departure, he has large vessels in port, two caravels and two brigantines, in all nine sail, having lost two since our arrival. He carries in them two hundred and thirty-seven horses, besides some of relief; three hundred and thirty foot, as well as those mounted; in all, five hundred and thirteen men, without the sailors. With these go more abundant subsistence than could have been gotten out of Spain for an armada. There are three thousand loads of caçabi, twenty-five hundred shoulders of bacon, and twenty-five hundred hanegas of maize: moreover, there are beasts on hoof for the settlement, and for the butcher, to be in readiness on the return of the vessels, through which we are to receive large supplies. With this object, the Adelantado has bought many grazing farms, at the cost of much money, to be employed solely in affording us sustenance.

In order that Your Majesty may entertain good hopes of that country of Florida, we report, that directly upon our arrival here, in order that Juan de Añasco might go with fifty men to look for some port on the coast, he was elected to be the royal Comptroller ; and although he passed through many hardships, because of the winter, he found the most convenient place that could be desired very near, only some seventy-five or eighty leagues from this land, inhabited and very secure. He brought four of the Indians, as interpreters, who are so intelligent that they already understand us, after a manner, and give grand expectations of that country, so much so, that all depart joyfully and contented.

The bearer of this letter is the Captain Hernan Ponçe de Leon, companion of the Adelantado, who has been a witness to all this, and is a person of whom Your Majesty can be informed in what-soever may most interest you.

We will say no more at present, save that on arriving in the land of Florida, we will, by Divine pleasure, take particular care to give a very long relation of all that shall hereafter occur.

Our Lord guard and increase the S. I. C. life of Your Majesty with augmentation of more and greater kingdoms and lordships, as the servants of Y. M. desire.

From the town of San X°bal of the Havana, the eighteenth day of May, of the year 1539.

From Y. S. I. C. M^{y'a}

Servants, who your Imperial feet kiss.

JUAN	JNO. DE AN	LUIS FERNANDEZ
GAYTAN	ASCO	DE BIEDMA
Rubrica.	*Rubrica.*	*Rubrica.*

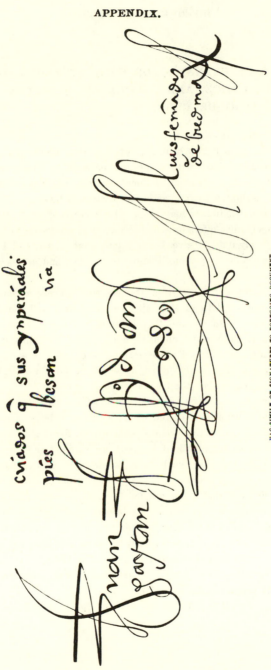

FAC-SIMILE OF SIGNATURES TO FOREGOING DOCUMENT.

LETTER OF HERNANDO DE SOTO AT TAMPA BAY TO THE JUSTICE AND BOARD OF MAGISTRATES IN SANTIAGO DE CUBA.

VERY NOBLE GENTLEMEN:

THE being in a new country, not very distant indeed from that where you are, still with some sea between, a thousand years appear to me to have gone by since any thing has been heard from you; and although I left some letters written at Havana, to go off in three ways, it is indeed long since I have received one. However, since opportunity offers by which I may send an account of what it is always my duty to give, I will relate what passes, and I believe will be welcome to persons I know favourably, and are earnest for my success.

I took my departure from Havana with all my armament on Sunday, the XVIIIth of May, although I wrote that I should leave on the XXVth of the month. I anticipated the day, not to lose a favourable wind, which changed, nevertheless, for calms, upon our getting into the Gulf; still these were not so continuous as to prevent our casting anchor on this coast, as we did at the end of eight days, which was on Sunday, the festival of Espiritu Santo.

Having fallen four or five leagues below the port, without any one of my pilots being able to tell where we were, it became necessary that I should go in the brigantines and look for it. In doing so, and in entering the mouth of the port, we were detained three days; and likewise because we had no knowledge of the passage—a bay that runs up a dozen leagues or more from the sea—we were so long delayed that I was obliged to send my Lieutenant-General, Vasco Porcallo de Figueroa, in the brigantines, to take possession of a town at the end of the bay. I ordered all the men and horses to be landed on a beach, whence, with great difficulty, we went on Trinity Sunday to join Vasco Porcallo. The Indians of the coast, because of some fears of us, have abandoned all the country, so that for thirty leagues not a man of them has halted.

At my arrival here I received news of there being a Christian in the possession of a Cacique, and I sent Baltazar de Gallegos, with XL. men of the horse, and as many of the foot, to endeavour to get him. He found the man a day's journey from this place, with eight or ten Indians, whom he brought into my power. We rejoiced no little over him, for he speaks the language; and although he had forgotten his own, it directly returned to him. His name is Juan Ortiz, an hidalgo, native of Sevilla.

In consequence of this occurrence, I went myself for the Cacique, and came back with him in peace. I then sent Baltazar de Gallegos, with eighty lancers, and a hundred foot-soldiers, to enter the country. He has found fields of maize, beans, and pumpkins, with other fruits, and provision in such quantity as would suffice to subsist a very large army without its knowing a want. Having been allowed, without interruption, to reach the town of a Cacique named Urripacoxit, master of the one we are in, also of many other towns, some Indians were sent to him to treat for peace. This, he writes, having been accomplished, the Cacique failed to keep certain promises, whereupon he seized about XVII. persons, among whom are some of the principal men; for in this way, it appears to him, he can best secure a performance. Among those he detains are some old men of authority, as great as can be among such people, who have information of the country farther on. They say that three days' journey from where they are, going by some towns and huts, all well inhabited, and having many maize-fields, is a large town called Acuera, where with much convenience we might winter; and that afterwards, farther on, at the distance of two days' journey, there is another town, called Ocale. It is so large, and they so extol it, that I dare not repeat all that is said. There is to be found in it a great plenty of all the things mentioned; and fowls, a multitude of turkeys, kept in pens, and herds of tame deer that are tended. What this means I do not understand, unless it be the cattle, of which we brought the knowledge with us. They say there are many trades among that people, and much intercourse, an abundance of gold and silver, and many pearls. May it please God that this may be so; for of what these Indians say I believe nothing but what I see, and must well see; although they know, and have it for a saying, that if they lie to me it will cost them their

37

lives. This interpreter puts a new life into us, in affording the means of our understanding these people, for without him I know not what would become of us. Glory be to God, who by His goodness has directed all, so that it appears as if He had taken this enterprise in His especial keeping, that it may be for His service, as I have supplicated, and do dedicate it to Him.

I sent eighty soldiers by sea in boats, and my General by land with XL. horsemen, to fall upon a throng of some thousand Indians, or more, whom Juan de Añasco had discovered. The General got back last night, and states that they fled from him; and although he pursued them, they could not be overtaken, for the many obstructions in the way. On our coming together we will march to join Baltazar de Gallegos, that we may go thence to pass the winter at the Ocale, where, if what is said be true, we shall have nothing to desire. Heaven be pleased that something may come of this that shall be for the service of our Divine Master, and whereby I may be enabled to serve Your Worships, and each of you, as I desire, and is your due.

Notwithstanding my continual occupation here, I am not forgetful of the love I owe to objects at a distance; and since I may not be there in person, I believe that where you, Gentlemen, are, there is little in which my presence can be necessary. This duty weighs upon me more than every other, and for the attentions you will bestow, as befits your goodness, I shall be under great obligations. I enjoin it upon you, to make the utmost exertions to maintain the repose and well-being of the public, with the proper administration of justice, always reposing in the Licentiate, that every thing may be so done in accordance with law, that God and the King may be served, myself gratified, and every one be content and pleased with the performance of his trust, in such a manner as you, Gentlemen, have ever considered for my honour, not less than your own, although I still feel that I have the weight thereof, and bear the responsibility.

As respects the bastion which I left begun, if labouring on it have been neglected, or perhaps discontinued, with the idea that the fabric is not now needed, you, Gentlemen, will favour me by having it finished, since every day brings change; and although no occasion should arise for its employment, the erection is provident for the well-being and safety of the town : an act that will yield me increased satisfaction, through your very noble personages.

That our Lord may guard and increase your prosperity is my wish and your deserving.

In this town and Port of Espiritu Santo, in the Province of Florida, July the IX in the year 1539.

The servant of you, Gentlemen.

El Adelantado Don Hernando De Soto.

This document, which exists in copy only, written in a firm, clear hand, is to be found in the *Archivo de Indias*, and doubtless is that which accompanied the letter of the Licentiate Bartolomé Ortiz, dated at Santiago, the eighth day of November, 1539, addressed to the Emperor and Council of the Indias. In it he says :

" Directly as the Governor left here I fell sick in bed, and remained so three months, on which account I could not finish the bastion and bulwark he commenced. * * * It may be a month since the Governor of this Island wrote from the Port of Espiritu Santo to the Board of this City, stating his arrival in Florida, and its occurrences, a copy of which I send. He strongly urges the completion of the bastion at this port, but the magistrates oppose it ; and, contrary to my commands, have ordered the assessment to cease, which is necessary for this purpose, and the following up of the wild Indians. * * * "

Notwithstanding the character in which the letter of the Adelantado is copied, the transcript seems to be faulty in omissions, and affords several evident mistakes of words.

LETTER TO CHARLES V. FROM THE JUSTICE AND BOARD OF MAGISTRATES OF SANTIAGO DE CUBA, GIVING A STATEMENT OF OCCURRENCES ON THE ISLAND.

[Original in the *Archivo General de Indias* at Sevilla.]

On the envelope is written :—

TO THE SACRED IMPERIAL CATHOLIC MAJESTY,
THE EMPEROR KING OUR MASTER.

S. I. C. M.

On the seventh day of June, of the present year, the Adelantado Don Hernando de Soto arrived at this port with five ships, bringing six hundred men for the conquest of Florida. He laid before us a provision bestowing on him the government of this Island, which we receive as favour. Being mindful that he goes to serve Your Majesty in the settlement of that country, his people have been entertained among the inhabitants of the place in the best manner possible, and he now makes ready for his departure. May our Lord guide him thither, and give the success most for His service and that of Your Highness.

According to Your Majesty's command, he presented for his Chief Judge the Licentiate Bartolomé Ortiz, a civilian, long resident in these parts, of whom we hope that he will see the inhabitants receive good treatment, with considerations of justice and honour.

On the 5th of April just past, a French vessel, having seventy-eight men, entered this port, with the intention of robbing the city, at a time when it pleased God there should be found here a vessel belonging to Diego Perez, resident of Sevilla, which opposed her, the two with bombards fighting together a day and night, each killing three or four men for the other, the most of the townspeople in the mean while going to their farmhouses and bringing together their women and property, as in the city there was no military defence or support of any sort. With this resistance, that vessel went out and went off. Now we have news that she sailed to San

Xeval of the Havana, on this Island, burned all the town, the church inclusive, taking a certain amount in gold, the property of persons deceased, and another of the Crusade, with one hundred and fifty dollars, the proceeds of gate duties, belonging to Your Highness, besides doing other injuries to individuals. When she left this city, they said she would return; and as it may be that these or some other Frenchmen might dare as much, we resolve to make this known to Your Majesty, that the remedy may be applied in affording the protection of some artillery with which to make defence at the wharf, and give that security which a half dozen of large calibre and a dozen culverins we think sufficient to insure. These we beg that Your Highness will order to be sent to us, and the necessary ammunition from the House of Contratacion in Sevilla, with the haste possible; for if this town be burned or destroyed, the Island is ruined, and the injury is great. God will not permit that the Church and other stone edifices shall be consumed. They have cost much to erect, and could not be rebuilt in a long time.

We likewise make known to Your Majesty that, eight months since, twenty or thirty wild natives insurged, and have committed many atrocities, killing Christians, Spaniards, negroes, domestic Indians, and herds, and setting farms on fire. Although this Board has from the first sent a force against them, which killed many, they continue to do harm; and the Adelantado, having got this information, directly upon his arrival in this city sent out a troop of Spaniards, with negroes and tame Indians, at the cost of the assessment we have made here; and having also ordered out another party, from the town of San Salvador, the two are now in their pursuit. We hope these may be overtaken and chastised, that the evil may cease. Nothing has been heard as yet. Since there are no arms here nor on the Island, and standing in much need of some, it will be necessary that Your Highness require that from Sevilla there be provided for us as many as fifty thousand maravedis, the half for crossbows, shafts, strings, and appurtenances, the other half in lances and bucklers. We ask Your Majesty will order that the money be laid out in the Contratacion of Sevilla, and the arms sent to us in the first ship that comes to this city, when directly as they arrive we will pay the royal officers the amount thus spent.

Money has been requisite to make this war upon the Indians, who do so great mischief, and to protect us from the French vessels. The Board, being without any for the purposes, was obliged to raise as many as three hundred dollars gold by assessment of the community. We entreat that Your Majesty be pleased to deem the act properly done, the greater part being paid by the principal persons of the Island; and that, should one or two hundred more be found necessary, Your Highness will favour us by directing that we be authorized and empowered to raise the sum, which, beyond our great obligations, is a necessary measure for the welfare of the land.

From what has been already said, it may be seen how greatly this Island and people need that Your Majesty should order that they be favoured and assisted, lest every thing be lost, and they go away to Florida, Peru, and other parts to find support, which occasion, to many residents, appears to be at hand. Should Your Highness be pleased to permit that all the gold which is got by the Indians and negroes pay the tenth part during seven or eight years, the mines would be sought out and worked unattended by the frauds and deceptions practised at the time of melting the metal, many perjuring themselves in statements that it is got by the negroes, when it is procured by Indians. So small is the quantity obtained, because of the hindrance, that it does not annually amount to thirteen thousand dollars; and, making this concession, every one would strive to discover mines, and not cease to look after gold, as many have done, to engage in fields of other labour and pursuits, whence the income of Your Majesty is less, and the inhabitants continue very poor.

We entreat that it may serve Your Highness to command this favour: that a stone fortress be directed to be built in the Havana; and all the citizens of this place, with the residents, beseech that, in consideration of the want also here of one for defence, it serve you to direct that a fortress be built at this port, to be a permanency in the Island, so that, though many French vessels come, it may be able successfully to prevent their entrance here. This fabric would be the avoidance of many evils, put the inhabitants in heart to remain and settle here; or otherwise, Your Majesty may be assured that this city is in danger of being pillaged and burned, whenever it is the disposition of the French that it should.

The Bishop of the Island arrived here ten or twelve days after the Adelantado came; consequently we have rejoiced much, his presence giving us great consolation, and we trusting in God that it will be very profitable, both for the Island and its inhabitants. As he writes to Your Majesty, nothing remains to be said more than refer to what he states.

Sacred I. C. Majesty our Master. Be the Imperial person of Your Majesty preserved, and your dominion enlarged, as we your vassals desire.

From the City of Santiago, of the Island of Fernandina, the XXVI. day of July, of the year 1539.

From Y. S. I. C. Majesty's humble vassals, who kiss your royal feet and hands.

JUAN DE LA TORRE.

INO. ARMANSA.

LOPE HURTADO.

ANDRES PARADA.

THORIBIO DE CASTRO.

By order of the Justice and Board of Magistrates:

X°VAL DE TORRES,

Notary Public, and of the Board.

MEMOIR OF THE NAMES OF PERSONS WHO CAME FROM FLORIDA, WHO THEY ARE, AND OF WHAT COUNTRIES NATIVE.

FROM SEVILLA.

Balthasar de Gallegos.
Rodrigo de Gallegos.
Jno. de Añasco.
Xpóval Espindola.
Trugillo.
Jno. Lopez Chachon.
Fuentes.
Villalobos.
Algalin, shoe-maker.
Bartholome Ruiz, stocking-maker.
Porras.
Tristan.
Coria.
Jno. de Mesa.
Morales.
Ynistrosa.
Rodon, sword-cutler.
Gº. Cartuyo, sailor.
Carrançe.
Galindo.
Alonso.
Rui Garcia, from Santlúcar Barrameda.
Jno. Diaz, from Sanlúcar.

FROM BADAJÓZ.

Pedro Calderon, and two sons.

Arias Tinoco, and two brothers, sons of Cardeñosa.

Luis Bravo, son of Balthasar Bravo.

Juan de Vega.

Balthasar Gen. notary.

Jno. Xuarez, companion of Luis Bravo.

Jno. Guttierrez.

Francisco Sanchez.

Andres Sanchez, brother.

Hernando de Vega.

Juan Gª. Rueda.

Jno. Carrion, tailor.

Ximon Perez.

Rodrigo Alonso.

Jno. Ruiz, carpenter.

Hernan Manzera.

Atanasio.

Villalobos.

FROM XERÉZ AND VILLANUEVA.

Alonso Vasquez, and Rodrigo Alvarez, his brother, from
    Xeréz.

Gonzalo Vazquez, from Villanueva.

Alonso Blasco, his brother.

Diego Garcia, brother of a prebend of Badajóz.

Jno. Carrasco, tailor.

Two Franciscos Vazquez.

Alonso de la Parra.

Alonso Botellon.

Pero Nuñez de Prado, from Llorena.

Jno. Gonçalez Alor.

Gonçalo Mendez.

Alonso Gomez.

Bacan de Xeréz.

Aguillar de Villanueva.

Gonçalo Alonso.

38

Zambrano.
Two Vargas.
Bolaños.
Andres Perez.
Francisco Perez.

FROM ZAFRA, ALMENDRALEJO, AND SEGURA.

The General Luis de Moscoso. and two brothers.
Gonzalo Quadrado.
Francisco de Tapia.
Jno. Coles, tailor.
Sayago, tailor.
Cortes, from Almendralejo.
Pero Alonso del Azuchal.
Rangel, from Almendralejo.
Ortiz, his brother.
Villegas, from Almendralejo.
Alonso Caro, from Almendralejo.
Andrez Marin, from Almendralejo.
The Father Pozo, from Segura.
Almendron, brother, from Segura.
Perez, farrier, from Segura.
Portillo, brother, from Segura.
Galvan.
Maçueles.
Madrigal.
Calçada.
Cornejo.
Francisco Martynez.
Pedro de Figueroa.

FROM MEDELLIN.

Alonso Caro.

Garcia de Godoy.
Jno. de Amarilla.
Gº. Martin.
Redondo.
Sagrado.
Sanabria.
Alonso Gutirrez.
Favian Rodriguez.

FROM ALBUQUERQUE.

Alvaro Nieto.
Jno. Nieto, his brother.
Domingo Landero, his brother.
Diego Sanchez.
Alonso Gutierrez.
Jno. Garcia Pechuga.
Caldera.
Jno. Fernandez.

FROM TOLEDO.

The Bachelor Herrera.
Verdejon.
Guzman.
Lope de Acuña, from Yllescas.
Rodrigo Corona, trumpeter.
Villagarcia, from La Mancha.
Castro del Castro, from Garciamuñóz.
Jno. Gaitan, from Talavera la Reina.
Treasurer of this Armada.
Carrauz, from Torrejon.

FROM UBEDA AND BAEZA.

Biedma, factor of this armament.

Rayo.
Francisco de Lera, tailor.
Cañete.
Jno. Rodriguez Lobillo, from Ronda.
Alonso de Torres.
Jno. Lopez Çabarron.
Another Jno. Lopez.
Carrion.

FROM CASTILLA LA VIEJA.

Tiedra, of Salamanca.
Pedro de Torres, from Medina del Campo.
Bonifacio, from Valladolid.
Luis Daçe.
Gin.
Alonso Hernandez.
Miranda de Soria.
Pedro de Soria.
Bustillon.
Baeça.
Verdugo.
Val de Olivas.
Pozo Salmeron.
Bautista and his brother.
Salamanca, tailor.
Tapia.
Calva Rasa.
Villegas, from Plazencia.
Velasco.
Ortiz.
Castro.
Alvañes.
Velasquez.
Salazar.
Salduendo.
Villa Roel.

Carrion, from Carrion de los Condes.
Valderas, from Leon.
Morales, from Soria.
Sancho de Torres.
Agostin.
Valtierra.
Jno. de la Calle, shoe-maker.
Jno. Duarte.
Diego Gallego.
Gaspar de Aguilar.
Diego de Oliva.

FROM ASTORGA.

Don Antonio, brother of the Marquis.
Reinoso.
Marban, notary.
Another Marban.
Alonso Gonçalez.
Jiraldo.
Otaço.
Argote.
Maestre Jno.
Castrejon.
Osorio Garcia.
Custreros.

FROM VIZCAYA, MEN OF THE SEA.

Juanes de a Vedi, seaman.
Miguel.
Pedro de Aroca.
Tolosa.
Min. Alrianes.
Jno. Perez.

Agostin.
Martucho.
Peria.
Bernaldo, calker.

THE AILING WHO REMAINED AT PANAMÁ.

Jno. Ruis, from Sevilla.
Enrriquez, from Astorga.
Viceinte Martinez.
Arias, a Galician.

FRIARS AND CLERGYMEN.

Three Friars.
One Clergyman, French.

FROM THE MOUNTAINS, AND STRANGERS.

Sin Ventura Salazar, from the Mountains.
Silvera, a Galician.
Sant Jorje, also.
Moreno, also.
Pedro de Rybera, also.
Hortuño, a Portuguese.
Jno. Cordero, also.
Alonso Gutierrez, also.
Pegado and his son, also.
Anton Martinez, also.
Manuel de Torres, also.
Gavian Lopez and his brother, also.
Domingo Sardina, also.
Jno. Alvarez, also.
Alvaro Alfonso, also.
Antonio Velazquez.
Jorge Matheos.
Viota, from Aragon.

Gº, a Galician.

Jno. Sedeños.

Jacome.

Antonio, a Galician.

Miguel de Andirrela.

This document, which, from the folds and look of the paper, appears to have been carried in the pocket some little time, is to be found in the *Archivo de Indias*, without any mark or indication of its origin, source, or authority. In the heading, "The ailing who remained at Panamá," there is probably in the proper name a mistake for Pánuco. The number of persons is two hundred and twenty-one.

LETTER TO THE KING FROM THE VICEROY OF NEW SPAIN, WITH TESTIMONY IN BEHALF OF GARCIA OSORIO, SOLICITING THE ROYAL FAVOUR.

HIS CATHOLIC MAJESTY:

At the request of Garcia Osorio, resident of the city, evidence has been taken in this Royal Audiencia, wherewith to inform Your Majesty touching his rank, merits, and past services, of his marriage with the daughter of a *conquistador*, and of the state of want he is in, to pray Your Majesty will favour him with some berth, that may become vacant in the Royal Treasury here, or in other way that may offer.

Besides this testimony, taken according to the order newly provided and commanded by Your Majesty, was received this official one on the subject. There appears from it that Garcia Osorio is a native of the City of Astorga, and housekeeper in this of Mexico, married to Doña Ysabel Marmolejo, daughter of Francisco Marmolejo, one of the first conquerors of this city, and of New Spain; and that he went in company with the Adelantado, Hernando de Soto, to Florida, where he was through the occurrences, in person, with arms, horses, and Spanish servants; and that he served Your Majesty likewise well, as a good soldier, in Italy, at the taking of Tunis, and also in the expedition to France; that to employ himself in Your Majesty's service he sold his patrimony, the town of Moleçuelas, in the kingdom of Castilla, and that he is a person of good standing, son of an hidalgo and man of quality.

Aside from what appears in the testimony, the Royal Audiencia deems Garcia Osorio a person of nice honour and character, reliable of trust, and, as such, some offices, of mayor and chief alcalde, have been given to him by me, the Viceroy, with one of which he is at present provided. In him combine qualities that make it desirable, with the pleasure of Your Majesty, that what can be given to him should be.

The foregoing letter in the *Archivo de Indias* at Sevilla, signed with the rubrics of the Viceroy, Don Luis de Velasco, and the *Oydores* of the Royal *Audiencia*, is from testimony taken in the year 1560, in New Spain, at the request of Garcia Osorio, a citizen of Mexico, concerning his merits, &c., wherein, as witnesses to the fact of the death of his brother, Francisco Osorio, in the march of Soto, appear Luis Daça, Diego de Silvera, Juan Lopez Cacho, Joan de Games, Francisco de Castrejon, and Gonçalo Mendez de Soto, merchant, all which are names to be found on the roll, or memoir of returned soldiers.

Castrejon swore that the brothers appeared in the expedition "like gentlemen, as they were, and with the consideration due to that grade were respected as such; they bore arms, and supported horses and Spanish soldiers at their own cost, and the said Garcia Osorio was captain of the arcabusiers, toiling, both he and his brother, to their best ability, in the service of His Majesty . . . ."

MEMORIAL OF ALONSO VAZQUEZ

TO THE KING OF SPAIN, PETITIONING FOR CERTAIN PRIVILEGES, AND
PERMISSION TO RESIDE IN FLORIDA, TOGETHER WITH THE TESTI-
MONY OF PERSONS AS TO HIS SERVICES IN THE ARMY OF HER-
NANDO DE SOTO, DURING THE INVASION OF THAT PROVINCE.

[MEMORIAL.]

HIS ROYAL MAJESTY:

Alonso Vazquez, native of the city of Xeréz, near Badajóz, says,
that in the year thirty-eight, gone by, he was with the Governor,
Don Hernando de Soto, in the armada brought together to go upon
the discovery of Florida, whither he went, the said Alonso Vazquez,
as soldier; and after they were arrived he was in the service of
Your Majesty in the exploration more than six years, during which
time he held command of over forty men, conferred for his good
example and his conduct; and thus he entered upon that first discovery accomplished in the province, where, in all that offered, he
served loyally and well, as likewise did his brother Rodrigo Vazquez, who accompanied him, enduring much hardship and hunger;
and he was injured of many wounds, was shoeless, and without
clothing; besides that he spent, in the aid he undertook to render the
Licentiate de la Gasca, in horses, in negroes, and arms, more than a
thousand ducats: And, in consideration of such his services, being
of the first that explored that Province of Florida, as will appear
from this memorial he presents; and knowing the country to which
he would return, taking with him his wife and household to live,
remain, and serve there (which is like what should be earliest done
for the royal interest, that persons should go thither who have been
in the country and know its character): and to the end of its
prosperity and of sustaining it, he asks and entreats that Your
Majesty be pleased, because he is of the first discoverers and conquerors, to command that your royal order issue to your Governor
and other justices (¹) in that province to give in *encomienda* Indians
39

of *repartimiento* due to his services and condition, whereby he may make support.

Also he begs that there be given him the command of a regiment of the chief city that shall be established there. (²)

Likewise, also, that license be ordered to issue permitting him to go to that province and taking his wife and household, four nephews of his, and two women belonging to his wife, and two men.(³)

Also, he begs that he be favoured with permission to transport eight slaves for his use, free of all duties, in consideration of their services.(⁴)

Also, that license be ordered to issue to him that he may transport a female slave of the India of the King of Portugal, which is of Brazil, and two girls, her children.(⁵)

Likewise, he says, that his said brother, Ro. Vazquez, was with him in the conquest, and remains in Florida, and that the Governor gave him the post of Alguazil-Mayor of the field and of the principal city that should be established; and he desires that upon his arrival, an equal privilege be extended to him,(⁶) since he goes to remain and to serve Y. M.; in the giving of which he will be favoured.

Gonzalo de Oribe.

On the margin are these original memoranda of the Orders in Council:

(¹) Recommendation.

(²) It is not permitted that the regiment should be there provided.

(³) Not being of the forbidden, and giving bonds that they go direct to Florida, and reside in the country ten years.

(⁴) According to the practice.

(⁵,⁶) Not allowed.

[PETITION.]

In the city of Xeréz, near Badajóz, the twelfth day of the month of June, one thousand five hundred and sixty years, before the magnificent Lord-licentiate Avila, Alcalde-Mayor of this said city, appeared Juan Guillen, householder thereof, and presented a power and a writing, and an interrogatory, which is the following:

Witnesses: SALVADOR MACON,
          DIEGO HERNANDEZ.

VERY MAGNIFICENT LORD:

I, Alonso Vazquez, native of the city of Xerez, appear before Your Worship, and say that respecting certain services that I have rendered to His Majesty, Don Felipe, our master, in wars and conquests, for the preservation of my rights in perpetual remembrance I find it necessary to take certain evidence. Accordingly, I ask and beg of Your Worship that you take the testimony of witnesses, which to that end I shall present, examining them by an interrogatory submitted, interposing therein through all your authority and initiatory decree, that the evidence to be taken in the matter shall everywhere find entire credence throughout and for whatsoever it should be most required . . . Your Worship I implore.

THE BACHELOR BAEÇA.

The Letter of Authority to be found in the Original is here omitted.

[INTERROGATORIES.]

I. First: if they know the aforesaid Alonso Vazquez?

II. Also, if they know, and is it also true, that in the year one thousand five hundred and thirty-eight, he went from Spain to the discovery and conquest of Florida, in the armament of Don Hernando de Soto, brought together by the consent and order of His Majesty, the said Alonso Vazquez going as a soldier known and admitted to be in the service of the King?

III. Also, if they know that the Adelantado Hernando de Soto debarked at Santiago de Cuba, and there and in the Havana he tarried a year, that said armament might be properly fitted out; and if the said Alonso Vazquez debarked with him, having been likewise in those towns the full time of a year, and at his own cost and maintenance?

IIII. Also, if they know that with that captain's rank the said Alonso Vazquez went to Florida, where he remained from five to six years with the said Adelantado?

V. Also, if that, directly after they debarked, the fidelity of said Alonso Vazquez being known, the Captain Juan Ruyz Lobillo gave him thirty, forty, and even as many as eighty men in charge, which he kept for a long time?

VI. Also, if at the end of twelve days, more or less, the said Alonso Vazquez went with Baltasar Gallegos, captain in the forces of that discovery, in the first entry made into the country, the Governor and the rest of the people remaining at the port?

VII. Also, if they went to a Province called Paracuxi, they found inhabited, and heard that it was a country abundant and plentiful in food; and that all the men, among whom was the said Alonso Vazquez, and his brother Rodrigo, who ever accompanied him in the service of His Majesty, suffered very great hunger for the space of a month, in which time they ate nothing but the green stalks of maize, suffering extremely?

VIII. Also, if the said Captain Baltasar de Gallegos sent to call the Governor Soto, in consequence of the news they had, who having come they went inland, among them being the said Alonso Vazquez, and Rodrigo his brother?

IX. Also, if, marching through that country with great toil and hunger, they arrived at a marsh, where they remained three days without eating, until, getting through it and coming out, they arrived at a province called Ocal, where there was some food, and the said Alonso Vazquez, and his brother, with the rest of the people, were somewhat restored?"

X. Also, if there the greater part of all the rest did not fear to enter the country, and told the Governor not to go forward, because in that direction a Governor named Narvaez had already been lost, and that they should return to embark?

XI. Also, if the Governor said that he desired to make the discovery of the country at the risk he might, and left in that place Luis de Moscoso, in command of all the camp?

XII. Also, if the Governor having told Alonso Vazquez that he should remain with the people of the camp, he answered that he should do little good to the King were he confined to incursions of little danger, and that his intent was entirely to serve His Majesty, and did not wish to remain at the camp, but to go on the enterprises; and that he did do so, going with the Governor, and explored the country, getting good news, in consequence of which, the people sent for and uniting with them, they directly marched inland?

XIII. Also, if in Mauvila the friendly and peaceful Indians planned to destroy them all, and did indeed kill fifteen or twenty men, and wounded one hundred and fifty; and if they know that in breaking down the palisade, where the Indians were in strength, many wounds were received by Alonso Vazquez, and particularly one in an ankle, which was broken by it, whence were extracted many bones, and which for more than a year could not bear his weight?

XIV. Also, if, at the time of the cry, in the affair of Tula, when the Indians fell upon them in mass, the Captain Juan Rruyz Lobillo did not say to Alonso Velazquez, and to two other soldiers, that they should go out and ascertain if the Indians were coming, while he put on arms; that he went with those soldiers, and saw the Indians and strove manfully with them, so that they were kept back until Captain Vasconcelos sallied with the cavalry and defeated them?

XV. If that, in the affair of Chicazulea, in the savanna, in another affray, he resisted courageously; doing all to him that was possible as a brave soldier, zealous of His Majesty's service, as likewise did his brother Rodrigo?

XVI. Also, if in the five or six years which the said Alonso Vazquez was in Florida, with the rest, he did not undergo great hunger and fatigue, bearing arms, unshodden, unclothed, as is public and notorious, in the toil and suffering that was undergone in the discovery of that land, in which he was through all?

XVII. Also, if all the while he had a company under his command, he kept the men well satisfied; and so much so, that, upon a time it being taken away from him, thereupon at once the soldiers, aggrieved at it, of themselves returned to ask it for him, so that in a month it was restored, and he remained with it, ever after being liked, affable, and conversable, was by the Governor himself liked, and by other captains and gentlemen was liked, honoured, and respected, and so was he held in the general intercourse?

XVIII. Also, if they know that, after he came with the survivors to Mexico, dressed in skins, in the succour which the Doctor de la Gasca asked, the said Alonso Vazquez went out with his brother Rodrigo, spending in horses, arms, and negroes, more than a thousand ducats?

XIX. Also, if he knows that the said Alonso Vazquez always kept in those parts a horse and groom, ever employing himself in the service of His Majesty faithfully and manfully?

XX. Also, if in all the different rencounters, Indian fights, and on whatsoever occasions that presented for the serving of His Majesty, the said Alonso Vazquez was not ever to be found among the first, from his own free and spontaneous will, being in that conquest from the beginning until the end?

XXI. Also, if in the pacification and colonization of that country, which His Majesty has desired and attempts, would Alonso Vazquez be of avail, from having travelled over and seen it, and knowing it as well as the best; could he be of great use to His Majesty from the certainty of what appears, that of those who have been in Florida, not more than three or four men have returned there, and none so capable as Alonso Vazquez, whence they know that he would greatly benefit the royal service were he in that country; for, besides knowing it all very well, is he not a man of excellent judgment?

XXII. Also, if all the foregoing is public and notorious, stating the reasons of the knowledge in such manner as to afford credence?

And thus propounded, the Alcalde-Mayor foregoing ordered that the witnesses be brought, intended to be examined, and commanded their testimony to be taken.

[TESTIMONY.]

Witness.   Then in the city of Xeréz aforesaid, on the fourteenth day of the month of June of the said year, the said Juan Guillen, in his behalf presented as a witness DOÑA YSABEL DE SOTO, wife of Don Carlos Enriquez, deceased, of said city, of whom the oath being taken in due form, answered to the foregoing questions as follows:

I. To the first inquiry, she said that she has known the said

Alonso Vazquez for a long time; she is neither his relative nor enemy, and she may be forty years of age, a little more or less.

II. That she knows what is stated: And being asked how she knows it, says: Because she was in that armada with the Captain Don Hernando de Soto, her uncle, who went as Adelantado to Florida, at the time that is mentioned, and with Don Carlos Enriquez, her lord, who accompanied him; and in which went Alonso Vazquez, as soldier, to the port of Havana, and thence he went to Florida; because she witnessed this to Havana, where she remained and saw him embark; and hence her knowledge.

III. That she knows what is stated to be true, because she witnessed it as aforesaid.

IV. That she saw Alonso Vazquez embark, and heard it said that he went to Florida with other people; and that he continued in that expedition until it came out by way of Mexico; which she heard Ana her serving-woman say, who went in it, and also many other persons with whom she has since spoken.

V. That she has so heard from many who were in the armada.

VI. That she does not know of this, beyond what she has said.

VII. That she knows only what many have said of the hunger they underwent.

VIII. That she had heard it said of him, by many of the expedition, and by the Adelantado himself, that he was beloved of him.

IX., X. That she has only heard it said by those persons.

XI. That she does not know it.

XII. That she only knows it so far as she supposes that Alonso Vazquez would have gone with the Adelantado, because he liked him much, and was on good terms with him.

XIII. That she has heard it said by Ana Mendez, her servant, who was there.

XIV., XV. That she does not know it.

XVI. That she was not present; and therefore does not know it except from hearing it said by persons who were there, and from letters that were written to her from Florida, concerning the trials that were undergoing.

XVII. That she reaffirms what she has said; that Alonso Vazquez is a respectable man, and that it appears to her that it should be as the inquiry states, since he was honoured by the Adelantado, who liked him, and was liked by every one.

XVIII. That they came out of Florida into Mexico, and were dressed in skins; for this witness was among them: of the rest she knows nothing.

XIX., XX. That she knows no more than she has already stated.

XXI. That (*because of the things stated*), it appears to her that any employment given him by His Majesty would be well bestowed.

XXII. That what she has stated is true, and what she knows of the matter upon which she is sworn, and signs it with her name.

DOÑA YSABEL DE SOTO.

After the foregoing, on the sixteenth day of the month aforesaid, Juan Guillen presented JUAN BOTELLO, householder, of the town of Villanueva de Varcarotta, being and dwelling in the valley of Matamoros, who being duly sworn, &c., answers as follows:

I. That he knows Alonso Vazquez by sight, intercourse, and conversation; that to the general questions, he is about forty-seven or forty-eight years of age, of no relationship to Alonso Vazquez, nor do any of the prohibitions contained forbid his testimony.

II. That he knows what is asked is so; that he was in the armament, and in the same ship where Alonso Vazquez went as soldier; and hence his knowledge.

III. That the Adelantado debarked at Santiago de Cuba; and there, and at Havana, and on the island, he was a year getting ready the armada; where Alonso Vazquez also was, at his own cost and maintenance. . . .

IV. That he knows it, for the reasons that he has stated.

V. That Captain Juan Ruyz Lobillo put thirty or forty men under the charge of Alonso Vazquez, and, witnessing his ability, he gave him others, taken from another soldier, so that he had near eighty men, though the number is not exactly enough remembered to be sworn to, from the long lapse of time since then.

VI., VII., VIII., IX., X. That he knows the facts stated, from having been present.

XI. That he knows it as one of the men going in the advance.

XII. That he, at the time the said Alonso Vazquez spoke the words, was not in the advance, and does not know.

XIII. That he knows Alonso Vazquez was struck by an arrow in the ankle at that fight, of which he remained lame for a long time; and this he knows, because he was present throughout.

XIIII. That he knows what is stated, for he was there present; and that though he only looked out for himself, Alonso Vazquez was a soldier of high character, and should have behaved well, for that he did everywhere.

XV. That in Chicaça, at the savanna, the Indians gave them battle, in which they sorely used many soldiers; and not being at that part where Alonso Vazquez was, but only present, for the Indians entered the town on three sides to engage them; still, he heard it said that he had behaved like a valiant soldier.

XVI. That he knows the truth of what is asked; but so great were the toils, and so excessive, that no man can find tongue to utter them, nor memory to recite them.

XVII. That the company of soldiers was taken away from Alonso Vazquez; but being a man of such worth, and affable, and they being so satisfied with him, that themselves asked the Governor that he would again put him over them, which he did; of which he has knowledge as a soldier, being present.

XVIII. That he desired and was assigned to go, as was his brother, to the assistance of the Doctor de la Gasca, in Peru, when the news came that aid would not be needed: and in so much he could not have failed to spend much money—how much, the witness is unable to say.

XIX., XX. That he reiterates what he has said.

XXI. That the being of Alonso Vazquez in Florida would be important, from his knowledge of the country; having travelled in it and having a knowledge of the Indians, of how they are to be treated, and how protect themselves in the settlement of the country. And this is what he knows of the matter, which he signs with his name.

He presented ANA MENDEZ, serving-woman of Doña Ysabel. . . .

I. That she has known Alonso Vazquez for a long time; that she is about thirty-one years of age, is not a relative.

40

II. That she knows the truth of what is said; for the Alonso Vazquez went in the armada, herself with Doña Ysabel de Soto, her mistress. . . .

III. That she knows the truth of the statement, having witnessed. . . .

IV. That Alonso Vazquez was there; she saw him, that he was among the men; that she was in all that took place at that time in Florida. . . .

V. That she knows the truth of the inquiry; Alonso Vazquez being a worthy man, the captain set him as chief officer of the squadron over the people at sea.

VI. That she reaffirms her statements, and of the rest knows nothing.

VII. That she knows its truth, as she witnessed it all.

VIII. That the truth is stated; for that she was present, and there went there the said Alonso Vazquez, and Rodrigo his brother.

IX. That she remembers crossing that swamp, there being much water in it, in places reaching to the knee, in others to the waist, and thence over the head, which they went through with much labour in three days; but has no recollection whether they passed the time without food or not.

X. That she knows it; for that she was present, and there was fear as stated.

XI. That she does not remember, but declares anew what she has stated.

XII. That she remembers it; that it was so.

XIII. That it is true; that she saw them fight and the Indians kill there Don Carlos, her master, and Alonso Vazquez was wounded by an arrow in an ankle, and was a long time lame.

XIV. That she heard some soldiers of Florida say it.

XV. That she does not remember with regard to the matter.

XVI. That it is true, and she was present.

XVII. That it is true that Alonso Vazquez was well beloved by all the people of the armada.

XVIII. That they went from Florida to Mexico, wearing skins; that she was with them, and the rest she does not know.

XIX., XX. That she says what she has said, and the rest she does not know.

XXI. That he knows well the Provinces of Florida; is a man respected, and from having been there, will better understand the things that will avail. . . .

XXII. That she repeats, &c.

(Unsigned; witness being unable to write.)

He presented GONZALO VAZQUEZ, resident of this city, dweller in the town of Matamoros, who was duly sworn:

I., II. That he has known the said Alonso Vazquez, for about the last twenty years; that he is fifty-four years of age, more or less; is not a relative. . . .

III. That he knows it; because Alonso Vazquez debarked with the rest of the soldiers of the armada, where stated, and was there at his own expense during the time mentioned.

IV. That he knows the truth of it; that he witnessed it; that he was in the company of Captain Juan Rruyz Lobillo; that they were there the full time.

V. That it is true; that Alonso Vazquez had charge of and commanded the men, in number more or less as stated; that he set the watches, and performed the other offices usual in military service.

VI. That he knows the facts; because he went with Baltasar de Gallegos and with the other soldiers to a country called Paracoxi, in Florida; Alonso Vazquez was with them and his brother Rodrigo, of which he was a witness—all going together.

VII. That it is true that they all endured the privation of food that is said, and they ate nothing but the stalks of corn, boiled or uncooked.

VIII., IX. That he knows it because he was present.

X. That he had heard it said: that it was talked about among the soldiers; but did not hear it from the Governor or the Captains.

XI. That he knows it, because he went with the people the Governor took with him, and returned with the rest of the soldiers to where Luis de Moscoso was; and breaking up the posts they united, and went on through Florida, advancing, Alonso Vazquez and his brother Rodrigo being of the company.

XII. That he does not know; that he did not hear him say it.

XIII. That he knows it; he was wounded in an ankle.

XIV. That he does not recollect.

XV. That they both behaved like good soldiers, as well there as at other places; for he found himself often with them.

XVI. That he knows it all; he was himself present.

XVII. That Alonso Vazquez associated with men of high standing; was beloved of all; and of the rest is ignorant.

XVIII. That they came there to Mexico habited in skins, when the Doctor de la Gasca sent for men, and an equipment was got ready to go to his assistance, that was not called into use; some soldiers in making ready, Alonso and Rodrigo Vazquez were of the number, could not have failed to spend much.

XIX. That Alonso Vazquez stood well there, and was respected. . . .

XX. That he was among the soldiers, ever doing his duty, of which the witness was an observer.

XXI. That he would be of great use in Florida. . . .

XXII. That he reaffirms; and it is what he knows of the matter. . . . .

This memorial and petition exists in the *Archivo de Indias*, with two certified copies of the testimony taken at Xeréz de los Caballeros, from which many redundancies and repetitions have been allowed to drop in making the translation.

INDEX.

41

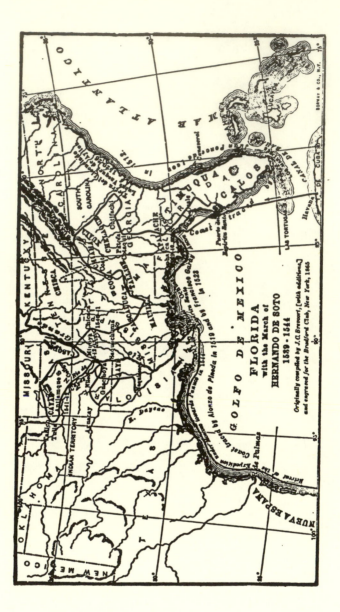

346

NARRATIVES *of the career*
of HERNANDO DE SOTO

IN THE

CONQUEST OF FLORIDA *as told by a* KNIGHT
OF ELVAS *and in a Relation by* LUYS HERNAN-
DEZ DE BIEDMA, *Factor of the Expedition*

TRANSLATED BY BUCKINGHAM SMITH
TOGETHER WITH AN ACCOUNT OF

DE SOTO'S EXPEDITION

BASED ON THE DIARY OF
RODRIGO RANJEL, HIS PRIVATE SECRETARY
TRANSLATED FROM OVIEDO'S HISTORIA GENERAL
Y NATURAL DE LAS INDIAS

EDITED WITH AN INTRODUCTION

By

EDWARD GAYLORD BOURNE
PROFESSOR OF HISTORY IN YALE UNIVERSITY

ILLUSTRATED

VOLUME II

NEW YORK
A. S. BARNES AND COMPANY
1904

RELATION

OF THE

CONQUEST OF FLORIDA

PRESENTED BY

LUYS HERNANDEZ DE BIEDMA

IN THE YEAR 1544

TO THE

KING OF SPAIN IN COUNCIL

———

TRANSLATED FROM THE ORIGINAL
DOCUMENT
BY BUCKINGHAM SMITH

A NARRATIVE

OF

DE SOTO'S EXPEDITION

BASED ON THE

DIARY OF RODRIGO RANJEL

HIS PRIVATE SECRETARY

BY

GONZALO FERNANDEZ DE OVIEDO Y VALDÉS

———

TRANSLATED BY

EDWARD GAYLORD BOURNE

AUTHOR'S PREFACE[1]

Let not the reader marvel that the historian goes over in exact detail the days' marches and rivers and crossings that this Commander and Governor Hernando de Soto encountered in these provinces and regions of the north, because among those gentlemen who were with the army all the time there was one named Rodrigo Ranjel, of whom mention has been made and will be made in the future, who served in this army and who, desiring to keep in mind what he saw and the course of his life, wrote down day by day at the end of his labours, every thing which happened, like a wise man, and also as a diversion, and also because every Christian ought to do so, to be able to confess, and to recall to memory his faults, especially those who are engaged in war; and also because those who have toiled and endured such heavy labours find comfort afterwards, as eyewitnesses, in sharing their experiences with

[1] From Oviedo's *Historia General y Natural de las Indias,* lib. XVII. cap. XXVI.

47

their friends, and in giving an account of themselves as they ought to. And so this Rodrigo Ranjel, after all these things had happened, which have been and shall be narrated, came to this city of Santo Domingo, in the Island of Española,[2] and gave an account to the royal audiencia of all these things, and it asked him and charged him that he should tell me in writing and give an account of everything in order that, as chronicler of their Majesties of these histories of the Indies, there might be gathered together and included in them this conquest and discovery in the North, that it might be known; since so many novelties and strange matters would be a delight for the judicious reader and a warning to many who are likely to lose their lives in these Indies following a governor who thus has control over the lives of others, as is apparent by these studies and writings of mine.

[2] This sentence makes it possible to fix the date before which Oviedo secured his material, for he left Santo Domingo in August, 1546.

48

CHAPTER I[1]

How Hernando de Soto was appointed to govern Cuba as Captain-General of their Majesties, and with the title of Adelantado of Florida.

THE Emperor, our lord, appointed as his Governor and Captain-General of the Island of Cuba and of the Province of Florida and the adjacent regions in the northern mainland, which had been discovered by the commander Johan Ponce de Leon, Hernando de Soto, who was one of the soldiers of the Governor Pedrarias de Ávila, of whom in the history of Terra-Firma[2] there has been frequent mention, since he was one of the pioneers in those parts and was in the lead in the capture of Atabaliba[3] when he was one of those who obtained a large share of the spoils. He brought so much to Spain that it was reported that he found himself in Castile with over one hundred thousand pesos de oro,[4] where, for his services and merits, he was very

[1] Chapter XXI. of Book XVII. of the *Historia General y Natural de las Indias* of Oviedo. Vol. I., pp. 544 ff.
[2] South America.
[3] Atahualpa, the Inca of Peru.
[4] The peso de oro was one-sixth of an ounce, and approximately equivalent to three dollars.

49

well received by the Emperor, our lord; and he made him Knight of the Order of St. James and bestowed other honours and made him Governor and Captain-General, as has been related.

And while he was in Castile he married one of the daughters of the Governor Pedrarias Dávila, whose name was Doña Isabel de Bovadilla, and, who, like her mother, was a woman both good and great and truly noble in mind and bearing. With her De Soto went to the island of Cuba where he arrived in the month of [June⁵] in the year 1539.⁶ And after he had viewed the island and its settlements, and made the provision needful for its well being and for the preservation of the land, he gave orders to arm and to pass over to the mainland to conquer and settle and reduce to peaceful life those provinces which his Majesty had bestowed upon him; and in this enterprise the events took place which will be narrated in the following chapters.

⁵ Blank in the text. A letter from the audiencia of Santiago de Cuba gives the date as June 7. The document itself is wrongly dated 1539, instead of 1538. (B. Smith's *Narratives of the Career of Hernando de Soto*, 288.)

⁶ So in the original, but it should be 1538. See Vol. I. Ch. V.

50

CHAPTER II

OF THE DEPARTURE OF THE GOVERNOR, HERNANDO DE
SOTO, FROM THE ISLAND OF CUBA OR FERNANDINA
FOR THE NORTHERN MAINLAND; AND OF THE FLEET
AND THE SOLDIERS WHICH HE TOOK FOR THE DIS-
COVERY; AND OF THE LABOUR OF LANDING AND
HOW MANY HORSES AND OTHER THINGS HE TOOK;
AND HOW THEY RESCUED A CHRISTIAN CALLED
JOHAN ORTIZ, WHO HAD BEEN LOST AND WENT
NAKED LIKE THE INDIANS.

ON Sunday, May 18, 1539, the Governor
Hernando de Soto departed from the City of
Havana with a noble fleet of nine vessels, five
ships, two caravels and two brigantines; and
on May 25, which was Whitsuntide, land
was seen on the northern coast of Florida;
and the fleet came to anchor two leagues
from shore in four fathoms of water or less;
and the Governor went on board a brigantine
to view the land, and with him a gentleman
named Johan de Añasco and the chief pilot
of the fleet whose name was Alonso Martin,
to discover what land it was, for they were
in doubt as to the port and where to find it;[1]
and not recognizing it, seeing that night was
approaching, they wished to return to the
ships, but the wind did not suffer them for it
was contrary; therefore they cast anchor near

[1] The port Juan de Añasco had found earlier during his reconnoisance. See Vol. I. p. 20.

51

the land and went on shore, where they came upon traces of many Indians and one of the large cabins that are seen in the Indies and other small ones. Later they were told that it was the village of Oçita.

The Governor and those with him were in no small peril, since they were few and without arms; and no less was the distress of those left in ships to see their General in such an evil case, for they could neither succour nor assist him if there were need. In fact, to take such great care, was really heedlessness and excessive zeal, or a lack of prudence on the part of the Governor; for such work belongs to other persons and not to him who has to govern and rule the army, and it is enough to send a captain of lower rank for such a reconnoissance and the protection of the pilot who has to go to examine the coast. And the ships there were in sore travail and the whole fleet too, in which there were 570 men, not counting the sailors; including them the number was fully 700. The next morning, Monday, the brigantine was far to the leeward of the ships and labouring to come up to them and was no wise able to. Seeing this, Baltasar de Gallegos shouted to the Admiral's ship that the Lieutenant-General, who was a knight named Vasco Porcallo, should go and see what had best be done.

52

and, when he heard him not, to bring aid to the Governor he ordered a large caravel to weigh anchor in which that gentleman went as captain, and which put out in the direction where the brigantine appeared; and although the Governor regretted it, yet it was well done since it was in his service and to succour his person. Finally the caravel came up to the brigantine, much to the satisfaction of the Governor.

In the meantime the harbour was recognized and the other brigantine stationed in the channel as sign for the ships, and the Governor's brigantine approached to station the caravel also in the channel of the harbour; and he ordered that it should take a position on one side of the channel and the brigantine on the other so that the ships might pass between them. This they now began to do under sail, for they were four or five leagues off. The Governor had to be there to show them the way, because the chief pilot was in the brigantine and because there were many shallows. In spite of all their pains two of the ships scraped bottom, but, as it was sandy, they received no damage. This day there were hard words between the Governor and Johan de Añasco, who came as the King's auditor, but the Governor restrained his feelings and was patient.

53

The ships entered the harbour constantly
sounding the lead, and sometimes they scraped
bottom, but, as it was mud, they passed on.
This took up five days, during which they did
not land except that some men went ashore
and brought water and forage for the horses.
Finally, since the ships with their loads could
not, on account of the shoals, proceed to
where the village lay, they anchored about
four leagues farther back.

On Friday, May 30, they began to put the
horses ashore. The place where they disem-
barked was due north of the Island of Tor-
tuga, which is in the mouth of the Bahama
channel. The chief of this land was named
Oçita,[2] and it is ten leagues west of the Bay
of Johan Ponce.[3]

As soon as some of the horses were on shore,
General Vasco Porcallo de Figueroa and
Johan de Añasco and Francisco Osorio rode
off to see something of the country; and they
lighted upon ten Indians with bows and
arrows who, in their turn, were coming as
warriors to get a look at these Christian
guests and to learn what manner of folk they

[2] Ucita in the Portuguese narrative.
[3] Tampa Bay. The landing place of De Soto
is usually identified as Tampa Bay. On the un-
certainty of the identification of De Soto's route
see Lowery (*Spanish Settlements in the United
States,* 461ff.).

54

357

were, and they shot two horses and the
Spaniards slew two Indians and put the rest
to flight.

There were in that expedition two hundred and forty-three horses. Of these nineteen or twenty died on the sea, but all the
rest were put ashore. The General and some
foot soldiers went in the brigantines to see
the village; and a gentleman named Gomez
Arias returned in one of them and gave a
good report of the country and likewise told
us how the people had gone away.

On Trinity Sunday, June 1, 1539, this
army marched by land toward the village,
taking as guides four Indians that Johan de
Añasco had captured when in search of the
harbour; and they lost their bearings somewhat, either because the Christians failed to
understand the Indians or because the latter
did not tell the truth. Thereupon the Governor went ahead with some horsemen, but
since they were unfamiliar with the land they
wearied the horses following deer and flound-
ering in the streams and swamps for twelve
leagues till they found themselves opposite
the village on the other side of the roadstead
of the harbour, which they could not pass
around. And that night worn out they slept
scattered about and not at all in order for
war. During all that week the ships gradu-

55

358

ally approached the village, being unloaded little by little with boats, and in that way they took ashore all the clothes and provisions which they carried.

Some paths were found, but no one knew or was able to guess which to take to find the natives of the country. The four Indians understood very little, and then only by signs, and it was not easy to guard them as they had no fetters. Tuesday, June 3, the Governor took possession of the country in the name of their Majesties, with all the formalities that are· required, and despatched one of the Indians to persuade and allure the neighbouring chiefs with peace. That same night two of the three Indians that remained ran away, and it was only by great good luck that all three did not get away, which gave the Christians much concern.

On Wednesday the Governor sent Captain Baltasar de Gallegos with the Indian that was left to look for some people or a village or a house. Toward sunset, being off their road, because the Indian, who was the guide, led them wandering and confused, it pleased God that they descried at a distance some twenty Indians painted with a kind of red ointment that the Indians put on when they go to war or wish to make a fine appearance. They wore many feathers and had their bows

56

359

and arrows. And when the Christians ran
at them the Indians fled to a hill, and one of
them came forth into the path lifting up his
voice and saying, "Sirs, for the love of God
and of Holy Mary, slay not me; I am a
Christian like yourselves and was born in
Seville, and my name is Johan Ortiz."

The delight of the Christians was very
great in God's having given them a tongue
and a guide, of which, at that time, they
were in great need; and, with every one very
much elated, Baltasar de Gallegos and all the
Indians who came with him, returned that
night very late to the camp; and the Spaniards
of the army were greatly wrought up, believing it was something else, and seized their
arms; but seeing what it was, great was the
joy that they felt, for they believed that by
means of that interpreter they could accomplish much more. Without loss of time, on the
Saturday following, the Governor resolved to
go with that Johan Ortiz, interpreter, to the
chief⁴ that had held him who was called
Mocoço, to make peace and to induce him to
make friends with the Christians. And he
awaited them in his village with his Indians,
his wives and his sons, not one missing, and
he made complaint to the Governor of the

⁴ The word *caçique* has been uniformly rendered
"chief."

57

chiefs Orriygua, Neguarete, Capaloey, and Eçita, all four of whom are chiefs of this coast, saying that they threatened him because he accepted our friendship and saw fit to give up this Christian as an interpreter to the Christians. The Governor made this same interpreter to say that he should have no fear of these chiefs or of others, since he would protect him; and that all the Christians and many more that were to come soon would be his friends and help him and show him favour against his enemies.

That same day Captain Johan Ruiz Lobillo went up into the country with about forty foot soldiers and came upon some huts, but were able to take only two Indian women. To rescue them, nine Indians followed him, shooting at him for three leagues; and they slew one Christian and wounded three or four, yet without his being able to do them any harm, although he had arquebusiers and crossbow-men, because these Indians are as agile and as good fighters as can be found among all the nations of the world.

58

CHAPTER III

How War began to kindle and was waged
cruelly; and how the Lieutenant-General
returned to the Island of Cuba; and how
the Governor set out from that Port of
Spiritu Sancto inland, and what befell him
and his folk up to August 10, 1539.

This Governor was much given to the
sport of slaying Indians, from the time that
he went on military expeditions with the Governor Pedrarias Dávila in the provinces of
Castilla del Oro and of Nicaragua; and likewise he was in Peru and present at the capture of that great Prince Atabalipa, where he
was enriched. He was one of the richest that
returned to Spain because he brought to
Seville, and put in safe keeping there, upwards
of one hundred thousand pesos of gold; and he
decided to return to the Indies to lose them
with his life and to continue the employment,
blood-stained in the past, which he had followed in the countries I mention.[1]

So then, continuing his conquest, he ordered
General Vasco Porcallo de Figueroa to go to
Oçita because it was reported that people had
come together there; and this captain having

[1] This paragraph records Oviedo's personal views
of De Soto, which were distinctly less favourable
than those of " The Gentleman of Elvas."

59

gone there, he found the people departed and
he burned the village and threw an Indian,
which he had for a guide, to the dogs. The
reader is to understand that *aperrear* (to
throw to the dogs), is to have the dogs eat
him, or kill him, tearing the Indian in pieces,
since the Conquistadores in the Indies have
always used to carry Irish greyhounds and
very bold, savage dogs. It is for this reason
that reference was made above to the chase[2]
of Indians. In this way this Indian guide
was killed because he lied and guided badly.

While Vasco Porcallo was doing what has
been related, the Governor despatched another
Indian as a messenger to the chief Orripara-
cogi,[3] and he did not return because an
Indian woman told him not to, and for this
reason she was thrown to the dogs. There
were among those in this army divers opinions
whether it would be well to settle there or not,
because the soil seemed to be barren, and such
in fact is its repute. For this reason the Governor resolved to send Captain Baltasar de
Gallegos to Orriparagi with eighty horse and
one hundred foot, and he set out on Friday,
June 20.

And the Governor likewise sent Johan de

[2] *Monteria*, translated " sport," p. 59 above.
[3] This name, which reappears in varying forms, is
the same as the Paracoxi of the " Gentleman of
Elvas."

60

Añasco in the ship's boats along the shore with some foot soldiers to disperse a gathering of the Indians, or to see and hear what was up. He found them on an island, where he had a fray with them and killed with the small cannons [4] that he carried nine of ten Indians and, they in turn, shot or cut down as many or more Christians. And since he could not dislodge them from the island he sent for help, and the messenger was a hidalgo named Johan de Vega, and he asked for horsemen to take possession of the mainland at the place where they were likely to come away; since with the force that he had and with the increase he expected to land and fight the Indians.

The Governor sent Vasco Porcallo with forty horse and some foot, but when this reinforcement arrived the Indians had gone; and the Spaniards, not to have come in vain, raided the land and captured some women whom they took to the camp. Vasco Porcallo, upon his return from this raid, had something of a clash with the Governor (which is concealed in this narrative) [5] nor was the historian able, on account of certain considerations, to find any one who could inform him what he said to him. And it

[4] *Versos de la artilleria.*
[5] Apparently Oviedo's note.

61

was accepted as a good settlement that Vasco
Porcallo should return to Cuba to look after
the affairs of the government there, and to
provide the Governor and his army when it
should be necessary with what they might
have need of. The departure of this cavalier
was regretted by many since he was a friend
of good men and did much for them.

The Governor had ordered Baltasar de
Gallegos even though he found no good land,
that he should write good news to encourage
the men; and, although it was not his nature
to lie since he was a man of truth, yet to obey
the order of his superior and not to dismay the
men, he always wrote two letters of different
tenor, one truthful, and the other of falsehoods, yet falsehoods so skilfully framed with
equivocal words that they could be understood one way or the other because they required it; and in regard to this, he said that
the true letter would have more force to ex-
culpate himself than the false one evil to
harm him.[6] And so the Governor did not
show the true letters, but announced beforehand that what he did not show was
very secret information which later on would
be made clear for the great advantage of
all. The ambiguous and deceptive letters he

[6] *I. e.,* the Governor. This sentence is blind in the
original.

62

365

showed and made such declarations as seemed best to him.

Those letters, although they promised no particular thing, gave hopes and hints that stirred their desires to go forward and emerge from doubts to certainty; wherefore as the sins of mankind are the reason that falsehood sometimes finds reception and credit, all became united and of one mind and requested the invasion of the land, which was just what the Governor was contriving; and those that were ordered to stay behind with Captain Calderon were heavy in spirit, and there were of them forty horse and sixty foot left in guard of the village and the stuff and the harbour and of the brigantines and boats that were left, for all the ships had been despatched to Havana.

The Governor, gratified at this agreement, set out from the village and harbour of Spiritu Sancto (so called from the day when the Governor and his fleet arrived). This departure took place on Tuesday, July 15, 1539, and that night they bivouacked on the river of Mococo, and they took with them a large drove of pigs which had been brought over in the fleet to meet any emergency. They made two bridges where the army crossed the river. The next day they were at the lake of the Rabbit, and they gave it this name because a rabbit suddenly started up in the camp and frightened all the horses, which ran back over a league, not one remaining; and all the Christians scattered to recover the loose horses; and if there had been any Indians around, even a few, they would have had the Spaniards at their mercy and, in return for their lack of caution, a shameful ending of the war would have been prepared for them.

The horses having been recovered, the next day they reached St. John's Lake, and the next day under a grievous sun they came to a plain, and the soldiers arrived much exhausted and a steward of the Governor's, who was named Prado, died of thirst; and many of the foot soldiers were hard pressed, and others must needs have followed the steward if they had not been helped with the horses. The next day they came to the plain of Guaçoco, and the soldiers went into the corn fields and gathered the green corn [7] with which they cheered themselves not a little, for it was the first they had seen in that country.

The next day, early, they came to Luca, a little village, and there Baltasar de Gallegos came to meet the Governor. The Monday following, July 21, they were joined by

[7] The Indian word *mahiz,* maize, "Indian corn," has been uniformly rendered corn in accordance with common American usage.

64

the soldiers that Baltasar de Gallegos had,
and the Governor sent a messenger to Urri-
paracoxi, but no reply was received; and on
Wednesday, July 23, the Governor set out
with his army and came to Vicela [8] and went
beyond it to sleep. On Thursday they slept
at another village called Tocaste which was
on a large lake. And this same day the Governor went on with some horsemen along the
road to Ocale [9] because he had great reports
of the riches he expected to find there. And
when he saw the roads broad he thought he
had his hands already on the spoil and ordered
one of his knights, named Rodrigo Ranjel, because, besides being a good soldier and a man
of worth, he had a good horse, to return to
the camp for more soldiers to accompany him;
and this esquire did so, although not without
misgiving of what might happen, since for the
Governor to stay with only ten horsemen
seemed to him too few; and he sent that
gentleman alone and through a land of
enemies and bad trails and where, if any
found him, he must die or rush through, if
he was not to return without response; and
since he felt ashamed to ask for company he
bowed his head and obeyed. But I do not
praise him for that determination since, indeed,

[8] Acela in the Portuguese narrative.
[9] Or Ocali.

65

368

in matters that are necessary and obvious, it is allowable that with reason one should submit to the prince who provides in order that he may be well served and his orders best carried into effect. What befell this messenger horseman on that day he did not wish to say, because what he said would be about himself. Suffice it to say that he well proved his resolution to be a brave man, and that he fell upon Indians enough that were on the trail of the Governor and got through. When he arrived at headquarters the Master of the Camp [10] gave him fourteen horse with which the number with the Governor was increased to twenty-six.

The next day, Friday, they moved the headquarters along the trail of the Governor, and on the road they came up with two horsemen whom the Governor had sent to the master of the camp, who was a knight named Luis de Moscoso, to order him not to

[10] The Spanish *Maestre de Cam,o* was a kind of adjutant-general, and had charge under the commanding officer of the administrative duties of the army. *Cf.* the " Gentleman of Elvas," Vol. I. p. 47. The *Maestre de Campo* was often placed in charge of an independent command, and his rank would then be equivalent at least to that of Brigadier-General. The Anglicized " Master of the Camp " has the sanction of Hakluyt and the other old translators.

66

move, and they returned to where they started from to sleep, because they had a brush,[11] which is the same as a skirmish, with the Indians who killed a horse belonging to Carlos Enriquez, the husband of the Governor's neice, a native of Xerez de Badajoz, and wounded some Christians. And there was much suffering from hunger so that they ate the ears of corn with the cobs or wood (which is *cassi*) on which the grains grow.

The next day, Saturday, the Governor found the roads broader and the aspect of the country fine, and he sent back two horsemen for thirty others and gave orders for the camp to follow him. And the Master of the Camp sent Nuño de Tovar with thirty horse and moved the headquarters as the Governor had ordered. The Governor, with the twenty-six horse that were with him, on St. Anne's day reached the river or swamp of Cale. The current was strong and broad and they crossed it with great difficulty, and where there was no need of a bridge they waded through the water up to their necks, with clothes and saddles on their heads, a distance of more than three cross-bow shots. The thirty horsemen that Nuño de Tovar took had crossed the following Sunday and the current carried off one horse which was drowned. Seeing

[11] Guaçabara.

that, the rest crossed with ropes just as those had done who were with the Governor.

These soldiers and the Governor came to the first village of Ocale, which was called Uqueten, where they took two Indians. Next the Governor sent back some of the horsemen with mules, that had been brought from Cuba, loaded with corn and other provisions for those that were behind, since he had come upon an abundance. This succour came in good time for they found them in that swamp eating herbs and roots roasted and others boiled without salt, and what was worse, without knowing what they were. They were cheered by the arrival of the food and their hunger and need gave it a relish and flavour most acceptable. From this refreshment their energies revived and strength took the place of weakness, and on the following Tuesday, the last of those lagging behind arrived at the Governor's camp. But some soldiers who had strayed had been wounded, and a crossbow-man named Mendoça had been slain. The camp was now at Ocale, a village in a good region for corn, and there, while they were sent to Acuera for provisions, the Indians, on two occasions, killed three soldiers of the Governor's guard and wounded others, and killed a horse; and all that through bad arrangements, since these Indians, al-

68

371

though they are archers and have strong bows and are skilful and sure marksmen, yet their arrows have no poison, nor do they know what it is.

CHAPTER IV

How the Governor, Hernando de Soto, following up his Conquest went on, and how the Indians desired to slay or to take him by guile to free a Chief whom he carried with him; and how a Chief gave the Governor a buffet that bathed his teeth in Blood; and of other matters appropriate to the Narrative of the History.

On August 11, the Governor set forth from Ocale with fifty horse and one hundred foot in search of Apalache, since it was reputed to be populous; and Luis de Moscoso remained behind with the remainder of the camp until it should appear how the advance section got on. That night they slept at Itaraholata,[1] a fine village with plenty of corn. There an Indian crowded up to Captain Maldonado and badly wounded his horse and he would have snatched his lance from his hands, had not the Governor by chance come up, although Maldonado was a good knight and one of the most valiant in that army; but the

[1] *Ytara* in the Portuguese narrative. See Vol. I. p. 38.

Indians of that land are very warlike and wild and strong.

The next day they were at Potano, and the the next, Wednesday, they reached Utina-mocharra,[2] and from there they went to the village of Bad Peace.[3] This name was given to it because when Johan de Añasco had captured on the way thirty persons belonging to that chief, he, in order that they might be surrendered, sent to say that he wished to make peace, and sent in his stead to treat, a vagabond, who was believed to be the chief himself, and his people were given to him. The sequel was that this Indian, escaping from the Christians another day, took refuge among the mass of Indians which were in a dense wood; and a blooded Irish greyhound which came up at the call, went in among the Indians, and, although he passed by many, he seized no one in the crowd except that fugitive; him he took by the fleshy part of the arm in such a way that the Indian was thrown and they took him.[4]

The next day the Christians arrived at a fair-sized village where they found much food and many small chestnuts dried and very delicious, wild chestnuts; but the trees that bear

[2] Utinama in the Portuguese narrative.
[3] *Mala-Paz.*
[4] *Cf.* the Portuguese narrative, Vol. I. p. 39.

70

373

them are only two palms high and they grow
in prickly burrs. There are other chestnuts
in the land which the Spaniards saw and ate,
which are like those of Spain, and grow on
as tall chestnut trees; and the trees themselves are big and with the same leaf and burrs
or pods, and the nuts are rich and of very
good flavour. This army went from there
to a stream which they named Discords, and
the reason therefor he desired to conceal who
prepared this narrative, because as a man of
worth, he did not purpose to relate the faults
or weaknesses of his friends.

On that day they built a bridge of pines
which abound there, and the next, Sunday,
they crossed that stream with as much or more
toil than was the case with the Ocale. The
next day, Monday, they arrived at Aguacaleyquen,[5] and Rodrigo Ranjel and Villalobos,
two gentlemen, equestrians, yet gentlemen (I
say equestrians because there were cavalry in
that army) captured an Indian man and an
Indian woman in a corn field; and she showed
where the corn was hidden, and the Indian
man took Captain Baltasar de Gallegos where
he captured seventeen persons, among them
the daughter of the chief, in order that it
might impel her father to make peace; but
he would have liked to free her without it,

[5] Caliquen. See Vol. I. p. 40.

71

if his deceptions and shrewdness had not been less than those of these conquerors.

On August 22, a great multitude of Indians appeared, and the Governor, seeing the land proved to be more populous and better supplied with provisions, sent eight horse in all haste to summon the Master of the Camp, Luis de Moscoso, to join him with all the force; and the Master of the Camp, took no small pains to comply with this order and arrived where the Governor was on September 4, and all rejoiced to be united once more, because, as they held the chief captive, there was alarm lest the Indians should make haste to get together, which was not far wrong, as presently appeared.

On September 9 they all departed in a body from Aguacaleyquen, taking with them the chief and his daughter, and an Indian of rank named Guatutima as guide, because he professed to know much of the country beyond and gave abundant information. And they made a bridge of pines to cross the river of Aguacaleyquen, and reached a small village for the night. The next day, Friday, they were at Uriutina, a village of pleasant aspect and abundant food, and there was in it a very large cabin with a large open court in the middle. The population there was considerable. When they left Aguacaleyquen

72

messengers were coming and going from
Ucachile, a great chief, playing upon a flute
for ceremony. On Friday, September 12,
these Christians came to a village which they
named Many Waters, because it rained so
much that they could not go on either Saturday or Sunday; the Monday following, the
15th, they proceeded and came upon a very
bad swamp and all the way was very toilsome,
and they slept at Napituca, which is a very
pleasant village, in a pretty spot, with plenty
of food.

There the Indians employed all their deceptions and devices to recover the chief of
Aguacaleyquen, and the affair reached a point
that put the Governor in great peril; but
their deceptions and tricks were seen through,
and he played them a greater one in this
fashion. Seven chiefs from the vicinity came
together, and sent to say to the Governor that
they were subjects of Uçachile, and that by
his order and of their own will, they wished
to be friends of the Christians and to help
them against Apalache, a mighty province
hostile to Uçachile and to themselves, and
that they had come to him persuaded and
requested by Aguacaleyquen (the chief that
the Christians had in captivity), and that they
were afraid to enter the camp and to be detained; therefore, let the Governor bring

73

Aguacaleyquen with him and go with them to a large plain that was there to negotiate this business. Their dealings were understood, and the message accepted and the Governor went forth to speak with them; but he gave command to the Christians to arm and to mount their horses and at the sound of the trumpet to rush upon the Indians. And having gone to the plain with only his guard and a saddle to sit upon,-and accompanied by the chief of Aguacaleyquen, hardly was the Governor seated and the discourse begun, than he saw himself suddenly surrounded with Indians with bows and arrows. From many directions countless others were coming, and immediately the peril was obvious, which the Governor anticipated; and before the trumpet sounded the Master of the Camp, Luis de Moscoso, struck the legs of his horse, shouting " Come on, Knights, Sanctiago, Sanctiago, at them! " And so in a jiffy the cavalry were thrusting many Indians with their lances; and their stratagem was of no use to them and enabled our men to get the start of them in the fighting; yet notwithstanding that they fought like men of great spirit and they killed the Governor's horse and- also that of a gentleman named Sagredo, and they wounded others.[6] And after the fighting had

[6] This account differs considerably from that of

74

lasted a considerable time, the Indians took flight and sought refuge in two ponds; and the Spaniards surrounded one, but the other they could not, and they held that enclosure, watching all the night and until morning, when the Indians surrendered, and they took out from there three hundred and five or six chiefs among them.

Uriutina remained to the last and would not go out until some Indians of Uçachile swam in to him and pulled him out, and as he came out he asked for a messenger for his country. When the messenger was brought before him, he said: "Look you, go to my people and tell them that they take no thought of me; that I have done as a brave man and lord what there was to do, and struggled and fought like a man until I was left alone; and if I took refuge in this pond, it was not to escape death, or to avoid dying as befits me, but to encourage those that were there and had not surrendered; and that, when they surrendered, I did not give myself up until these Indians of Uçachile, which are of our nation, asked me to, saying that it would be best for all. Wherefore, what I enjoin upon

the "Gentleman of Elvas." See Vol. I. p. 42. The account in Garcilaso would seem to be quite imaginary. *Cf.* Irving's reproduction of it *(Conquest of Florida,* Ed. 1851, pp. 105ff.).

75

them and ask is, that they do not, out of regard for me or for any one else, have anything to do with these Christians who are
devils and will prove mightier than they; and
that they may be assured that as for me, if I
have to die, it will be as a brave man."

All of this was immediately reported and
declared to the Governor by Johan Ortiz, the
interpreter, that Christian who was found in
the land, as the history has related. The Indians that were taken in the manner described
were carried and put in a wigwam with their
hands tied behind their backs; and the Governor went among them to recognize the chiefs,
encouraging them in order to induce them to
peace and harmony; and he had them released that they might be treated better than
the common Indians. One of those chiefs,
as they untied him, while the Governor was
standing by, threw back his arm and gave the
Governor such a tremendous blow that he
bathed his teeth in blood and made him spit
up much. For this reason they bound him and
the others to stakes and shot them with
arrows.[7] Other Indians did many other deeds

[7] The divergence between the "Gentleman of
Elvas" and Ranjel in relating this incident is considerable. *Cf.* Vol. I. p. 43. Juan Coles, whose
written recollections Garcilasco quoted, says that De
Soto lost two teeth by this blow *(La Florida, 67)*.

76

which cannot be fully described, as the historian said, who was present. Wherefore, the Governor seeing that the Christians with so few Indians and without arms were so hard pressed, not being less so himself, spoke as follows: "Would to God that those lords of the Council were here to see what it is to serve his majesty in this country!" And it is because they do know it, says the Chronicler,[8] that they have ordered the tyrannies and cruelties to cease, and that the pacification of the Indians shall be carried on in a better way, in order that God our Lord and his Imperial Majesty may be better served, and the consciences of the conquerors be more at peace, and the natives of the country no longer maltreated.

Tuesday, September 23, the Governor and his army departed from Napituca and came to the river of the Deer. This name was given to it because there the messengers from Uça-chile brought thither some deer, of which there are many fine ones in that land; and across this river they made a bridge of three great pine-trees in length and four in breadth. These pines are well proportioned and as tall as the tallest in Spain. After the whole army had finished crossing this river, which was on the 25th of this month, they passed through on

[8] *I. e.,* Oviedo.

77

the same day two small villages and one very large one, which was called Apalu, and they came by nightfall to Uçachile. In all these villages they found the people gone, and some captains went out to forage and brought in many Indians. They left Uçachile on the following Monday, the 29th, and having passed by a high mountain, they came at nightfall to a pine wood. And a young fellow named Cadena went back without permission for a sword, and the Governor was going to have him hanged for both offences; and by the intervention of kind persons he escaped. Another day, on Tuesday, the 30th of September, they came to Agile,[9] subject to Apalache and some women were captured; and they are of such stuff that one woman took a young fellow named Herrera, who staid alone with her and behind his companions, and seized him by his private parts and had him worn out and at her mercy; and perhaps, if other Christians had not come by who rescued him the Indian woman would have killed him. He had not wanted to have to do with her in a carnal way, but she wanted to get free and run away.

On Wednesday, the first of October, the Governor Hernando de Soto, started from Agile and came with his soldiers to the river

[9] Axille in the Portuguese narrative.

or swamp of Ivitachuco,[10] and they made a bridge; and in the high swamp grass on the other side there was an ambuscade of Indians, and they shot three Christians with arrows. They finished crossing this swamp on the Friday following at noon and a horse was drowned there. At nightfall they reached Ivitachuco and found the village in flames, for the Indians had set fire to it. Sunday, October 5, they came to Calahuchi, and two Indians and one Indian woman were taken and a large amount of dried venison. There the guide whom they had ran away. The next day they went on, taking for a guide an old Indian who led them at random, and an Indian woman took them to Iviahica,[11] and they found all the people gone. And the next day two captains went on further and found all the people gone.

Johan de Añasco started out from that village and eight leagues from it he found the port where Pamphilo de Narvaez had set sail in the vessels which he made. He recognized

[10] Uitachuco in the Portuguese narrative. Garcilaso made Vitachuco the Indian hero of his account of the attempted destruction of the Spaniards, and also the one who struck De Soto in the face.

[11] Anhayca Apalache in the Portuguese narrative, and Iniahico in Biedma's Relation. Possibly Oviedo or his editor misread v for n. The place is supposed to have been not far from Tallahassee.

79

it by the headpieces of the horses and the place
where the forge was set up and the mangers
and the mortars that they used to grind corn
and by the crosses cut in the trees.

They spent the winter there, and remained
until the 4th of March, 1540, in which time
many notable things befell them with the
Indians, who are the bravest of men and
whose great courage and boldness the discern-
ing reader may imagine from what follows.
For example, two Indians once rushed out
against eight men on horseback; twice they
set the village on fire; and with ambuscades
they repeatedly killed many Christians, and
although the Spaniards pursued them and
burned them they were never willing to make
peace. If their hands and noses were cut off
they made no more account of it than if each
one of them had been a Mucius Scaevola of
Rome. Not one of them, for fear of death,
denied that he belonged to Apalache; and
when they were taken and were asked from
whence they were they replied proudly:
" From whence am I? I am an Indian of
Apalache." And they gave one to understand that they would be insulted if they were
thought to be of any other tribe than the
Apalaches.[12]

The Governor decided to go further inland,

[12] See the extracts from the *Peregrinaçion* of

because an Indian lad gave great reports of what there was in the interior; and he sent Johan de Añasco with thirty horse for Captain Calderon and the soldiers left in the harbour; and they burned the supplies which they left and the village; and Captain Calderon came by land with all the soldiers, and Johan de Añasco came by sea with the brigantines and boats to the harbour of Apalache.

On Saturday, November 19,[13] Johan de Añasco arrived at the harbour and immediately Maldonado was despatched along shore with the brigantines to discover a harbour to the west. At the same time Captain Calderon arrived with all his force, less two men and seven horses, that the Indians killed on the way. Maldonado discovered an excellent harbour and brought an Indian from the province adjacent to this coast which was called Achuse, and he brought a good blanket of sable fur. They had seen others in Apalache but none like that. Captain Maldonado was sent to Havana and left Apalache the 26th of February, 1540, with the instructions and

Alonzo de Carmona on the Apalache indians, p. 151, below.

[13] November 19, 1539, came on Wednesday. This is the first error in chronology noted in Ranjel's narrative. Apparently the date given by the "Gentleman of Elvas," Sunday, December 28, is the correct one. See Vol. I. p. 49.

81

command of the Governor that he should
return to the port that he had discovered and
to that coast where the Governor expected to
arrive. The Province of Apalache is very
fertile and abundantly provided with supplies
with much corn, kidney beans, pumpkins,
various fruits, much venison, many varieties
of birds and excellent fishing near the sea;
and it is a pleasant country, though there are
swamps, but these have a hard sandy bottom.

CHAPTER V

How the Governor, Hernando de Soto, and his
Army Set out from Iviahica in search of Capachequi; how the Guide that they carried,
when he knew nothing further about the
Road, made believe that he was possessed of
the Devil; and also about various other
notable Incidents.

THE departure from Iviahica in search of
Capachequi began on Wednesday, March 3,
1540, and by night the Governor came to the
river Guacuca; and departing from there they
came to the river Capachequi, where they arrived early the following Friday; and they
made a canoe or barge to cross it. And the
river was so broad that Christopher Mos-
quera, who was the best thrower, was not

82

385

able to throw across it with a stone. And they took the chains in which they were bringing the Indians, and with some " S " hooks of iron, fastened them together and made one chain of them all. They fastened one end of the chain to one bank and the other to another in order to take over the barge, and the current was so strong that the chain broke twice. Seeing this, they fastened many ropes together and made of them two, and they fastened one to the stern and the other to the bow and drawing the barge first one way and then the other, they got the people and the baggage across. To get the horses over they made long ropes and tied them about their necks and although the current carried them down, by pulling on the ropes they drew them over, yet with toil and some were half drowned.

On Wednesday, March 9,[1] the whole force finished crossing the river Capachequi and went on to sleep in a pine wood. The next day, Thursday, they came to the first village of Capachequi, which contained an abundance of supplies. They passed through much undergrowth or land closely covered with bushes, and then came by nightfall to another village further along where they struck a bad swamp close to the village with a strong current, before they arrived. And they crossed

[1] Wednesday was the 10th.

a great stretch of water up to the girths and saddlepads of the horses; and it was not possible for all the force to get across that day, on account of the hard passage. And there a hundred [2] soldiers with swords and bucklers strayed off, and as many Indians beset them and killed one of them and would have killed all if they had not been rescued.

On the 17th of March they left Capachequi and at nightfall came to White Spring. This was a very beautiful spring with a large flow of good water and containing fish.[3] The next day they came at nightfall to the river Toa [4] where they made two bridges; and the horse belonging to Lorenzo Suarez, son of Vasco Porcallo was drowned. On the following Sunday, March 21, they came to cross the river Toa, and they twice made a bridge of pines and the strong current broke them. Another bridge was made with timbers criss-

[2] Evidently there is an error of transcription in Oviedo's text; *cinco* should be substituted for *cient.* See the Portuguese narrative, Vol. I. p. 52. Garcilaso de la Vega, who uniformly indulges in large numbers, mentions only seven, of whom six were killed. (*La Florida*, 109, Ed. 1723. Irving, *Conquest of Florida*, 1851, 194.)

[3] *Cf.* Bartram's description of one of the large springs in this region. (*Travels through North and South Carolina*, etc., Ed. 1793, 229.)

[4] Toalli in the Portuguese narrative, Vol. I. p. 52.

84

crossed in a way suggested to them by a gentleman named Nuño de Tovar, at which
everybody laughed; but it was true what he
said, and after it was made they passed over
very well by that means; and Monday all
the force got across and came by nightfall to
a pine wood, although separated into many
sections and in bad order. On Tuesday morning they arrived early at Toa, a large village,
and the Governor wanted to go on further,
but they would not suffer him. On Wednesday, the 24th, the Governor went off at
midnight in secret with about forty horse,
knights and gentlemen and some others, who
for various reasons had not wished to be under
another captain. And they went on all that day
until night, when they came to a bad passage
of water quite deep. Although it was night,
they got over it, and that day they went twelve
leagues. And the next day, in the morning,
which was Holy Thursday, they arrived at the
settlement of Chisi[5] and they crossed a
branch of a big river, very broad, wading and
a good part of it swimming. And they came
to a village, which was on an island in this
river, where they captured some people and
found some provisions; and, as it was a perilous place, before canoes should appear, they
turned to go back the way they came; but

[5]Achese in the Portuguese narrative, Vol. I. p. 54.

first they breakfasted on some fowl of the country, which are called *guanaxas*[6] and some strips of venison which they found placed upon a framework of sticks,[7] as for roasting on a gridiron. And though it was Holy Thursday there was no one so strict a Christian that he scrupled to eat flesh; and there the lad Perico, whom they brought from Apalache as a guide, took them, and they passed on to other villages and to a bad passage through a swamp where some horses nearly got drowned. The horses swam with their saddles, while their masters crossed on a beam stretched over the channel, and in so crossing, one Benito Fernandez, a Portuguese, fell off the log and was drowned. This day they came to a village where some principal Indians appeared as messengers from Ichisi; and one of them addressed the Governor and said three words, one after the other, in this manner: " Who are you, what do you want, where are you going? " And they brought presents of skins, the blankets of the country, which were the first gifts as a sign of peace. All of this took place on Holy Thursday and

[6] Turkeys.
[7] *En barbacoa.* The *barbacoa,* whence the word "barbecue," was usually a kind of scaffold or framework on posts, used for drying meat, for a burial place, or as a look-out. It is also used for our familiar corncrib. *Cf.* Vol. I. pp. 44, 53.

86

on the Day of the Incarnation. To the questions of the Indian the Governor replied that he was a captain of the great King of Spain; that in his name he had come to make known to them the holy faith of Christ; that they should acknowledge him and be saved and yield obedience to the Apostolic Church of Rome and to the Supreme Pontiff and Vicar of God, who lived there; and that in temporal affairs they should acknowledge for king and lord the Emperor, King of Castile, our Lord, as his vassals; and that they would treat them well in every thing and that he would maintain toward them peace and justice just the same as towards all his Christian vassals.

Monday, March 29, they went from there to Ichisi; and it rained very hard and a small stream rose so much that if they had not made great haste in crossing all the army would have been in danger. This day Indian men and women came forth to receive them, and the women were clothed in white and made a fine appearance; and they gave the Christians corn cakes and some bunches of young onions just like those of Castile, as big as the end of the thumb and larger. And from now on, this food was of great assistance to them and they ate the onions with the cakes roasted and boiled and raw, and they

87

390

were a great refreshment, for they are very
good. The white clothing, with which the
Indian women were clothed, were mantles,
apparently of homespun linen and some of
them were very thin. They make the thread
of them from the bark of the mulberry tree,
not the outside, but the intermediate layers;
and they know how to make use of it and to
spin it, and to dress it as well and to weave
it. They make very fine mantles, and they
wear one from the girdle down and another
fastened on one side with the end over the
shoulders like those Bohemians, or gypsies,
who wander sometimes through Spain; and
the thread is of such a quality that one who
was there assured me that he saw the women
spin it from that mulberry bark and make it
as good as the best thread from Portugal that
women can get in Spain for their work, and
finer and somewhat like it and stronger. The
mulberry trees are quite like those of Spain,
just as tall and larger, but the leaf is softer
and better for silk, and the mulberries are
better eating and larger than those of Spain,
and they were very frequently of great advantage to the Spaniards for food.

That day they came to a village of a
chief, a subject of Ichisi, a small village with
abundant food; and he gave of what he had
with good will. They rested there Tuesday

33

and on Wednesday the last of March the
Governor set out with his army and came to
Great River, where they took many canoes,
in which they crossed easily and came to the
village of the lord, who was one-eyed and he
gave them much food and fifteen Indians as
porters. As he was the first that came to
them in peace they did not wish to burden him
overmuch. They were there Thursday, the
first of April, and they set up in the mound
of the village a cross and interpreted to them
the holiness of the cross, and they received it
and worshipped it devoutly to all appearance.
On Friday, April 2, the army departed from
that place and slept in the open country. On
the next day they came to a considerable
stream and found deserted cabins, and there
messengers came from Altamaha and took
them to a village where they found an abundance of food; and a messenger came from
Altamaha with a present and the next day
they brought many canoes and the army
crossed very comfortably. And from there
the Governor sent to call the chief Camumo,
and they told him that he always ate and slept
and went about armed; that he never laid
aside his arms because he was on the borders
of another chief named Cofitachequi, his
enemy; and that he would not come without
them; and the Governor replied and said: that

89

he might come as he pleased; and he came, and the Governor gave him a large plume adorned with silver. And the chief took it very gladly and said to the Governor: " You are from Heaven, and this plume of yours which you have given me, I can eat with it; I shall go to war with it; I shall sleep with my wife with it; " and the Governor said, yes, he could do all that. And this Camumo and the others were subjects of a great chief whose name was Ocute. And the chief with the plume asked the Governor to whom he should give tribute in the future, whether to the Governor or to Ocute; and the Governor suspected that this question was put with cunning; and he replied that he regarded Ocute as a brother and that he should pay his tribute to Ocute until the Governor ordered otherwise.

From there he sent messengers to summon Ocute, and he came thither; and the Governor gave him a cap of yellow satin and a shirt and a plume; and he set up a cross there in Altamaha and it was well received. The next day, Thursday, April 8, the Governor departed from that place with his army and took with him Ocute, and they passed the night in some cabins; and Friday he came to the village of Ocute; and the Governor was angry with him and he trembled

90

with fear. Soon a large number of Indians came with supplies and offered as many Indians as porters as the Christians needed; and a cross was set up and they received it very devoutly to all appearances and worshipped it on their knees as they saw the Christians do. Monday, April 12, they departed from Ocute and reached Cofaqui and the leading men came with gifts. This chief Cofaqui was an old man, with a full beard, and his nephew governed for him. Hither came the chief Tatofa and another principal Indian; and they gave their present, both food and tamemes, all that they had need of. And in that language tameme means the same as carrier. Thursday, the 15th of this month, Perico, who was the Indian lad whom they took for a guide from Apalache, began to lose his bearings because he no longer knew anything of the country. And he made believe that he was possessed of the devil, and he knew how to act the part so well that the Christians believed it was real, and a priest whom they brought with them named Friar John, the Evangelist, said it was so. The upshot of it was that they had to take guides that Tatofa gave them to go to Cofitachequi through a desert country some nine or ten days' march.

I have wondered many times at the venture-

91

someness, stubbornness, and persistency or firmness, to use a better word for the way these baffled conquerors kept on from one toil to another, and then to another still greater; from one danger to many others, here losing one companion, there three and again still more, going from bad to worse without learning by experience. Oh, wonderful God! that they should have been so blinded and dazed by a greed so uncertain and by such vain discourses as Hernando de Soto was able to utter to those deluded soldiers, whom he brought to a land where he had never been, nor put foot into, and where three other leaders, more experienced than he, had ruined themselves: Johan Ponce, Garay, and Pamphilo de Narvaez, any one of whom had more experience than he in the affairs of the Indies, and inspired more confidence than he; for he neither in the islands nor in the mainland of the north had knowledge except of the government of Pedrarias, in Castilla del Oro and Nicaragua, and in Peru, which was quite another sort of embroilment with Indians. He thought that that experience in the South was sufficient to show him what to do in the North, and he was deceived as the history will tell. Let us return now to the narrative and the march of this captain or Governor, whom I knew very well, and with whom I talked and

92

associated, as well as with the other three mentioned above, and with the Lawyer Ayllón.[8]

On Friday, the 16th of the month, this Governor and his army spent the night by a small stream on the way to Cofitachequi; and the next day they crossed a very large river, divided into two branches, wider than a long shot from an arquebuse. And the fords were very bad, with many flat stones, and the water came up to the stirrups and in places to the saddlepads. The current was very strong and none of the horsemen dared to take a foot soldier on the croup. The foot soldiers crossed the river further up where it was deeper in this way. They made a line of thirty or forty men tied together and so they crossed over supporting each other; and although some were in much danger, it pleased God that none was drowned, for the horsemen helped them with their horses and gave them the butt of the lance or the tail of the horse, and in that way they all got out and passed the night on a hill. That day they lost many pigs of those which they had brought tame from Cuba, as they were carried down by the current.

The next day, Sunday, they came to an-

[8] This paragraph presents the views of Oviedo, not of Ranjel. Judged by his actual achievement, De Soto far outranks Ponce, Garay, or Pamphilo de Narvaez as an explorer.

other hill or grove to stop, and the next day, Monday, they marched without any trial and crossed another very large river. Tuesday they passed the night beside a small stream and Wednesday reached another very large river and hard to cross which was divided into two streams which were very difficult to enter and worse to get out of. The Christians now were without provisions and with great labour they crossed this river and reached some huts of fishermen or hunters. And the Indians whom they carried had now lost their bearings and no longer knew the way; nor did the Spaniards know it, or in what direction they should go; and among them were divers opinions. Some said they should turn back; others said they ought to go on in a different direction; and the Governor proposed, as he always had done, that it was best to go on, without knowing, either himself or they, what they were aiming at or whither they were wandering. And being at a loss in this labyrinth, on Friday, the 23d of April, the Governor sent to look for roads or villages in the following manner: Baltasar de Gallegos was to go up the river northwest, and Johan de Añasco was to go along the river southeast, each with ten horsemen [9] and rations of

[9] Garcilaso de la Vega says that these scouting parties were each accompanied by one thousand In-

94

397

ten days. And on that day other captains
returned from searching and they had found
nothing. And on Saturday the Governor
sent Johan Ruiz Lobillo with four horsemen
to the north, with ten days' rations, and he
ordered that some of the grown pigs in the
army should be slaughtered, and they gave as
rations to each man a scant pound of flesh and
with it herbs and blite [10] that they gathered.
And so as best they could they supplied their
needs, not without great struggle and toil, the
horses without any food; they and their masters dying of hunger; with no trail, drenched
with continual rain, the rivers always rising
and narrowing the land, and without hope of
villages or knowledge where to find them,
lamenting and calling on God for mercy.
And our Lord did bring the succour in the
following manner. That Sunday, April 25,
Johan de Añasco came with news that he had
found a village and food, and he greatly
cheered the soldiers, and he brought an interpreter and guide. And so they stopped the rations of flesh and each one helped himself out
as he could with unknown herbs and blite
that the flesh might be left for a reserve.

dians, an interesting example of his romancing (*La
Florida,* 119. Irving, *Conquest of Florida,* 212).

[10]*Bledo.* Blite is the English equivalent, but perhaps " greens " is sufficiently exact. Wild spinach
was one of the plants called blite.

95

398

And the Governor decided immediately to set out, and writing some letters and putting them in some pumpkins he buried them in a secret place and wrote on a tall tree some directions where to find them. And so they set out with Johan de Añasco on Monday, April 26. That day the Governor, with some of the horse, although a few, reached the village which was called Hymahi; [11] and the army remained two leagues behind, the horses exhausted. There was found in the village a barbacoa covered with corn and more than thirty bushels of *pinol* prepared, which is parched corn. And the next day the main force arrived and rations of corn and *pinol* were distributed. And there was no end of mulberries, because there were many trees and it was their season; and this was a great help. And likewise there were found in the plains some berries such as in Italy grow on vines close to the ground and are like madroños, [strawberries] very savoury, palatable, and fragrant and they also grow abundantly in Galicia. In the Kingdom of the Naples this fruit is called *fraoles* [strawberries] and it is a finer delicate fruit and highly thought of. And besides those, they found there along the trails countless roses growing wild like those

[11]Aymay in the Portuguese narrative, see Vol. I. p. 63.

96

in Spain; and although they have not so many
leaves since they are in the woods they are
none the less fragrant and finer and sweeter.
This village they named Succour.

The next day Captain Alonso Romo came
who likewise had been out reconnoitring, and
he brought four or five Indians, and not one
would show any knowledge of his lord's
village or discover it, although they burnt
one of them alive before the others, and all
suffered that martyrdom for not revealing it.
The next day Wednesday, Baltasar de Gallegos came with an Indian woman and news
of a populated region. The next day Lobillo
returned with news of trails, and he had left
behind two companions lost; and the Governor rated him soundly and without suffering him to rest or to eat made him go back
to look for them under pain of death, if he
brought them not back. And that was a
better order and a better deed and judgment
than burning alive the Indian that Alonso
Romo brought for not consenting to reveal
his lord; for to such a one as him the Romans
set up a memorable statue in the Forum; and
to Christians no such cruelty is allowable
toward any one and especially toward an Indian who was ready to die to be loyal to his
country and to his lord. But later on the
account was squared.

97

CHAPTER VI

How the Governor Hernando de Soto came to the
village of Jalameco; how the woman Chief,
Lady of this Land, welcomed him and placed
upon his neck a string of pearls that she
wore around the neck; and how they found
many other Pearls; and how, by the fault
of the Governor, they failed to find all
that they wanted to; and how later Pearls
were found in Streams of fresh Water; and
many other Details, appropriate to the
course of this Narrative.

·   ·   ·   ·   ·

LET us return to the sequel and continuation of what we have in hand and are here narrating. Friday the last day of April the Governor took some horse, those that were most refreshed, and the Indian woman that Baltasar de Gallegos brought for a guide, and went along the road to Cofitachequi, and spent the night near a large, deep river; and he sent on Johan de Añasco with some horsemen to secure some interpreters and canoes for crossing the river, and he got some. The next day the Governor came to the crossing opposite the village, and the chief Indians came with gifts and the woman chief,[1] lady

NOTE—The passage omitted is given as Oviedo's Preface, p. 47 above.

[1] *La Cacica,*

98

of that land whom Indians of rank bore on their shoulders with much respect, in a litter covered with delicate white linen. And she crossed in the canoes and spoke to the Governor quite gracefully and at her ease. She was a young girl of fine bearing; and she took off a string of pearls which she wore on her neck, and put it on the Governor as a necklace to show her favour and to gain his good will. And all the army crossed over in canoes and they received many presents of skins well tanned and blankets, all very good; and countless strips of venison and dry wafers, and an abundance of very good salt. All the Indians went clothed down to their feet with very fine skins well dressed, and blankets of the country, and blankets of sable fur and others of the skin of wild cats which gave out a strong smell. The people are very clean and polite and naturally well conditioned.[2]

Monday, May 3, all the rest of the force came up; but all were not able to get across until the next day, Tuesday, nor then without the cost and loss of seven horses that were drowned, from among the fattest and strongest ones which struggled against the current.

[2] Cofitachequi has usually been identified with Silver Bluff on the Savannah River, about twenty-five miles south of Augusta, Ga. *Cf.* Lowery (*Spanish Settlements*, 228).

99

The thin ones that let themselves go with the stream got across better. On Friday, May 7, Baltasar de Gallegos, with the most of the soldiers of the army, arrived at Ilapi to eat seven barbacoas of corn, that they said were there stored for the woman chief. That same day the Governor and Rodrigo Ranjel entered the mosque and oratory of this heathen people, and opening some burying places they found some bodies of men fastened on a barbacoa. The breasts, belly, necks and arms and legs full of pearls; and as they were taking them off Ranjel saw something green like an emerald of good quality and he showed it to the Governor and was rejoiced and he ordered him to look out of the enclosure and to have Johan de Añasco called, the treasurer of their majesties; and Ranjel said to him: "My lord, let us not call any one. It may be that there is a precious stone or jewel?" The Governor replied, somewhat angry, and said: "Even if there should be one, are we to steal it?" When Johan de Añasco came they took out this emerald and it was glass, and after it many beads of glass and rosaries with their crosses. They also found Biscayan axes of iron from which they recognized that they were in the government or territory where the lawyer Lucas Vazquez de Ayllón came to his ruin. They took away from there some two

100

hundred pounds of pearls; and when the woman chief saw that the Christians set much store by them, she said: " Do you hold that of much account? Go to Talimeco, my village, and you will find so many that your horses cannot carry them." The Governor replied: " Let them stay there; to whom God gives a gift, may St. Peter bless it." And there the matter dropped. It was believed that he planned to take that place for himself, since it was the best that they saw and with the land in the best condition, although there did not appear to be much people or corn, nor did they delay to look for it there. Some things were done there as in Spain, which the Indians must have been taught by the followers of the lawyer Lucas Vazquez de Ayllón; since they make hose and moccasins and leggings with ties of white leather, although the leggings are black, and with fringes or edging of coloured leather as they would have done in Spain. In the mosque, or house of worship, of Talimeco there were breastplates like corselets and head-pieces made of rawhide, the hair stripped off; and also very good shields. This Talimeco was a village holding extensive sway; and this house of worship was on a high mound and much revered. The *caney,* or house of the chief, was very large, high and broad,

101

all decorated above and below with very fine
handsome mats, arranged so skilfully that
all these mats appeared to be a single one;
and, marvellous as it seems, there was not
a cabin that was not covered with mats.
This people has many very fine fields and a
pretty stream and a hill covered with walnuts,
oak-trees, pines, live oaks, and groves of
liquidamber, and many cedars. In this river,
Alaminos, a native of Cuba (although a
Spaniard), was said to have found a trace
of gold, and rumour of this spread abroad
among the Spaniards in the army, and from
this it was believed that it was a land of
gold and that good mines would be found
there.

Wednesday, May 13,[3] the Governor went
on from Cofitachequi, and in two days came
to the territory of Chalaque; but they were
not able to come upon the village of the
chief, nor was there an Indian that would
reveal it. And they bivouacked in a pine
wood, whither many Indian men and women
began to come in peace with presents and
gifts; and they were there on Whitsuntide,
and from there the Governor sent a letter
to Baltasar de Gallegos with some Indians
to the barbacoas where, as has been said above,

[3] The date should be Thursday, May 13, or
Wednesday, May 12.

they had gone to eat the corn, requesting
him to come on behind the Governor. On
Monday, the 17th of this month, they departed thence, and spent the night at a
mountain; and on Tuesday they came to
Guaquili, and Indians came forth in peace
and gave them corn, although little, and many
fowls roasted on a barbacoa, and a few little
dogs which were good eating. These are
dogs of a small size that do not bark; and
they breed them in their homes for food.[4]
Likewise they gave them tamemes, which are
Indians to carry their burdens. On Wednesday, the next day, they came to a region full
of reeds, and Thursday to a small plain
where one of the horses died, and some of the
foot soldiers who had been with Baltasar de
Gallegos came up to inform the Governor
that he would come soon. The next day,
Friday, they were at Xuala,[5] which is a
village in a plain between two rivers, and the
chief was so prosperous that he gave the
Christians whatever they asked—tamemes,
corn, dogs, *petacas,* and as much as he had.

[4] Conjectured to be opossums.
[5] Ordinarily located in northern Georgia, but
James Mooney places it in western North Carolina
near the head of the Broad River. *Cf.* Lowery
(*Spanish Settlements,* 230, and note to map opposite
p. 480).

103

Petacas are baskets covered with leather and likewise ready to be so covered with their lids, for carrying clothes or whatever they want to. And on Saturday Baltasar de Gallegos came there with many sick and lame who must needs be restored whole, particularly in view of the mountain ranges before them. In that Xuala region it seemed that there were more indications that there were gold mines than in all the country they had traversed and viewed in that northern region.

Tuesday, May 25, they left Xuala, and on that day went over a very high range [6] and at nightfall they encamped at a little mountain; and the next day, Wednesday, in a plain where they suffered from severe cold, although it was the 26th of May. There they crossed the river, wading up to their shins, by which later they were to depart in the brigantines they had made. This, when it reaches the sea, the chart indicates to be the Rio del Spiritu Santo (River of the Holy Spirit), which, according to the maps of the geographer Alonso de Chaves, empties into a great bay; and the mouth of this river, where the water is salt, is in 31 degrees north of the equator. [7]

[6] The Blue Ridge.
[7] The map of Alonso de Chaves, which was con-

Returning to my narrative, from this place where, as was said, they waded across the river, the woman chief of Cofitachequi, whom they carried with them in return for the good treatment which they had received from her, escaped; and that day there remained behind, it was supposed intentionally, Mendoça de Montanjes and Alaminos of Cuba. And since Alonso Romo kept that day the rearguard and left them, the Governor made him return for them, and they waited for them one day. When they arrived, the Governor wished to hang them. In that region of Xalaque was left a comrade whose name was Rodriquez, a native of Peñafiel; and also an Indian slave boy from Cuba, who knew Spanish, and belonged to a gentleman named Vi-

structed in 1536, is no longer extant. It is described by Oviedo, whose data are summarized by Harrisse *(Discovery of North America,* 633-34). J. G. Shea (in Winsor, *Narrative and Critical History,* II., 247) assumed that De Soto had this map and studied it; but in the judgment of the present editor the remarks in the text about Chaves' map are by Oviedo, and not derived from Ranjel's diary, and consequently by no means warrant the notion that De Soto and his officers "pored over the cosmography of Alonso de Chaves." The river which Oviedo erroneously identified as the Mississippi is supposed to have been either the Chattahoochee or the Coosa. *Cf.* Lowery *(Spanish Settlements,* 231).

105

408

llegas; and there was also left a slave belonging to Don Carlos, a Berber, well versed in Spanish; and also Gomez, a negro belonging to Vasco Gonçalez who spoke good Spanish. That Rodriquez was the first, and the rest deserted further on from Xalaque. The next day they passed the night in an oak grove, and the day following along a large stream, which they crossed many times. The next day messengers of peace appeared and they arrived early at Guasili, and they gave them many tamemes, many little dogs and corn; and since this was a fine stopping place, the soldiers afterwards in throwing dice called out " the house of Guasuli," or, a good throw.

Monday, which was the last day of May, the Governor left Guasili and came with his army to an oak wood along the river; and the next day they crossed by Canasoga, and at night they slept in the open country. Wednesday they slept near a swamp, and that day they ate an enormous amount of mulberries. The next day, Thursday, they went along a large stream near the river which they had crossed in the plain where the woman chief went off. It was now very large. The next day, Friday, they came to a pine wood on the stream, where appeared peaceful Indians fom Chiaha and brought

106

corn. The next day, Saturday, in the morning the Spaniards crossed one arm of the
river, which was very broad, and went into
Chiaha, which is on an island in the same
river.

It was Saturday, the 5th of June, that
they entered Chiaha,[8] and since all the way
from Xuala had been mountainous and the
horses were tired and thin, and the Christians
were also themselves worn out, it seemed best
to tarry there and rest themselves; and they
were given an abundance of corn, of which
there was plenty of good quality, and they
were also given an abundance of corn cakes,[9]
and no end of oil from walnuts and acorns,
which they knew how to extract very well,[10]
which was very good and contributed much
to their diet. Yet some say that the oil from
nuts produces flatulence. However, it is

[8] In northern Georgia. Formerly placed near
Rome, but by Mooney near Columbus. Lowery,
231.

[9] *Maçamorras.* The editor of Oviedo explains it
as a kind of mush or porridge. For the various
kinds of corn cakes made by the Southern Indian
cf. C. C. Jones' *Antiquities of the Southern Indians,* 45 and 316; also see Bartram *(Travels,* 239),
for a kind of jelly made from the roots of the
China briar.

[10] Cf. Bartram *(Travels,* 380) for the process. The
Indian name was hiccory milk.

107

very delicious. The Indians spent fifteen days with the Christians in peace, and they played with them, and likewise among themselves. They swam with the Christians and helped them very much in every way. They ran away afterwards on Saturday, the 19th of the month, for something that the Governor asked of them; and, in short, it was because he asked for women. The next day in the morning the Governor sent to call the chief and he came immediately; and the next day the Governor took him off with him to make his people come back, and the result was they came back. In the land of this Chiaha was where the Spaniards first found fenced villages. Chiaha gave them five hundred carriers, and they consented to leave off collars and chains.

Monday, June 28, the Governor and his soldiers departed from Chiaha, and, passing through five or six villages, they spent the night in a pine grove near a village. There they had much labour in crossing a river which flowed with a strong current, and they made a bridge or support of the horses in the following manner, so that the foot soldiers should not be endangered, and it was this way: They put the horses in the river in line, head and tail, and they were as steady as they could be, and on each one his master, and they re-

108

411

ceived the force of the stream, and on the lower side, where the water was not so violent, the foot soldiers forded, holding on to the tails and stirrups, breast-pieces, and manes, one after the other. And in this way the whole army got across very well.

The next day, Tuesday, they passed through a village and took corn and went beyond to sleep in the open country. Wednesday they passed over a river and through a village and again over the river and slept in the open country. On Thursday the chief of Coste came out to receive them in peace, and took the Christians to sleep in a village of his; and he was offended because some soldiers provisioned themselves from, or, rather, robbed him of, some barbacoas of corn against his will. The next day, Thursday, on the road leading toward the principal village of Coste, he stole away and gave the Spaniards the slip and armed his people. Friday, the 2d of July, the Governor arrived at Coste. This village was on an island in the river, which there flows large, swift, and hard to enter.

And the Christians crossed the first branch with no danger to any of the soldiers, yet it was no small venture, and the Governor entered into the village careless and unarmed,

109

with some followers unarmed. And when the soldiers, as they were used to do, began to climb upon the barbacoas, in an instant the Indians began to take up clubs and seize their bows and arrows and to go to the open square.

The Governor commanded that all should be patient and endure for the evident peril in which they were, and that no one should put his hand on his arms; and he began to rate his soldiers and, dissembling, to give them some blows with a cudgel; and he cajoled the chief, and said to him that he did not wish the Christians to make him any trouble; and they would like to go out to the open part of the island to encamp. And the chief and his men went with him; and when they were at some distance from the village in an open place, the Governor ordered his soldiers to lay hands on the chief and ten or twelve of the principal Indians, and to put them in chains and collars; and he threatened them, and said that he would burn them all because they had laid hands on the Christians. From this place, Coste, the Governor sent two soldiers to view the province of Chisca, which was reputed very rich, toward the north, and they brought good news. There in Coste they found in the trunk of a tree as good honey and even better than could be had in Spain.

In that river were found some mussels that they gathered to eat, and some pearls. And they were the first these Christians saw in fresh water, although they are to be found in many parts of this land.

Friday, July 9, the commander and his army departed from Coste and crossed the other branch of the river and passed the night on its banks. And on the other side was Tali, and since the river flows near it and is large, they were not able to cross it. And the Indians, believing that they would cross, sent canoes and in them their wives and sons and clothes from the other side, away from the Christians; but they were all taken suddenly, and as they were going with the current, the Governor forced them all to turn back, which was the reason that this chief came in peace and took them across to the other side in his canoes, and gave the Christians what they had need of. And he did this also in his own land as they passed through it afterwards, and they were there Saturday and were given carriers and they set out Sunday and passed the night in the open country.

Monday they crossed a river and slept in the open country. Tuesday they crossed another river and Wednesday another large river and slept at Tasqui. During all the days of their march from Tali the chief of

111

414

Tali had corn and mazamorras[11] and cooked
beans and every thing that could be brought
from his villages bordering the way. Thursday they passed another small village, and then
other villages, and Friday the Governor
entered Coça.[12]

This chief is a powerful one and a ruler
of a wide territory, one of the best and most
abundant that they found in Florida. And
the chief came out to receive the Governor
in a litter covered with the white mantles of
the country, and the litter was borne on the
shoulders of sixty or seventy of his principal
subjects, with no plebeian or common Indian
among them; and those that bore him took
turns by relays with great ceremonies after
their manner.

There were in Coça many plums like the
early ones of Seville, very good; both they and
the trees were like those of Spain. There
were also some wild apples like those called
canavales in Extremadura, small in size.
They remained there in Coça some days, in
which the Indians went off and left their
chief in the power of the Christians with some
principal men, and the Spaniards went out
to round them up, and they took many, and
they put them in iron collars and chains. And

[11] *Cf.* above, p. 107.
[12] Generally placed in Talledega County, Ala.

verily, according to the testimony of eye-wit-
nesses, it was a grievous thing to see. But
God failed not to remember every evil deed,
nor were they left unpunished, as this history
will tell.

On Friday, August 20, the Governor and
his people left Coça, and there stayed behind
a Christian named Feryada, a Levantine; and
they slept the next night beyond Talimachusy,
and the next day in a heavy rain they went to
Itaba, a large village along a fine river, and
there they bought some Indian women, which
were given them in exchange for looking-
glasses and knives.

Monday, August 30, the Governor left
Itaba, and came by nightfall to an oak wood;
and the next day they were at Ulibahali, a
very fine village close to a large river. And
there were many Indians lying in wait for
them planning to rescue the chief of Coça
from the Christians because they were his
subjects, and in order that the land should not
rise in revolt nor refuse them supplies they
took him with them, and they entered the
village very cautiously.

And the chief of Coça ordered the Indians
to lay aside their arms, and it was done; and
they gave them carriers and twenty Indian
women and were peaceful. A gentleman of
Salamanca named Mancano left them there,

113

416

and it was not known whether he did so
of his own will or whether he lost his way,
as he kept by himself walking alone and
melancholy. He had asked the other soldiers
to leave him to himself before they missed
him. This was not known for certain, but
it was reported in the camp after he was
gone. A negro, who spoke Spanish and who
belonged to Captain Johan Ruiz Lobillo, was
also missing.[13] His name was Johan Biscayan. The day that they left this village
they ate many grapes as good as those grown
in the vineyards of Spain. In Coça and further back they had eaten very good ones, but
these of Ulibahali were the best. From this
village of Ulibahali the Spaniards and their
Governor departed on Thursday, September 2, and they passed the night at a small
village near the river, and there they waited
a day for Lobillo, who had gone back without permission to look for his negro. On his
return the Governor rated him soundly. Sunday, they went on and spent the night in the
open country, and the next day, Monday,
they came to Tuasi, where they were given

[13] This negro and one of the other deserters lived
among the Coças ten or twelve years, as the members of a Spanish expedition which came to the
Coça country in 1560 were informed (Lowery,
Spanish Settlements, 365).

114

417

carriers and thirty-two Indian women. Monday, the 13th of September, the Governor departed thence, and they slept in the open country. Tuesday they made another day's march and again spent the night in open country, but Wednesday they came to an old village that had two fences and good towers, and these walls are after this fas.. : They drive many thick stakes tall and straight close to one another. These are then interlaced with long withes, and then overlaid with clay within and without. They make loopholes at intervals and they make their towers and turrets separated by the curtain and parts of the wall as seems best. And at a distance it looks like a fine wall or rampart and such stockades are very strong.

The next day, Thursday, they slept at a new village close by a river, where the Spaniards rested the following day. On the next day, Saturday, they were at Talisi and they found the chief and his people gone. This village is extensive and abounding in corn and near a large river. And there a messenger came to them from Tascaluça, a powerful lord and one much feared in that land. And soon one of his sons appeared and the Governor ordered his men to mount and the horsemen to charge and the trumpets to be blown (more to inspire fear than to make

115

merry at their reception). And when those Indians returned the Commander sent two Christians with them instructed as to what they were to observe and to spy out so that they might take counsel and be fore-warned.

September 25, came the chief of Talisi, and he gave what they asked, such as carriers, women, and supplies; and from that place they sent and released the chief of Coça, so that he might return to his land; and he went in anger and in tears because the Governor would not give up a sister of his that they took, and because they had taken him so far from his country.

Tuesday, October 5, they went on from Talisi and came to Casiste for the night. This was a small village by the river. The next day, Wednesday, they came to Caxa, a wretched village on the river banks on the direct line from Talisi to Tascaluça. And the next day, Thursday, they slept by the river; and on the other side of the stream was a village called Humati; and the next day, Friday, they came to another settlement, a new one named Uxapita; and the next day, Saturday, the force encamped in the open country, a league this side of the village of Tascaluça. And the Governor dispatched a messenger, and he returned with the reply that

116

he would be welcome whenever he wished to come.

The historian asked a very intelligent gentleman who was with this Governor, and who went with him through his whole expedition in this northern country, why, at every place they came to, this Governor and his army asked for those tamemes or Indian carriers, and why they took so many women and these not old nor the most ugly; and why, after having given them what they had, they held the chiefs and principal men; and why they never tarried nor settled in any region they came to, adding that such a course was not settlement or conquest, but rather disturbing and ravaging the land and depriving the natives of their liberty without converting or making a single Indian either a Christian or a friend. He replied and said: That they took these carriers or tamemes to keep them as slaves or servants to carry the loads of supplies which they secured by plunder or gift, and that some died, and others ran away or were tired out, so that it was necessary to replenish their numbers and to take more; and the women they desired both as servants and for their foul uses and lewdness, and that they had them baptized more on account of carnal intercourse with them than to teach them the faith; and that if they held the

117

chiefs and principal men captive, it was because it would keep their subjects quiet, so that they would not molest them when foraging or doing what they wished in their country; and that whither they were going neither the Governor nor the others knew, but that his purpose was to find some land rich enough to satiate his greed and to get knowledge of the great secrets this Governor said he had heard in regard to those regions according to much information he had received;[14] and as for stirring up the country and not settling it, nothing else could be done until they found a site that was satisfactory.

Oh, wicked men! Oh, devilish greed! Oh, bad consciences! Oh, unfortunate soldiers! that ye should not have understood the perils ye were to encounter, and how wasted would be your lives, and without rest your souls! That ye were not mindful of that truth which the blessed St. Augustine uttered in lamenting the miseries of this life, saying, this life is a life of misery, frail, and uncertain, full of toil and stain; a life, Lord, of ills, a kingdom of pride, full of miseries and terror, since it is not really life, nor can be called so, but rather death, for in a moment it is ended by various changes of fortune and

[14]*E. g.,* from Cabeça de Vaca. See Vol. I. p. 5.

118

divers kinds of deaths! Give ear, then, Catholic reader, and do not lament the conquered Indians less than their Christian conquerors or slayers of themselves, as well as others, and follow the adventures of this Governor, ill governed, taught in the School of Pedrarias de Avila, in the scattering and wasting of the Indians of Castilla del Oro; a graduate in the killing of the natives of Nicaragua and canonized in Peru as a member of the order of the Pizarros; and then, after being delivered from all those paths of Hell and having come to Spain loaded with gold, neither a bachelor nor married, knew not how nor was able to rest without returning to the Indies to shed human blood, not content with what he had spilled; and to leave life as shall be narrated, and providing the opportunity for so many sinners deluded with his vain words to perish after him. See what he wanted most of what that queen or woman chief of Cofitachequi, lady of Talimeco, offered him when she told him that in that place of hers he would find so many pearls that all the horses in the army could not carry them off; and, when she received him so courteously, see how he treated her. Let us proceed, and forget not this truth which you have read, how as a proof of the number of pearls which were offered him, this Governor and his

119

422

people took over two hundred pounds, and you will know what enjoyment they got out of them in the sequel.

CHAPTER VII

In which is related what happened to the Commander Hernando de Soto, in his intercourse with the Chief of Tascaluça named Actahachi, who was such a tall Man that he seemed a Giant; and also of the Skirmishes and tough Battles, and the Assault made upon the Christians in the Village called Mabila and further on in Chicaca. And other Incidents noteworthy and appropriate to the History narrated in this Chapter.

Sunday, October 10, the Governor entered the village of Tascaluça, which is called Athahachi, a recent village. And the chief was on a kind of balcony on a mound at one side of the square, his head covered by a kind of coif like the almaizal, so that his head-dress was like a Moor's which gave him an aspect of authority; he also wore a *pelote* or mantle of feathers down to his feet, very imposing; he was seated on some high cushions, and many of the principal men among his Indians were with him. He was as tall as that Tony of the Emperor, our lord's guard, and well proportioned, a fine and

120

comely figure of a man. He had a son, a
young man as tall as himself but more slender.
Before this chief there stood always an Indian
of graceful mien holding a parasol on a handle
something like a round and very large fly
fan, with a cross similar to that of the Knights
of the Order of St. John of Rhodes, in the
middle of a black field, and the cross was
white. And although the Governor entered
the plaza and alighted from his horse and went
up to him, he did not rise, but remained
passive in perfect composure and as if he had
been a king.

The Governor remained seated with him a
short time, and after a little he arose and said
that they should come to eat, and he took him
with him and the Indians came to dance; and
they danced very well in the fashion of rustics
in Spain, so that it was pleasant to see them.
At night he desired to go, and the commander
told him that he must sleep there. He understood it and showed that he scoffed at such
an intention for him, being the lord, to receive
so suddenly restraints upon his liberty, and
dissembling, he immediately despatched his
principal men each by himself, and he slept
there notwithstanding his reluctance. The
next day the Governor asked him for carriers
and a hundred Indian women; and the chief
gave him four hundred carriers and the rest

121

424

of them and the women he said he would give at Mabila, the province of one of his principal vassals. And the Governor acquiesced in having the rest of that unjust request of his fulfilled in Mabila; and he ordered him to be given a horse and some buskins and a scarlet cloak for him to ride off happy. And now that the chief had given him four hundred carriers. or rather slaves, and was to give him in Mabila a hundred women, and what they were most in need of, see how happy he could be made with those buskins and the cloak and with riding on a horse when he felt as if he were mounted on a tiger or a most savage lion, since this people held horses in the greatest terror!

At last, Tuesday, October 12, they departed from that village of Atahachi, taking along the chief as has been said and with him many principal men and always the Indian with the sunshade attending his lord, and another with a cushion. And that night they slept in the open country. The next day, Wednesday, they came to Piachi, which is a village high above the gorge of a mountain stream; and the chief of this place was evil intentioned, and attempted to resist their passage; and as a result, they crossed the stream with effort, and two Christians were slain, and also the principal Indians who

122

425

accompanied the chief. In this village, Piachi, it was learned that they had killed Don Teodoro and a black, who came from the ships of Pamphilo de Narvaez.

Saturday, October 16, they departed thence into a mountain where they met one of the two Christians whom the Governor had sent to Mabila, and he said that in Mabila there had gathered together much people in arms. The next day they came to a fenced village, and there came messengers from Mabila bringing to the chief much bread made from chestnuts, which are abundant and excellent in that region.

Monday, October 18, St. Luke's day, the Governor came to Mabila,[1] having passed that day by several villages, which was the reason that the soldiers stayed behind to forage and to scatter themselves, for the region appeared populous. And there went on with the Governor only forty horsemen as an advance guard, and after they had tarried a little, that the Governor might not show weakness, he entered into the village with the chief, and all his guard went in with him. Here the Indians immediately began an areyto,[2] which is their fashion for a ball with dancing and

[1] Placed somewhat above the head of Mobile Bay. Cf. Lowery (Spanish Settlements, 233).
[2] A West Indian word for an Indian dance.

123

song. While this was going on some soldiers saw them putting bundles of bows and arrows slyly among some palm leaves, and other Christians saw that above and below [3] the cabins were full of people concealed. The Governor was informed of it and he put his helmet on his head and ordered all to go and mount their horses and warn all the soldiers that had come up. Hardly had they gone out when the Indians took the entrances of stockade, and there were left with the Governor, Luis de Moscoso and Baltasar de Gallegos, and Espindola, the Captain of the Guard, and seven or eight soldiers. And the chief went into a cabin and refused to come out of it. Then they began to shoot arrows at the Governor. Baltasar de Gallegos went in for the chief, he not being willing to come out. He disabled the arm of a principal Indian with the slash of a knife. Luis de Moscoso waited at the door, so as not to leave him alone, and he was fighting like a knight and did all that was possible until, not being able to endure any more, he cried: " Señor Baltasar de Gallegos, come out, or I will leave you, for I cannot wait any longer for you." During this, Solis, a resident of Triana of

[3] See Bartram's *Travels*, 189-90, for a description of the cabins of the Alachua Indians, which had an open loft at one end.

124

Seville, had ridden up, and Rodrigo Ranjel, who were the first, and for his sins Solis was immediately stricken down dead; but Rodrigo Ranjel got to the gate of the town at the time when the Governor went out, and two soldiers of his guard with him, and after him came more than seventy Indians who were held back for fear of Rodrigo Ranjel's horse, and the Governor, desiring to charge them, a negro brought up his horse; and he told Rodrigo Ranjel to give aid to the Captain of the Guard, who was left behind, for he had come out quite used up, and a soldier of the Guard with him; and he with a horse faced the enemy until he got out of danger, and Rodrigo Ranjel returned to the Governor and had him draw out more than twenty arrows which he bore fastened in his armour, which was a loose coat quilted with coarse cotton. And he ordered Ranjel to watch for Solis, to rescue him from the enemy that they should not carry him inside. And the Governor went to collect the soldiers. There was great valour and shame that day among all those that found themselves in this first attack and beginning of this unhappy day; for they fought to admiration and each Christian did his duty as a most valiant soldier. Luis de Moscoso and Baltasar de Gallegos came out with the rest of the soldiers by another gate.

125

As a result, the Indians were left with the village and all the property of the Christians, and with the horses that were left tied inside, which they killed immediately. The Governor collected all of the forty horse that were there and advanced to a large open place before the principal gate of Mabila. There the Indians rushed out without venturing very far from the stockade, and to draw them on the horsemen made a feint of taking flight at a gallop, withdrawing far from the walls. And the Indians believing it to be real, came away from the village and the stockade in pursuit, greedy to make use of their arrows. And when it was time the horsemen wheeled about on the enemy, and before they could recover themselves, killed many with their lances. Don Carlos wanted to go with his horse as far as the gate, and they gave the horse an arrow shot in the breast. And not being able to turn, he dismounted to draw out the arrow, and then another came which hit him in the neck above the shoulder, at which, seeking confession, he fell dead. The Indians no longer dared to withdraw from the stockade. Then the Commander invested them on every side until the whole force had come up; and they went up on three sides to set fire to it, first cutting the stockade with axes. And the fire in its course burned the

126

429

two hundred odd pounds of pearls that they had, and all their clothes and ornaments, and the sacramental cups, and the moulds for making the wafers, and the wine for saying the mass; and they were left like Arabs, completely stripped, after all their hard toil. They had left in a cabin the Christian women, which were some slaves belonging to the Governor; and some pages, a friar, a priest, a cook, and some soldiers defended themselves very well against the Indians, who were not able to force an entrance before the Christians came with the fire and rescued them. And all the Spaniards fought like men of great courage, and twenty-two died, and one hundred and forty-eight others received six hundred and eighty-eight arrow wounds, and seven horses were killed and twenty-nine others wounded. Women and even boys of four years of age fought with the Christians; and Indian boys hanged themselves not to fall into their hands, and others jumped into the fire of their own accord. See with what good will those carriers acted. The arrow shots were tremendous, and sent with such a will and force that the lance of one gentleman named Nuño de Tovar, made of two pieces of ash and very good, was pierced by an arrow in the middle, as by an auger, without being split, and the arrow made a cross with the lance.

127

On that day there died Don Carlos, and Francis de Soto, the nephew of the Governor, and Johan de Gamez de Jaen, and Men Rodriguez, a fine Portugues gentleman, and Espinosa, a fine gentleman, and another named Velez, and one Blasco de Barcarrota, and many other honoured soldiers; and the wounded comprised all the men of most worth and honour in the army. They killed three thousand of the vagabonds without counting many others who were wounded and whom they afterwards found dead in the cabins and along the roads. Whether the chief was dead or alive was never known. The son they found thrust through with a lance.

After the end of the battle as described, they rested there until the 14th of November, caring for their wounds and their horses, and they burned over much of the country. And up to the time when they left there, the total deaths from the time the Governor and his forces entered the land of Florida, were one hundred and two Christians, and not all, to my thinking, in true repentance.

Sunday, November 14, of the year already mentioned, the Governor left Mabila, and the Wednesday following came to a fine river. Thursday, the 28th,[4] their way lay over bad places and through swamps, and they

[4] This should be the 18th.

found a village with corn which was named Talicpacana. The Christians had discovered on the other side of the river a village which appeared to them from a distance to be finely situated.

On Sunday, the 21st of November, Vasco Gonçalez found a village half a league distant from this named Moçulixa, from which they had transported all the corn to the other side of the river and had piled it in heaps covered with mats; and the Indians were across the river, and were making threats. A barge was constructed which was finished the 29th of the month, and they made a large truck to carry it to Moçulixa; and when it was launched in the water sixty soldiers embarked in it. The Indians shot countless darts, or rather arrows. But when this great canoe reached the shore they took flight, and not more than three or four Christians were wounded. The country was easily secured, and they found an abundance of corn.

The next day, Wednesday, the whole force came to a village which was called Zabusta, and there they crossed the river in the boat and with some canoes that they had found in that place; and they tarried for the night in another village on the other side, because up above they found a fine one, and took the chief, whose name was Apafalaya, and carried

129

432

him along as guide and interpreter; and this
stream was called the river Apafalaya. From
this river and town the Governor and his
army set out in search of Chicaça on Thursday, December 9. The following Tuesday
they arrived at the river of Chicaça, having
traversed many bad passages and swamps and
cold rivers.

And that you may know, reader, what sort
of a life these Spaniards led, Rodrigo Ranjel,
an eye-witness, says that among many other
great hardships that men endured in this undertaking he saw a knight named Don Antonio
Osorio, brother of the Lord Marquis of
Astorga, wearing a short garment of the
blankets of that country, torn on the sides,
his flesh showing, no hat, bare-headed, bare-
footed, without hose or shoes, a buckler on his
back, a sword without a shield, amidst heavy
frosts and cold. And the stuff of which he
was made and his illustrious lineage made him
endure his toil without laments such as many
others made, for there was no one who could
help him, although he was the man he was,
and had in Spain two thousand ducats of income through the Church. And the day that
this gentleman saw him he did not believe that
he had eaten a mouthful, and he had to dig for
it with his nails to get something to eat.

I could hardly help laughing when I heard

130

that this knight had left the Church and the
income above mentioned to go in search of
such a life as this, at the sound of the words
of De Soto; because I knew Soto very well,
and, although he was a man of worth, I did
not suppose that he was so winning a talker
or so clever, as to be able to delude such persons. What was it that a man like him[5]
wanted of a land unexplored and unknown?
Nor did the Captain that took him know anything more than that in this land had perished
Johan Ponce de Leon and the lawyer Lucas
Vazquez de Allyón and Pamphilo de Narvaez
and others abler than Hernando de Soto.
And those that follow such guides have to go
in that manner,[6] since they found regions
where they were able to make a settlement
and rest and gradually push in and make their
inferences and learn the country. But let
us proceed, for the toil of this knight is little
compared with those that are dying and
escape.[7]

The river of Chicaça they found overflowing
its bed, and the Indians on the other side in
arms with many white flags. Orders were

[5] *I. e.*, Osorio.
[6] There seems to be an ellipsis of something like
this: but it need not have been so with a different
leader since, etc.
[7] À respecto de los que mueren, sino se salvan.

131

434

given to make a barge, and the Governor sent
Baltasar de Gallegos with thirty horsemen,
swimmers, to search the river up above for a
good crossing place, and to fall suddenly upon
the Indians; and it was perceived, and they
forsook the passage and they crossed over very
comfortably in the barge on Thursday, the
16th of the month. And the Governor went
on ahead with some horsemen, and they arrived
late at night at a village of the lord which
had been deserted by all the people. The
next day Baltasar de Gallegos appeared with
the thirty that went with him, and they spent
that Christmas in Chicaça,[8] and there was a
snowstorm with a heavy fall of snow, just
as if they had been in Burgos, and the cold
was as severe, or more so. On Monday,
January 3, 1541, the chief of Chicaça came
proffering peace, and promptly gave the
Christians guides and interpreters to go to
Caluça, a place of much repute among the
Indians. Caluça is a province of more than
ninety villages not subject to any one, with
a savage population, very warlike and much
dreaded, and the soil is fertile in that section.
In Chicaça the Governor ordered that half
of his army make war on Sacchuma; and on
their return the Chief Miculasa made peace,

[8] In Mississippi, near the headwaters of the Yazoo
and Tombigbee rivers. *Cf.* Lowery, 236.

and messengers came from Talapatica. In the meantime, while this war was going on, the time came to march, and they asked the chief for carriers; and the Indians raised such a tumult among themselves that the Christians understood it; and the settlement was that they would give them on the 4th of March, when they had to start, and that on that day they would come with them. On the evening of that day the Governor mounted his horse and found the Indians evilly disposed, and realizing their dangerous intentions he returned to the camp and said in public: "To-night is an Indian night. I shall sleep armed and my horse saddled." And they all said that they would do the same, and he called the Master of the Camp, who was Luis de Moscoso, and told him that they should take extra precautions that night in regard to the sentinels, since it was the last. The Governor as he went away from where he left those soldiers to whom he had given these warnings, lay down undressed on his couch, and neither was his horse saddled nor any other, and all those in the camp lay down to sleep without precautions and unarmed. The Master of the Camp put on the morning watch three horsemen, the most useless and with the poorest horses in the army. And on the day before mentioned, the 4th of March,

133

when the Indian carriers had been promised
them, at dawn, the Indians, fulfilling their
word, entered the camp in many detachments,
beating drums as if it had been in Italy, and
setting fire to the camp, they burned and captured fifty-nine horses, and three of them they
shot through both shoulders with arrows.

And the Christians were like heedless people
on this occasion; and few arms, coats-of-mail,
lances and saddles remained after the fire; and
all the horses had run off, escaping the fire
and the noise. Only the commander was able
to mount his horse, and they did not fasten
the horse's girth, nor did he buckle his coat of
arms, and Tapia de Valladolid was with him;
and he fell over the first Indian that he thrust
at who had thrust at him, saddle and all,[9] and
if the Indians had known how to follow up
their victory, this would have been the last
day of the lives of all the Christians of that
army, and made an end of the demand for
carriers.[10]

Next the Spaniards went to a plain, a league
from that village where they were; and they
had cabins and supplies, and they set up the

[9] Garcilaso characteristically makes De Soto fight
an hour with the saddle girth unfastened! (*La
Florida*, 167.)

[10] See below, p. 153, for Alonso de Carmona's account of another narrow escape the Spaniards had
three days later.

134

camp on a sloping hillside. And they made haste to set up a forge, and they made bellows of bear skins, and they retempered their arms, and made new frames for their saddles, and they provided themselves with lances for there were in that place very good ash-trees. And within a week they had everything repaired. There were slain in Chicaça and burned alive twelve Christians.

Tuesday, March 15, the morning watch, the Indians returned upon the Christians, determined to finish them up, and attacked them on three sides; and as necessity had made them cautious, and, as they were informed and on the watch, they fought with them bravely and put the Indians to flight. And it pleased God that the Christians should not suffer much loss, and few Indians perished. Some Spaniards displayed great valour that day, and no one failed to do his duty. And unfortunate was he on that occasion who did not well defend his life and who failed to prove to the enemy the quality and arms of the Christians.

135

CHAPTER VIII

IN WHICH THE HISTORY NARRATES ANOTHER EN-
COUNTER AT A BARRICADE, IN WHICH THE COM-
MANDER FOUGHT WITH THE INDIANS; AND HOW
HE CAME TO A VERY LARGE RIVER WHICH THE
CHRISTIANS CROSSED; AND OF THE NARRATION
AND DISCOURSE WHICH THE CHIEF OF CASQUI
DELIVERED IN FAVOUR OF THE CROSS AND THE
FAITH IN THE PRESENCE OF THE COMMANDER AND
THE CHRISTIANS; AND OF THE CONTENTION OF
THIS CHIEF WITH ANOTHER, HIS ENEMY, NAMED
PACAHA, AS TO WHICH OUGHT TO HAVE PRECE-
DENCE. THEIR DEPARTURE FROM UTIANGÜE, AND
MANY OTHER NOTABLE INCIDENTS.

TUESDAY, April 26, in the year aforesaid,
1541, the Governor Hernando de Soto set
out from the plain of Chicaça, and arrived at
Limamu for the night; and there they searched
for corn, because the Indians had hidden it,
and they had to pass over a desert. And
Thursday they came to another plain where
the Indians had taken the position, having
made a very strong barricade, and within it
there were many Indian braves, painted red
and decorated with other colours which appeared very fine (or rather, very bad, at least
it meant harm to the Christians). And they
entered the barricade by force, and with some
loss by death and wounds on the part of the
Commander and his army, and with a loss

136

greater beyond comparison on the part of the conquered; and it would have been still more if the Indians had not taken flight.

Saturday, the last of April, the army set out from the place of the barricade and marched nine days through a deserted country and by a rough way, mountainous and swampy, until May 8, when they came to the first village of Quizqui, which they took by assault and captured much people and clothes; but the Governor promptly restored them to liberty and had everything restored to them for fear of war, although that was not enough to make friends of these Indians. A league beyond this village they came upon another with abundance of corn, and soon again after another league, upon another likewise amply provisioned. There they saw the great river.[1] Saturday, May 21, the force went along to a plain between the river and a small village, and set up quarters and began to build four barges to cross over to the other side. Many of these conquerors said this river was larger than the Danube.

On the other side of the river, about seven thousand Indians had got together, with about two hundred canoes, to defend the passage. All of them had shields made of canes joined, so strong and so closely inter-

[1] The Mississippi.

137

woven with such thread that a cross-bow could hardly pierce them. The arrows came raining down so that the air was full of them, and their yells were something fearful. But when they saw that the work on the barges did not relax on their account, they said that Pacaha, whose men they were, ordered them to withdraw, and so they left the passage free. And on Saturday, June 8,[2] the whole force crossed this great river in the four barges and gave thanks to God because in His good pleasure nothing more difficult could confront them.[3] Soon, on Sunday, they came to a village of Aquixo.

Tuesday, June 21, they went from there and passed by the settlement of Aquixo, which is very beautiful, or beautifully situated. The next day, Wednesday, they passed through the worst tract for swamps and water that they had found in all Florida, and on that day the toil of the soldiers was very heavy.

The next day following, Thursday, they entered the land of Quarqui, and passed through small villages; and the next day, Friday, St. John's day, they came to the village of the Lord of Casqui, who gave food and clothing to the army. It was Saturday when

[2] This should be June 18.
[3] The crossing is supposed to have taken place below Memphis and above the mouth of the Arkansas.

138

they entered his village, and it had very good cabins, and, in the principal one, over the door, were many heads of very fierce bulls, just as in Spain, noblemen who are sportsmen mount the heads of wild boars or bears. There the Christians planted the cross on a mound, and they received it and adored it with much devotion, and the blind and lame came to seek to be healed. Their faith, says Rodrigo Ranjel, would have surpassed that of the conquerors if they had been taught, and would have brought forth more fruit than those conquerors did.

Sunday, June 26, they departed thence to go to Pacaha, an enemy of Casqui; and after passing several villages, they spent the night in one. And the following day they crossed a swamp over which the Indians had thrown a well-constructed bridge, broad and very cleverly built. On Wednesday they came to the village of Pacaha, a village and lord of wide repute and highly thought of in that country.

This town was a very good one, thoroughly well stockaded; and the walls were furnished with towers and a ditch round about, for the most part full of water which flows in by a canal from the river; and this ditch was full of excellent fish of divers kinds. The chief of Casqui came to the Christians when they

139

442

were entering the village and they entertained him bravely. In Aquixo, and Casqui, and Pacaha, they saw the best villages seen up to that time, better stockaded and fortified, and the people were of finer quality, excepting those of Cofitachequi. The Commander and his soldiers remaining some days in Pacaha, they made some incursions further up country.

And the chief of Casqui, on one occasion, when he saw a chance for it, went off without seeking permission, on account of which the Governor tried to secure peace with Pacaha; and he came to the camp to recover a brother of his whom the Christians had taken when they entered the village; and an agreement was made with Pacaha that they should war against Casqui, which was very gratifying to Pacaha. But Casqui got wind of this resolve and came with fifty Indians of his in fine array, and he brought a clown for display, who said and did much that was amusing, making those who saw him laugh a good deal. The Governor assumed an air of irritation and sternness to please Pacaha, and sent word that Casqui should not come into the village. Casqui replied that he would not refrain from coming even if they cut off his head. Pacaha asked the Governor to allow him to give Casqui a slash in the face with a knife that he had in his hand, which the Christians had

140

given him. But the Governor told Pacaha
that he should do no such thing, nor do him
any harm, for he would be angry at him; and
he ordered Casqui to come so as to see what
he wanted, and because he wished to ask him
the reason why he had gone without his permission. Casqui came and spoke to the Governor as follows:—as it was reported by the
interpreter Johan Ortiz and the other Indian
interpreters that the Governor and the Christians had—"How is it, my Lord, possible,
that after having given me the pledge of
friendship, and without my having done any
harm to you, or given any occasion, you desire
to destroy me, your friend and brother? You
gave me the cross for a defence against my
enemies, and with it you seek to destroy me."
(This he said because the Indians of Pacaha,
his enemy, that went with the Christians,
against him, wore crosses on their heads,
high up, that they might be seen.) "Now,
my Lord," said Casqui, "when God has
heard us by means of the cross; when the
women and boys and all those of my country
threw themselves on their knees before it to
pray for water to the God who you said suffered on it; and He heard us and gave us
water in great abundance and refreshed our
corn-fields and plantations; now, when we
had the most faith in it and in your friend-

141

ship, you desired to destroy these boys and
women that are so devoted to you and your
God. Why did you desire to use us with
such cruelty without our deserving it from
you? Why did you desire to destroy the
faith and confidence which we had in
you? Why did you desire to offend your
God and us, when for Him, and in His name,
you gave us assurances and received us for
friends, and we gave you entire confidence
and trust in the same God and His cross, and
have it for our safeguard and protection, and
hold it in the reverence and veneration which
is proper? With what object or purpose
were you actuated to do, or even to think of
a thing so grievous against a people without
blame, and friends of the cross and of yours?"

This said, he held his peace. The Governor, his eyes melting and not without trace
of tears, considering the faith and words of
this chief, replied to him, through the interpreters, in the presence of many of the Christian soldiers, who, attentively, and not without tears, overcome by such goodness and
faith, had heard what was said, and spoke as
follows: "Look you, Casqui, we are not
come to destroy you, but to do for you what
you know and understand is the work of the
cross and our God, as you tell me. And these
favours, which it has bestowed upon you, are

142

445

a small thing in comparison with many others
and very great ones, which it will secure you
if you love it and believe in it. Be assured
of this, and you will find it so and realize it
better every day. And when you ran off
without my permission I thought that you held
the teaching we had given you of little account, and for that contempt that you had
for it I wanted to destroy you; supposing
that in pride you had gone off, for that is the
thing which our God most abhors, and for
which He punishes us the most. Now that
you have come in humility, be assured that I
wish you more good than you think; and if
you have need of anything from me, tell me
of it and you will see, since we do what our
God commands us, which is not to lie; and,
therefore, believe that I tell you the truth,
since to speak a lie is a very great sin amongst
us. For this good-will be not grateful to me
or mine, since if you hold what you say, God,
our Lord, commands that we love you as a
brother, and that we treat you as such because you and yours are our brethren, and
such is the injunction of our God."

The Indians, as much as the Christians,
had heard with ·wonder what Casqui had
said. It was now the hour for dinner and
the commander sat down and ordered both
chiefs to be seated. And between them there

143

446

was much contention, as to which of them should sit on the right hand of the Governor. Pacaha said to Casqui: "You know well that I am a greater lord than you, and of more honourable parents and grandparents, and that to me belongs a higher place." Casqui replied as follows: "True it is that you are a greater lord than I, and that your forbears were greater than mine. And since this great lord here tells us that we must not lie, I will not deny the truth. But you know well that I am older and mightier than you, and that I confine you in your walls whenever I wish, and you never have seen my country." Finally this was left to the Governor to settle and he ordered that Pacaha should be seated on his right hand because he was a greater lord and more ancient in rank, and he showed in his good customs more of the manners of the courtier after their fashion.

Casqui had brought a daughter, a fine young girl, to the Governor. Pacaha gave him one of his wives, blooming, and very worthy; and he gave him a sister and another Indian woman of rank. The Governor made them friends and embraced them and ordered that there should be merchandising and business between one country and the other, and they agreed to it. And after this the Governor departed thence the 29th of July.

144

But I could wish that along with the ex-
cellencies of the cross and of the faith that
this Governor explained to these chiefs, he
had told them that he was married, and that
the Christians ought not to have more than
one wife, or to have intercourse with another,
or to commit adultery; that he had not taken
the daughter whom Casqui gave him, nor the
wife and sister and the other woman of rank
whom Pacaha gave him; and that they had
not got the idea that the Christians, like the
Indians, could have as many wives and concu-
bines as they desired, and thus, like the Indians,
live as adulterers.

Let us pass on. To my thinking it would
have been better after baptizing a chief of so
much intelligence as Casqui, and making him
and his people Christians, to have remained
there, than to go on to what the history will
relate. Nor do I approve of their having gone
further than to Cofitachequi, for the same
reason, and on account of what was said of
that land. However, this army and its Governor having departed, they came by nightfall
to a village of Casqui. And the next day to
the principal village of the same lord of
Casqui, which they had already passed. And
they departed from there Sunday, the last day
of that month and came to a village of that
province. And Monday, August 1, they came

145

to another village, which is on the river of Casqui, which is a branch of the great river of Pacaha, and this branch is as large as the Guadalquivir. Thither came Casqui and assisted them across the river in canoes, August 2.

On Wednesday, they slept in a burned village. The next day, Thursday, in another near the river, where there were many pumpkins and an abundance of corn, and beans. And the next day, Friday, they came to Quiguate, which is the largest village which they saw in that country, situated on the river of Casqui; and it was later known that the banks of this river were thickly populated further down (although they did not find it out there) and along it they took the trail of Coligua which was not peopled in the intervening country.

Friday, August 26, they left Quiguate in search of Coligua and passed the night by a swamp, and from swamp to swamp they made a journey over four swamps and days' marches; and in these swamps, or pools, there was no end of fish, because all that country is flooded by the great river when it overflows its banks. And, Tuesday, they came to the river of Coligua, and, Wednesday, likewise, to the same river. And the next day, Thursday, September 1, to the town of Coligua; and

146

449

they found it populated, and from it they took much people and clothes, and a vast amount of provisions and much salt. It was a pretty village, between some ridges along the gorge of a great river. And from there, at midday, they went to kill some cows, of which there are very many wild ones.

Tuesday, the 6th of September, they left Coligua and crossed the river again, and Wednesday they passed some mountains and came to Calpista, where there was an excellent salt spring which distilled very good salt in deposits. The Thursday following they came to Palisma, and on Saturday, September 10, they went on to encamp by a water; and Sunday they came to Quixila, where they rested over Monday. Tuesday they went on to Tutilcoya, and Wednesday, to a village along a large river. And Thursday they encamped near a swamp. And the Governor went on ahead with some horsemen, and came to Tanico, and the next day they came to the same settlement of Tanico, which was built in a somewhat scattered fashion, but was very abundantly provided with supplies. Some would have it that it was Cayase, of which they had heard much, a large stockaded town, but they were never able to see that place or discover it; and subsequently they were told that they had left it near the river.

147

From there the Governor, with thirteen horsemen and fifty foot, went on to see Tula, and he returned from there in a hurry, and the Indians killed one horse and wounded four or five, and he resolved to go there with the army. One ought not to omit and leave in forgetfulness that in Cayase our Spaniards gathered baskets of dry sand from the river and strained water through it, and there came out a brine, and they boiled it down, and let it harden, and in that way made excellent salt, very white and of very good flavour.

Wednesday, October 5, they departed from the station of Tanico, and came, Friday, to Tula, and found the inhabitants gone, but abundant provisions. On Saturday, in the morning, the Indians came to give them a brush, or a battle, and they had large, long poles, like lances, the ends hardened by fire, and they were the best fighting people that the Christians met with, and they fought like desperate men, with the greatest valour in the world. That day they wounded Hernandarias, the grandson of the marshal of Seville, and, thank God, the Christians defended themselves so valiantly that they did not receive much damage, although the Indians tried to round up the whole force.

Wednesday, October 19, the army and the Governor departed from Tula, and passed the

148

night at two cabins. And the next day, Thursday, at another cabin, and Friday, at another, where Hernandarias de Saavedra, who had been wounded at Tula, died in convulsions; and he died like a Catholic knight, commending his soul to God. The next day they came to Guipana, which is between ridges of mountains near a river; and from there they went for the night to a place where they could cross over, and all the country was mountainous from Tula. The next day they left the mountain and came on to the plains and Monday the last day of the month, they came to a village called Quitamaya, and Tuesday, the 1st of November, they went through a small village; and Wednesday, the 2d. of November, they came to Utiangüe, which was a plain well peopled and of attractive appearance.[8] .   .   .   .

[8] The manuscript of Book XVII. of Oviedo's *Historia General y Natural de las Indias* breaks off at this point, leaving the chapter unfinished.

149

THE CAÑETE FRAGMENT:
ANOTHER NARRATIVE OF HERNANDO DE SOTO

Eugene Lyon, Editor and Translator

St. Augustine Foundation
St. Augustine, Florida

1982

On Tuesday, August 14, 1565, in San Juan, Puerto Rico, one Rodrigo Ramirez, notary public, copied the Royal contract of Pedro Menéndez de Avilés. Menéndez, just named Adelantado of Florida and on his journey to its conquest, had come to San Juan on his voyage from Spain, and had some need for another copy of his contract. The legajo, or document bundle, of Seville's Archive of the Indies in which this document appears, and the particular piece in which it is found, seem to have been a depository for miscellany about Pedro Menéndez and the Florida conquest, ranging in date from 1565 to 1580.

Ramirez wrote across the bottom of the last sheet of the contract copy the following words:

There is in most parts of Florida much worked copper as in thin sheets (hoja de Milán); there are in the inland mountains great veins of silver, of very rich metal. Those who entered from Mexico by Copala toward Florida discovered great things, and found a place of more than twenty thousand citizens, and strong and high houses of seven floors and very strong walls. They found dies where they worked silver and many jewels of it and of gold; they had notice of kings crowned with golden crowns, far inland. . .

He added that this information had been gathered for the Spaniards in Menéndez' entourage, but "without hope of it."[1] There then follows the one-page Cañete fragment of a larger narrative about the journeys of Hernando de Soto, and several pages about the discoveries of Miguel de Legazpi in the Philippines. It can only be assumed that Pedro Menéndez de Avilés and his followers sought, as they prepared for their landing in Florida, to utilize past knowledge of the continent; it can further be assumed that Ramirez, or Menéndez, had access to the full Cañete narrative at the time when he was copying materials at San Juan.

RELATION OF FRAY SEBASTIAN DE CAÑETE

Some of the things which are contained in the relation which Fray Sebastián de Cañete and the Captain gave, of the things they saw in Florida, going with Soto. In the province of Mocozo they found a Spaniard who was fourteen years among (the) Indians, and he had forgotten his (own) language. He had gone in search of Narváez. The lord of the province of Tascaluco was as large as a Spaniard mounted on a horse. The Adelantado Soto died in the River of the Holy Spirit in the province of Guachoya.

The clothing which the Indians ordinarily wear are blankets of mulberry-roots and of marten, very fine, and this in most parts; and hides of bears, wolves, lions, tigers, and of cows (probably buffalo: translator) near the plains. In all parts they found an abundance of food of the land, (such) as corn, beans and squash----infinite fruits of the land of those of Spain; there were four kinds of nuts---hazel-nuts and chestnuts; in all the land a great quantity of grapes, and in some parts muscatel grapes, as sweet and flavorful as those of Spain. There are many acorns, and of this they make butter, and of nuts. (There is a) great quantity of woods and greater of

---

[1] From Archivo General de Indias Patronato Real 19, No. 1, No. 15.

plums, very good, and from them they make loaves like quince-sweet (carne de membrillo), and in most parts of all Florida they found much gold which the Indian men and women have and they offered it to the Spaniards.

There are not a number of pearls, because (he found? word partly destroyed at page margin) in the house of an idol they called El Cu in Cofitachiqui, they found more than 12 horse-loads of pearls, and the caciques of that town who were embalmed in El Cu, they had great sacks of pearls at the neck. They found much worked copper like fine sheets (hola de millión--sic--hoja de Milán).

The people are very bright and well-featured and of acute judgement in the places that they are accustomed (word off page end)....

They not only gave what was necessary to wear and eat for the men but to the horses they gave feather blankets, and in the houses there is variety, according to the regions; in some parts toward the mountains there are houses with stoves (estufas; sweat-houses?), and in other parts they are of flat roofs as in Andalusia. There are elevated (álzados? the word is on a page edge and partly torn) places, and very great, and in Tanlo_rado (partly torn?) one hundred; (in?) the province of Coza they travelled along the banks of a river four leagues through populated areas. (The) arms they ordinarily carry are (bows and) arrows, wooden clubs (macanas, here spelled machanas), and they are so skilled and spirited that in a skirmish which Soto had in Macula where they killed twenty-five soldiers of his, was an Indian who went looking for the most valiant and best armed Spaniard in order to kill himself with him. In Chicaza they came by night upon the Spaniards and took from them whatever they had, with the pearls.

In Cofitachiqui and in other places there were raisins from grapes and mulberries, of which there is a great quantity in all Florida. There are some plains in a certain part which extend more than three hundred leagues, all filled with small cows (vacas pequeñas--probably buffalo) of very good meat, and there is trade in the hides inland. In all parts there are many turkeys (gallinal de papada--literally chickens with dewlap), deer, hares, rabbits, an infinite number of partridge, turtle-doves (passenger-pigeons?), and many other kinds of very good birds. There are many squirrels, bears, lions, tigers (panther?); in all the rivers many fish and shellfish, mainly flounder (catfish?). There are wild-olive trees with fruit, liquidambar trees, chinilla (china? a species of sarsaparilla); sumac to tan the hides (cortir--sic--curtir), even though they do not tan the deer hides with it, of which there are a great number in all the land. They greatly abominate those who lie and steal and married women who are bad. When they marry, they go to the house of the maiden's parents--he who wishes to marry with her--and says that they shall gather together, her relatives, that he wishes to talk to them. Being gathered together and the marriage being carried out, they all give her to him. If, afterwards, she is an adulteress, they return her, the same relatives of the husband, and having gathered her relatives together, the husband says to them "You gave me this woman as good, and she is bad, and all of you as well; therefore (word off page) beware, patience; you all have to pay," and beginning with the adulteress, they kill them all. There is in everything much justice and reason, as in Spain....

*****

Examination of the text of Cañete fragment and comparison of its contents with the texts of the four major Soto narratives: (Hernando Luis de Biedma, Rodrigo Ranjel, the "Gentleman of Elvas," and Garcilaso de la Vega---"The Inca") raises many points of interest. In general the other narratives subordinate description to the running tale of exploration, rapine, battle, and disaster. By contrast, the Cañete fragment, even though quite short, devotes much of its space to description of the land, fruits, fauna, and even the mores of its native people. The thirtieth chapter of the Ranjel diary, not extant in the Oviedo y Valdés version, appears to have contained some of this type of material, but the Cañete fragment is rich in it. As examples, one may cite the deity El Cu of the temple at Cofitachiqui, and the description of marriage customs and the treatment of adultery in the Cañete relation.

The research question of most import here is: can the full narrative of Sebastián de Cañete be found? Judging by the promise of the fragment, the search for it seems most worth doing.

TITLES IN THE SERIES